The
BLACK
FEMINIST
READER

To Barbara Christian, to my sister, Tracy, and to all the women who taught me to think critically, imaginatively, and with courage.
JJ

This one is for my father – male feminist that he is – who raised me to become the feminist thinker that I am.
TDSW

The
BLACK
FEMINIST
READER

EDITED BY

Joy James and
T. Denean Sharpley-Whiting

First published 2000
2 4 6 8 10 9 7 5 3 1

Blackwell Publishers Inc.
350 Main Street
Malden, Massachusetts 02148
USA

Blackwell Publishers Ltd
108 Cowley Road
Oxford OX4 1JF
UK

Library of Congress Cataloging-in-Publication Data
The Black feminist reader / edited by Joy James and Tracey Denean Sharpley-Whiting.
  p. cm.
Includes bibliographical references and index.
ISBN 0-631-21006-7 -- ISBN 0-631-21007-5 (pbk.)
  1. American literature--Afro-American authors--History and criticism--Theory, etc. 2.
American literature--Women authors--History and criticism--Theory, etc. 3. English
literature--Black authors--History and criticism-- Theory, etc. 4. English
literature--Women authors--History and criticism-- Theory, etc. 5. Feminism and
literature--English-speaking countries. 6. Afro-American women in literature. 7.
Women, Black, in literature. I. James, Joy, 1958- II. Sharpley-Whiting, T. Denean.
PS153.N5 B5536 2000
305.48'896073--dc21   99-051385

British Library Cataloguing in Publication Data

A CIP catalogue record for this book is available from the British Library.

Typeset in 10/13 pt Sabon
by SetSystems Ltd, Saffron Walden, Essex
Printed in Great Britain by
TJ International, Padstow, Cornwall

This book is printed on acid-free paper

Contents

CONTENTS
········

Contributors

Michael Awkward is Professor of English and Afro-American Studies at the University of Pennsylvania. He is author of *Inspiriting Influence* and *Negotiating Difference: Race, Gender, and the Politics of Positionality*.

Barbara Christian is Professor of African American Studies at the University of California at Berkeley. She is author of *Black Women Novelists: The Development of Tradition, 1892–1976*, winner of the Before Columbus Book Award, and *Black Feminist Criticism: Perspectives on Black Women Writers*. She is co-editor of the *Norton Anthology of African American Literature*.

Patricia Hill Collins is the Charles Phelps Taft Professor of Sociology and Professor of African American Studies at the University of Cincinnati. She is author of *Black Feminist Thought: Knowledge, Consciousness, and the Politics of Empowerment*, winner of the C. Wright Mills Award by the American Sociological Association, and *Fighting Words: Black Women and the Search for Justice*.

Kimberlé Crenshaw is Professor of Law at Columbia University and the University of California at Los Angeles. She is the author of numerous legal articles and editor of several collections, including *Critical Race Theory: The Key Writings that Formed the Movement*.

Angela Y. Davis is University Professor in the History of Consciousness Program at the University of California at Santa Cruz. She is author of *Women, Race and Class*; *Women, Culture, and Politics*; and *Blues Legacies and Black Feminism*; and she is co-editor with Bettina Aptheker of *If They Come in the Morning: Voices of Resistance*. Her collected essays, spanning three decades, appear in *The Angela Y. Davis Reader*.

bell hooks (Gloria Watkins) is Distinguished Professor of English at New York's City College. hooks has written extensively on social justice and popular culture. Her numerous publications have made her name synonymous with black feminism. Her works include: *Ain't I a Woman: Black Women and Feminism*; *Feminist Theory: From Margin to Center*; *Black Looks: Race and Representation*; *Talking Back: Thinking Feminist*, *Thinking Black*; *Yearning: Race, Gender, and Cultural Politics*; and *Killing Rage*.

Joy James is author of *Resisting State Violence*; *Transcending the Talented Tenth: Black Leaders and American Intellectuals*; and *Shadowboxing: Representations of Black Feminist Politics*. She is also editor of *The Angela Y. Davis Reader* and *States of Confinement: Policing, Detention, and Prisons*. James is Distinguished Visiting Scholar in the Institute for Research in African American Studies at Columbia University.

Toni Morrison, Nobel Prize-winning novelist, is Goheen Professor of Humanities at Princeton University. The recipient of the National Book Foundation Medal for Distinguished Contributions to American Letters, she is author of *The Bluest Eye*, *Song of Solomon*, *Beloved*, *Sula*, and *Paradise* among other creative works and works of criticism, and co-editor of several anthologies on culture and politics

T. Denean Sharpley-Whiting is Director of the African American Studies and Research Center at Purdue University. She is author of *Black Venus* and *Frantz Fanon: Conflicts and Feminisms*, and co-editor of *Spoils of War* and *Fanon: A Critical Reader*.

Hortense J. Spillers is Professor of English at Cornell University. She has published widely on black feminist criticism and psychoanalysis. She is co-editor of *Conjuring: Black Women, Fiction, and Literary Tradition* and author of several short stories that have appeared in *Essence* and *The Black Scholar*.

Sylvia Wynter is a Caribbean novelist, playwright, and literary critic, and Professor Emerita of Spanish and Portuguese Literature and former Director of Africana Studies at Stanford University. Wynter is the author of numerous works including the novel *The Hills of Hebron*.

Preface

The Black Feminist Reader restricts itself to a select number of feminist writers. Space does not permit us to reproduce the extensive body of literature by the numerous scholars and activists who have influenced the growth and development of black feminism. Given their scope and length, in our estimation the following essays best reflect the literary, social, and political critiques that mark this area of feminism as singular, controversial, and transformative. The ten essays reprinted here were written during the last twenty-five years by intellectuals who address key themes within black feminisms: the intersections of sex, gender, and race, sometimes class and ideology. These analyses promote critical thinking about language, culture, democratic justice, and humanity. Hence the *Reader* is organized thematically and paradigmatically rather than historically and is divided into two sections: Part I, Literary Theory; and Part II, Social and Political Theory. These chapters coalesce around community and identity (especially Barbara Christian's and Sylvia Wynter's essays, which examine the erasure or marginalization of the community of African American *and* Caribbean women in literature and language). Each essay in its own way represents a theoretical paradigm for a trajectory or strand of black feminism.

The editors' introduction provides a brief historical overview of black feminism. That several of the contributors may not be readily recognized as black feminists reflects the restrictive perceptions surrounding this body of work. Nonetheless, the following authors have furthered critical theory while emphasizing key themes within black feminism. The reader will find that not all the writers are women, which reflects the evolving notions of who and what qualifies as "feminist" as well as the interest black feminism continues to generate among women *and* men. By incorporating the work of male feminists, Marxists, legal scholars, and literary, cultural, and social theorists, we intend to convey the expansive range of black feminism while presenting *The Black Feminist Reader* as a volume that is organizationally and conceptually unique. We anticipate that this anthology will add to the growing body of work that introduces more and more readers and scholars to black feminism.

Part I of *The Black Feminist Reader* opens with Barbara Christian's influential article, "The Race for Theory." This essay explores the re-inscription of Western philosophical methods of inquiry in literary studies, postmodernism's exclusionary uses of language, and the erasure of "theorizing" by people of color, particularly women who, as Christian argues, have "continuously speculated about the nature of life through pithy language that unmasked the power relations of their world." Christian writes, "It is this language . . . that I find celebrated, refined, critiqued in the works of writers like Morrison . . ." As does Christian, Toni Morrison, in chapter 2, reflects on community and language. In "Unspeakable Things Unspoken: The Afro-American Presence in American Literature," a lecture presented at the University of Michigan in 1988, she analyzes several of her novels to emphasize community and the individual's relationship to it, examining how language activates and is activated in African American culture.

Chapter 3, Hortense J. Spillers's "Mama's Baby, Papa's Maybe: An American Grammar Book," describes an enslaved African American female who shares the conditions of all "captive flesh . . . as the entire captive community becomes a living laboratory." For such women, Spillers argues, the theft and mutilation of the (black) body create a singular condition in which gender difference is lost, and the female body and the male body become "a territory of cultural and political maneuver" that is neither gender-related nor gender-specific.

Spillers's essay greatly influenced the chapter that follows, "A Black Man's Place in Black Feminist Criticism." In chapter 4, Michael Awkward presents a feminist manifesto in which he posits that the value of male black feminism lies in its anti-patriarchal stance and self-reflexivity in its relations to, rather than reproduction of, a feminism that focuses on black female subjectivity.

In chapter 5, "Beyond Miranda's Meanings: Unsilencing the 'Demonic Ground' of 'Caliban's Woman'," Sylvia Wynter offers an explication of Shakepeare's play *The Tempest*. Wynter's essay was originally published as the Afterword to *Out of the Kumbla*, an anthology on black women and Caribbean literature edited by Carole Boyce

Davies and Elaine Savory Fido. Undergirded by a reworking of Martini-
quan poet Aimé Césaire's rereading of the Shakespeare play, Wynter's
analysis discloses the erasure of the black female body/sexuality and the
silencing of voice. The absence of Caliban's woman, the African American and Caribbean woman necessary to reproduce Caliban's "vile race,"
represents an ontological absence, a negation of an entire people.

Continuing the themes of absence and negation, Part II, Social and
Political Theory, presents writings from the fields of cultural and legal
studies, sociology, and political philosophy. bell hooks, a cultural studies
feminist, theorizes the need for a "revolutionary feminism" in "Black
Women: Shaping Feminist Theory," chapter 6. Discussing the limitations
of bourgeois feminism, hooks's work seeks to repoliticize feminism as
"a commitment to reorganizing society so that the self-development of
people can take precedence over imperialism, economic expansion, and
material desires."[1]

The pioneering essays on the intersections of race, class, and gender
by Angela Y. Davis, the black feminist most associated with Marxism,
first appeared during her incarceration as a political prisoner in the early
1970s.[2] In chapter 7, written while she was imprisoned and originally
published for a symposium on dialectical materialism, Davis's "Women
and Capitalism: Dialectics of Oppression and Liberation" presents a
Marxist analysis that incorporates gender and race as central components to her criticism of capitalism.

Building upon Alice Walker's definition of womanist as culturally
specific to women of color, Patricia Hill Collins's "The Social Construction of Black Feminist Thought," chapter 8, presents an Afrocentric
womanism that empowers women and men to actualize a humanist
vision and develop an emancipatory theory reflective of black female
struggles.[3] This essay provides the foundation for Collins's *Black Feminist Thought*, a widely read text in women's studies.

Chapter 9 provides a legal studies analysis of the binary opposition
that constrains theory and practice in regard to women of color.
Kimberlé Crenshaw's "Demarginalizing the Intersection of Race and
Sex: A Black Feminist Critique of Antidiscrimination Doctrine, Feminist
Theory, and Antiracist Politics" explores politics, law, and theory within
the context of black women's lives. A leading proponent of feminist
critical race theory, Crenshaw examines the inability or unwillingness of
the law, and its practitioners, to conceptualize the convergence of gender
and race within law.

In chapter 10, Joy James probes the negative impact of state practices and corporate institutions on gender, race, and culture. Arguing that black feminism is generally progressive but not inherently radical or transformative, James's "Radicalizing Feminism" examines liberal and radical politics within a multiplicity of black feminisms.

The Black Feminist Reader concludes with an appendix that contains three key writings and manifestoes by black women over the last quarter-century. The 1977 Combahee River Collective Statement illustrates the emergence of the contemporary wave of black feminism out of the civil rights and black liberation movements of the 1950s, 1960s, and 1970s. The African American Women in Defense of Ourselves manifesto, issued during the 1991 hearings for the confirmation of Clarence Thomas as Supreme Court Justice, in which Anita Hill raised charges of sexual harassment, challenges the continuing sexual objectification and abuse of black women in both media and government. Finally, the 1998 Open Letter from Assata Shakur highlights the critical juncture that black women face concerning political struggles, liberation, and state repression. A former US political prisoner currently in exile in Cuba, Shakur has produced literature and a memoir that have provided an avenue for revolutionary black feminism, a strand of feminism that is often not fully pursued but one that has nevertheless made an indelible mark on black feminist theorizing.[4]

Minor cosmetic editorial changes have been made to some of the readings in pursuit of consistency and ease of reading.

Notes

1   bell hooks, *Feminist Theory: From Margin to Center* (Boston: South End Press, 1984), 24.

2   For information on her case and political repression of black dissidents, see: Angela Davis, *Angela Davis: An Autobiography* (New York: Random House, 1974); Bettina Aptheker, *The Morning Breaks: The Trial of Angela Davis* (Ithaca, NY: Cornell University Press, 1999); and Joy James, ed., *The Angela Y. Davis Reader* (Oxford: Blackwell, 1998).

3   Patricia Hill Collins, *Black Feminist Thought: Knowledge, Consciousness, and the Politics of Empowerment* (Cambridge, MA: Unwin Hyman, 1990) 32, 139–61.

4   See Assata Shakur, *Assata: An Autobiography* (Chicago: Lawrence Hill, 1987).

Acknowledgments

The editors would like to thank Andrew McNeillie and the editorial and production staff at Blackwell Publishers (UK), as well as Loretta Wahl and Sabrina Hodges, former research assistants at the University of Colorado at Boulder. Many thanks also to Rita Hillman and Carolyn Johnson in the African American Studies and Research Center at Purdue University.
JJ
TDSW

The editors and publishers gratefully acknowledge the following for permission to reproduce copyright material: "African American Women in Defense of Ourselves," in *Kitchen Table*, copyright © 1992 Women of Color Press, Lutham; Michael Awkward, "A Black Man's Place in Black Feminist Criticism," from *Negotiating Difference*, copyright © 1995 The University of Chicago Press, Chicago, reprinted by permission of the publishers; Barbara Christian, "The Race for Theory," in *Cultural Critique*, copyright © 1987 Oxford University Press; Kimberlé Crenshaw, "Demarginalizing the Intersection of Race and Sex: A Black Feminist Critique of Antidiscrimination Doctrine, Feminist Theory, and Antiracist Politics," copyright © 1989 The University of Chicago Legal Forum, Chicago; Angela Y. Davis, "Women and Capitalism: Dialectics of Oppression and Liberation," in Howard Parsons et al., eds, *Marxism, Revolution, and Peace*, copyright © 1977 B. R. Grüner Publishing Co., Amsterdam, reprinted by permission of John Betjamins Publishing Company; Patricia Hill Collins, "The Social Construction of Black Feminist Throught," from *Signs*, 4, copyright © 1989 The University of Chicago Press, Chicago, reprinted by permission of the publishers; bell hooks, "Black Women: Shaping Feminist Theory," in *Feminist Theory: From*

Margin to Center, copyright © 1984 South End Press, Boston, reprinted by permission of the publisher; Gloria Hull, "Combahee River Collective Statement," in *All The Women Are White, All The Blacks Are Black, But Some Of Us Are Brave*, copyright © 1982 The Feminist Press, New York; Joy James, "Radicalizing Black Feminism," in *Race and Class*, vol. 40, no. 4, copyright © 1999 Institute of Race Relations, London, reprinted by permission of the publishers; Toni Morrison, "Unspeakable Things Spoken: The Afro-American Presence in American Literature," in *Michigan Quarterly Review*, pp. 1–34, copyright © 1989 University of Michigan, Ann Arbor; Assata Shakur, "Open Letter," in Black Radical Congress Website, www.blackradicalcongress.com; Hortense J. Spillers, "Mama's Baby, Papa's Maybe," *Diacritics* 17. 2 (Summer 1987): pp. 65–81, © 1987 The John Hopkins University Press, reprinted by permission of the publisher; Sylvia Wynter, "Beyond Miranda's Meaning," in Carole Boyce Davies and Elaine Savory Fido Trenton, eds., *Out of the Kumbla: Caribbean and Literature*, copyright © 1990 Africa World Press, New Jersey.

The publisher apologize for any errors or omissions in the above list and would be grateful to be notified of any corrections that should be incorporated in the next edition or reprint of this book.

Editors' Introduction

Joy James and T. Denean Sharpley-Whiting

Since their forced migration to the Americas, women of African descent have struggled with the multiple realities of gender, racial, and economic or caste oppression shaped by the American experience. In the process, they have created both space for a more viable democracy and a body of extraordinary literature. Although struggles for power and equality as well as political analyses and artistic achievement exist wherever women of African descent exist, the best-known documentation of these endeavours is found in the historical and contemporary works of black women in the United States.

In the antebellum years there were a number of prominent black women abolitionists. Self-named and self-emancipated former slave Sojourner Truth is perhaps one of the best recognized, largely because of her symbolic use among white feminists dating from the mid-nineteenth century. A contemporary of abolitionist and women's rights advocate Frederick Douglass and white suffragettes, Truth had a profound impact on expanding notions of womanhood and delivered two significant speeches: the 1851 "Woman's Rights" and the 1867 "When Woman Gets Her Rights Man Will Be Right."[1] Her lesser-known contemporary Maria W. Stewart, a free Black Bostonian and associate of David Walker – the black abolitionist allegedly poisoned for his antislavery agitation – became one of the first American women to establish a reputation as a public, political speaker, merging the issues of women's rights with abolitionism. Stewart's fiery advocacy led her to the pulpit; she would later be ousted from the church and public speaking by African American male clergy who found her claims of direct communion with God as the inspiration for her activism heretical. During the Civil War, Stewart also served in the medical corps, tending wounded soldiers. Another contemporary, Harriet Tubman, who had herself escaped slavery and led thousands of black people to freedom through the Underground Railroad before the war, fought as a soldier and officer during the conflict. As the first American woman to lead black and white troops in battle, Tubman headed the Intelligence Service in the Department of the South. Known as the "Black Moses" because of her leading black slaves from bondage to freedom in the North, her courage and skill as a military strategist during the Civil War garnered her another title: "General Tubman."

Amid the militant emancipation speeches and military campaigns of the nineteenth century, a black feminist literature was born. Fictionalized slave narratives, such as Harriet Wilson's *Our Nig*, and autobiographies couched in the thematics of the sentimental novel, like Harriet Jacob's *Incidents in the Life of a Slave Girl* and Frances E. W. Harper's *Iola Leroy*, emerged to challenge Victorian notions of true womanhood and rigid racial categories. Such works aroused sympathy for the slave who dared to love her children as any mother would, and exposed the sexual oppression unique to enslaved women.

Decades after the war and the aborted Reconstruction that followed, African American women became formidable chroniclers and commentators on society, politics, and equality. In 1892 educator Anna Julia Cooper published *A Voice from the South: By a Black Woman from the South*. One of two black women delegates from the United States to attend the first Pan-African Congress held in 1900 in London, Cooper would two years later become principal of the celebrated M Street High School in Washington, DC. Her contemporaries, antilynching crusaders Ida B. Wells and Mary Church Terrell, chronicled their experiences and understandings of justice in the nineteenth and early twentieth centuries respectively in *Crusade for Justice: The Autobiography of Ida B. Wells* (published in 1970) and *A Colored Woman in a White World* (1940). Active in the national black women's club movement where Terrell ascended to the presidency of the National Association of Colored Women, both women achieved international prominence through their antiracist and antilynching efforts, political speeches on the "Negro Question" in the United States, and writings that established them as critical intellectuals and activists for their era.

The Harlem Renaissance (1919–40) marked another milestone in black women's literary production. The works of Jessie Redmon Fauset, Nella Larsen, and Zora Neale Hurston among others continued to deftly interrogate the intersections of race, sex, class, and color within the

United States as well as abroad. Bold articles edited by Amy Jacques Garvey on the "Woman's Page" of the United Negro Improvement Association's (UNIA) *Negro World* called for women's liberation and participation in public service, while denouncing imperialism and advocating pan-Africanism. The writings of Jacques Garvey, second wife of the orator and UNIA founder Marcus Garvey, and other lesser-known women, as well as the writings of the Harlem Renaissance, proved inspirational to the cultural nationalism and new race-conscious literature advocated by French-speaking black women like Jane and Paulette Nardal, Suzanne Césaire, and Suzanne Lacascade. Indeed, Paulette Nardal would go on to co-found the bilingual *Review of the Black World/Revue du monde noir* in Paris in the 1930s.

The era of the Second World War and the postwar boom – reflected variously in the new literary traditions of Realism and Modernism (1940–60) – revealed another important dimension of black feminist inquiry. The emergent feminism found expression in a number of works, including those by the short-story writer, novelist, and editor Dorothy West; poet Gwendolyn Brooks, whose *Annie Allen* won the Pulitzer in 1950; and playwright Lorraine Hansberry, whose 1959 *A Raisin in the Sun* became the first play written by an African American woman to debut on Broadway. Such creative endeavors helped to bring the struggles of black people and black women before many Americans.

The literary inventions and interventions of the 1920s through the 1950s co-existed with civil rights activism, fostered by organizations like the National Association for the Advancement of Colored People (NAACP) and the Southern Christian Leadership Council (SCLC) headed by the Reverend Dr. Martin Luther King, Jr. By the late 1960s, black women had played key roles in the NAACP, the SCLC, the Student Nonviolent Coordinating Committee (SNCC), the Congress on Racial Equality (CORE), the Organization of Afro-American Unity (OAAU), and the Black Panther Party (BPP). Activism filtered through and focused their emergent feminism. Names such as Septima Clark, Fannie Lou Hamer, Ella Baker, Ruby Doris Smith-Robinson, Kathleen Cleaver, and Assata Shakur have become, in black feminist scholarship, synonymous with the political leadership and commitments of these organizations.

In the 1960s and 1970s, black women as individuals and in collectives issued cogent calls for a transformative black feminism.[2] Even if the words "black feminism" were rarely used, questions and debates about black women's sexuality, the intersections of race and sex, and the nature of black women's political, economic, and social roles were certainly not in short supply, as witnessed in the writings of Sonia Sanchez, June Jordan, Audre Lorde, and *The Black Woman: An Anthology* edited by Toni Cade. At times these writings, when issued by black Marxist and socialist feminists, held strong criticisms of capitalism. Indeed, Gloria Joseph's "Black Feminist Pedagogy and Schooling in Capitalist White America"[3] and Angela Davis's *Women, Race and Class* set out critical analyses of capitalism's impact on democratic politics and culture.

As a result of the highly politicized activities of the civil rights and Black Power eras, the Black Arts Movement, and the wealth of African American literary achievements, black studies and women's studies programs exploded onto the university scene. By the late 1970s and early 1980s, a flurry of writings by black women sought to correct the racial bias of women's studies and communities and the gender bias of black studies and communities within and outside of the academy. Influential texts that initially were most strongly received by women's studies programs included: Toni Morrison's *The Bluest Eye*, which according to Morrison was reissued in the 1980s largely at the insistence of white, women's studies teachers; Alice Walker's *In Search of Our Mothers' Gardens: Womanist Prose* and *The Color Purple*; Ntozake Shange's Broadway play *For Colored Girls*; Michele Wallace's polemical *Black Macho and the Myth of the Superwoman*; bell hooks's *Ain't I a Woman?*; Gloria T. Hull, Patricia Bell Scott, and Barbara Smith's anthology *All the Women Are White, All the Blacks Are Men, But Some of Us Are Brave: Black Women's Studies*; Barbara Smith's edited collection *Home Girls: A Black Feminist Anthology*; and Paula Giddings's historical narrative *When and Where I Enter: The Impact of Black Women on Race and Sex in America*.

The 1980s also saw male academics and writers promoting works by and about black women writers and feminists. For example, Henry Louis Gates's anthology *Reading Black, Reading Feminist* and his editing of the New York Public Library's Schomburg series on black women writers proved influential, introducing readers to relatively obscure women authors from the nineteenth and early to mid-twentieth centuries who embodied black feminist sensibilities and politics.

The interest generated by black women's writings sparked discussions of black feminist criticism. In effect, theories of reading and notions of tradition were created by significant black feminist works like Barbara

Christian's *Black Women Novelists: The Development of Tradition, 1892–1976*, Mae Gwendolyn Henderson's "Speaking in Tongues," Barbara Smith's "Towards a Black Feminist Criticism," Deborah McDowell's follow-up to Smith entitled "New Directions for Black Feminist Criticism," and Sherley Anne Williams's "Some Implications of 'Womanist' Theory."

In the early 1980s, noted author Alice Walker contrasted black feminism with white or Eurocentric feminism, using the term "womanist" to render the adjective "black" superfluous for gender-progressive "women of color" and positing a culturally specific womanism that extends beyond women of African descent but is identifiably different from the dominant feminism of white (bourgeois) women.[4] Walker's ideology influenced the Afrocentric womanism of black women theorists and black and latina female theologians. Partly in response to the dominance of male voices stemming from the late 1960s in fostering black theology as pioneered by James Cone, in the late 1980s black female theologians began to issue race *and* gender critiques of theology's overwhelming white and male hegemony. Katie G. Cannon's *Black Womanist Ethics*, Jacquelyn Grant's *White Women's Christ and Black Women's Jesus*, and Delores S. Williams's *Sisters in the Wilderness: The Challenge of Womanist God-Talk* ushered black feminism into protestant theology.

Although works in literature, history, political and popular culture, and, to a lesser extent, theology are more widely read in black feminism, in the 1990s critical race feminism developed within legal studies to offer incisive analyses. Emphasizing the theoretical and practical concerns of women of color under the law, critical race feminism emerged out of critical race theory – itself an outgrowth of the critical theory movement in law that challenged the conservatism of hegemonic legal theory without addressing its racism. The most prominent writers in critical race theory who analyze gender include Derrick Bell, Patricia Williams, Richard Delgado, Mari Matsuda, Cheryl Harris, and Kimberlé Crenshaw. In 1998 New York University Press published the first anthology of writings by or about gender and race in legal studies, Adrien Wing's *Critical Race Feminism*. One impetus for the emergence of critical race feminism was the highly controversial and publicized 1991 Senate hearings for the confirmation of Clarence Thomas as a justice for the US Supreme Court. The hearings became an interrogation session for Anita Hill, who had raised charges of sexual harassment against Thomas. Televised and drawing a large audience, the proceedings sparked a number of publications, such as Toni Morrison's anthology *Race-ing Justice, En-gendering Power* and Robert Chrisman and Robert L. Allen's *Court of Appeal*, as well as widespread organizing among black women. African American Women in Defense of Ourselves, an ad hoc organization that formed during the Thomas confirmation hearings, issued a document criticizing the gender and racial biases of the hearings in a *New York Times* advertisement.

In the mid- to late 1990s it became evident that the varied ideological, cultural, and literary contributions by black women belie any attempt to formulate a monolithic or homogeneous black feminism. A diversity in outlook and writing, and a lack of ideological uniformity despite the shared concerns for racial and gender equality, give this school of thought its complexity. Nevertheless, the influence of historical women on black feminism has proved enduring. As the Combahee River Collective – a militant black feminist collective whose name is derived from Harriet Tubman's 1863 guerrilla foray into South Carolina's Port Royal or Combahee River region – maintain in their 1977 "Black Feminist Statement":

> There have always been Black women activists – some known, like Sojourner Truth, Harriet Tubman, Frances E. W. Harper, Ida B. Wells Barnett and Mary Church Terrell, and thousands upon thousands unknown – who have had a shared awareness of how their sexual identity combined with their racial identity to make their whole life situation and the focus of their political struggles unique. Contemporary Black feminism is the outgrowth of countless generations of personal sacrifice, militancy, and work by our mothers and sisters.[5]

Increasingly, new literature and activism explore black feminist contributions, creativity, and ideological debates. Growing amid diverse tendencies and tensions, which fuel its insights, the significance of black feminism as a tool for critical inquiry within American and global culture is undeniable.

Notes

1   Sojourner Truth's speeches are reprinted in Beverly Guy-Sheftall, ed., *Words of Fire: An Anthology of African-American Feminist Thought* (New York:

The New Press, 1995), 36–8. For a comprehensive biography that examines Frances D. Gages attributing the rhetorical question "Arn't I a woman?" to Truth in the latter's 1851 Akron, Ohio, Arn't I A Woman? speech, see Nell Painter, *Sojourner Truth: A Life, a Symbol* (New York: W. W. Norton, 1996).

2   For anthologies documenting the emergence of black feminism in the late 1960s and early 1970s, see: Barbara Smith, ed., *Home Girls: A Black Feminist Anthology* (New York: Kitchen Table/Women of Color Press, 1983); Toni Cade Bambara, ed., *The Black Woman* (New York: New American Library, 1970); and Guy-Sheftall, ed., *Words of Fire*.

3   See Mike Cole, ed., *Bowles and Gintes Revisited: Correspondence and Contradiction in Education Theory* (London and New York: Falmer, 1988).

4   See Alice Walker, *In Search of Our Mothers' Gardens* (San Diego: Harcourt Brace Jovanovich, 1988), xi. Walker notes that white women feel no need to preface "feminist" with "white," understanding the term as stemming from their racial/ethnic culture. For a discussion of Afrocentricity, see E. Frances White, "Africa on My Mind: Gender, Counterdiscourse, and African American Nationalism," *Journal of Women's History* 2 (Spring 1990), 73–97.

5   Combahee River Collective, "Black Feminist Statement," in Gloria T. Hull, Patricia Bell Scott, and Barbar Smith, eds, *All the Women are White, All the Blacks Are Men, But Some of Us Are Brave: Black Women Studies* (Westbury, NY: Feminist Press, 1982), 273.

PART ONE

Literary Theory

ONE

The Race for Theory

Barbara Christian

I have seized this occasion to break the silence among those of us, critics, as we are now called, who have been intimidated, devalued by what I call the race for theory. I have become convinced that there has been a takeover in the literary world by Western philosophers from the old literary élite, the neutral humanists. Philosophers have been able to effect such a takeover because so much of the literature of the West has become pallid, laden with despair, self-indulgent, and disconnected. The New Philosophers, eager to understand a world that is today fast escaping their political control, have redefined literature so that the distinctions implied by that term, that is, the distinctions between everything written and those things written to evoke feeling as well as to express thought, have been blurred. They have changed literary critical language to suit their own purposes as philosophers, and they have reinvented the meaning of theory.

My first response to this realization was to ignore it. Perhaps, in spite of the egocentrism of this trend, some good might come of it. I had, I felt, more pressing and interesting things to do, such as reading and studying the history and literature of black women, a history that had been totally ignored, a contemporary literature bursting with originality, passion, insight, and beauty. But unfortunately it is difficult to ignore this new takeover, since theory has become a commodity which helps determine whether we are hired or promoted in academic institutions – worse, whether we are heard at all. Due to this new orientation, works (a word which evokes labor) have become texts. Critics are no longer concerned with literature, but with other critics' texts, for the critic yearning for attention has displaced the writer and has conceived of himself as the center. Interestingly in the first part of this century, at least in England and America, the critic was usually also a writer of poetry, plays, or novels. But today, as a new generation of professionals develops, he or she is increasingly an academic. Activities such as teaching or writing one's response to specific works of literature have, among this group, become subordinated to one primary thrust, that moment when one creates a theory, thus fixing a constellation of ideas for a time at least, a fixing which no doubt will be replaced in another month or so by somebody else's competing theory as the race accelerates. Perhaps because those who have effected the takeover have the power (although they deny it) first of all to be published, and thereby to determine the ideas which are deemed valuable, some of our most daring and potentially radical critics (and by our I mean black, women, third world) have been influenced, even coopted, into speaking a language and defining their discussion in terms alien to and opposed to our needs and orientation. At least so far, the creative writers I study have resisted this language.

For people of color have always theorized – but in forms quite different from the Western form of abstract logic. And I am inclined to say that our theorizing (and I intentionally use the verb rather than the noun) is often in narrative forms, in the stories we create, in riddles and proverbs, in the play with language, since dynamic rather than fixed ideas seem more to our liking. How else have we managed to survive with such spiritedness the assault on our bodies, social institutions, countries, our very humanity? And women, at least the women I grew up around, continuously speculated about the nature of life through pithy language that unmasked the power relations of their world. It is this language, and the grace and pleasure with which they played with it, that I find celebrated, refined, critiqued in the works of writers like Morrison and Walker. My folk, in other words, have always been a race for theory – though more in the form of the hieroglyph, a written figure which is both sensual and abstract, both beautiful and communicative. In my own work I try to illuminate and explain these hieroglyphs, which is, I think, an activity quite different from the creating of the hieroglyphs themselves. As the Buddhists would say, the finger pointing at the moon is not the moon.

In this discussion, however, I am more concerned with the issue raised by my first use of the term, *the race for theory*, in relation to its academic hegemony, and possibly of its inappropriateness to the energetic emerging literatures in the world today. The pervasiveness of this academic hegemony is an issue continually spoken about – but usually in hidden groups, lest we, who are disturbed by it, appear ignorant to the reigning academic élite. Among the folk who speak in muted tongues are people of color, feminists, radical critics, creative writers, who have struggled for much longer than a decade to make their voices, their various voices, heard, and for whom literature is not an occasion for discourse among critics but is necessary nourishment for their people and one way by which they come to understand their lives better. Clichéd though this may be, it bears, I think, repeating here.

The race for theory, with its linguistic jargon, its emphasis on quoting its prophets, its tendency towards "Biblical" exegesis, its refusal even to mention specific works of creative writers, far less contemporary ones, its preoccupations with mechanical analyses of language, graphs, algebraic equations, its gross generalizations about culture, has silenced many of us to the extent that some of us feel we can no longer discuss our own literature, while others have developed intense writing blocks and are puzzled by the incomprehensibility of the language set adrift in literary circles. There have been, in the last year, any number of occasions on which I had to convince literary critics who have pioneered entire new areas of critical inquiry that they did have something to say. Some of us are continually harassed to invent wholesale theories regardless of the complexity of the literature we study. I, for one, am tired of being asked to produce a black feminist literary theory as if I were a mechanical man. For I believe such theory is prescriptive – it ought to have some relationship to practice. Since I can count on one hand the number of people attempting to be black feminist literary critics in the world today, I consider it presumptuous of me to invent a theory of how we *ought* to read. Instead, I think we need to read the works of our writers in our various ways and remain open to the intricacies of the intersection of language, class, race, and gender in the literature. And it would help if we share our process, that is, our practice, as much as possible since, finally, our work is a collective endeavor.

The insidious quality of this race for theory is symbolized for me by the very name of this special issue – Minority Discourse* – a label which is borrowed from the reigning theory of the day and is untrue to the literatures being produced by our writers, for many of our literatures (certainly Afro-American literature) are central, not minor, and by the

---

* This essay was originally written for a special issue of *Cultural Critique* on "Minority Discourse," published in spring 1987.

titles of many of the articles, which illuminate language as an assault on the other, rather than as possible communication, and play with, or even affirmation of another. I have used the passive voice in my last sentence construction, contrary to the rules of Black English, which like all languages has a particular value system, since I have not placed responsibility on any particular person or group. But that is precisely because this new ideology has become so prevalent among us that it behaves like so many of the other ideologies with which we have had to contend. It appears to have neither head nor center. At the least, though, we can say that the terms "minority" and "discourse" are located firmly in a Western dualistic or "binary" frame which sees the rest of the world as minor, and tries to convince the rest of the world that it is major, usually through force and then through language, even as it claims many of the ideas that we, its "historical" other, have known and spoken about for so long. For many of us have never conceived of ourselves only as somebody's *other*.

Let me not give the impression that by objecting to the race for theory I ally myself with or agree with the neutral humanists who see literature as pure expression and will not admit to the obvious control of its production, value, and distribution by those who have power, who deny, in other words, that literature is, of necessity, political. I am studying an entire body of literature that has been denigrated for centuries by such terms as *political*. For an entire century Afro-American writers, from Charles Chestnutt in the nineteenth century through Richard Wright in the 1930s, Imamu Baraka in the 1960s, Alice Walker in the 1970s, have protested the literary hierarchy of dominance which declares when literature is literature, when literature is great, depending on what it thinks is to its advantage. The Black Arts Movement of the 1960s, out of which Black Studies, the Feminist Literary Movement of the 1970s, and Women's Studies grew, articulated precisely those issues, which came *not* from the declarations of the New Western philosophers but from these groups' reflections on their own lives. That Western scholars have long believed their ideas to be universal has been strongly opposed by many such groups. Some of my colleagues do not see black critical writers of previous decades as eloquent enough. Clearly they have not read Wright's "Blueprint for Negro Writing," [Ralph] Ellison's *Shadow and Act*, Chesnutt's resignation from being a writer, or Alice Walker's "Search for Zora Neale Hurston." There are two reasons for this general ignorance of what our writer-critics have said. One is that black writing has been generally ignored in this country. Since we, as Toni Morrison has put it, are seen as a discredited people, it is no surprise, then, that our creations are also discredited, but this is also due to the fact that until recently dominant critics in the Western world have also been creative writers who have had access to the upper middle class institutions of education; and until recently our writers have decidedly been excluded from these institutions and in fact have often been opposed to them. Because of the academic world's general ignorance about the literature of black people and of women, whose work too has been discredited, it is not surprising that so many of our critics think that the position arguing that literature is political begins with these New Philosophers. Unfortunately, many of our young critics do not investigate the reasons *why* that statement – literature is political – is now acceptable when before it was not; nor do we look to our own antecedents for the sophisticated arguments upon which we can build in order to change the tendency of any established Western idea to become hegemonic.

For I feel that the new emphasis on literary critical theory is as hegemonic as the world which it attacks. I see the language it creates as one which mystifies rather than clarifies our condition, making it possible for a few people who know that particular language to control the critical scene – that language surfaced, interestingly enough, just when the literature of peoples of color, of black women, of Latin Americans, of Africans began to move to "the center." Such words as *center* and *periphery* are themselves instructive. *Discourse, canon, texts,* words as latinate as the tradition from which they come, are quite familiar to me. Because I went to a Catholic Mission school in the West Indies I must confess that I cannot hear the word "canon" without smelling incense, that the word "text" immediately brings back agonizing memories of Biblical exegesis, that "discourse" reeks for me of metaphysics forced down my throat in those courses that traced *world* philosophy from Aristotle through Thomas Aquinas to [Martin] Heidegger. "Periphery" too is a word I heard throughout my childhood, for if anything was seen as being at the periphery, it was those small Caribbean islands which had neither land mass nor military power. Still I noted how intensely important this periphery was, for US troops were continually invading one island or another if any change in political control even seemed to be occurring. As I lived among folk for whom language was an absolutely necessary way of validating our existence, I was told that the minds of the world lived only in the small continent of Europe. The metaphysical language of the New Philosophy, then, I must admit, is repulsive to me and is one reason why I raced from philosophy to literature, since the latter seemed to me to have the possibilities of rendering the world as large and as complicated as I experienced it, as sensual as I knew it was. In literature I sensed the possibility of the integration of feeling/knowledge, rather than the split between the abstract and the emotional in which Western philosophy inevitably indulged.

Now I am being told that philosophers are the ones who write literature, that authors are dead, irrelevant, mere vessels through which their narratives ooze, that they do not work nor have they the faintest idea what they are doing; rather they produce texts as disembodied as the angels. I am frankly astonished that scholars who call themselves Marxists or post-Marxists could seriously use such metaphysical language even as they attempt to deconstruct the philosophical tradition from which their language comes. And as a student of literature, I am appalled by the sheer ugliness of the language, its lack of clarity, its unnecessarily complicated sentence constructions, its lack of pleasurableness, its alienating quality. It is the kind of writing for which composition teachers would give a freshman a resounding F.

Because I am a curious person, however, I postponed readings of black women writers I was working on and read some of the prophets of this new literary orientation. These writers did announce their dissatisfaction with some of the cornerstone ideas of their own tradition, a dissatisfaction with which I was born. But in their attempt to change the orientation of Western scholarship, they, as usual, concentrated on themselves and were not in the slightest interested in the worlds they had ignored or controlled. Again I was supposed to know *them*, while they were not at all interested in knowing *me*. Instead they sought to "deconstruct" the tradition to which they belonged even as they used the same forms, style, language of that tradition, forms which necessarily embody its values. And increasingly as I read them and saw their substitution of their philosophical writings for literary ones, I began to have the uneasy feeling that their folk were not producing any literature worth mentioning. For they always harkened back to the masterpieces of the past, again reifying the very texts they said they were deconstructing. Increasingly, as *their* way, *their* terms, *their* approaches remained central and became the means by which one defined literary critics, many of my own peers who had previously been concentrating on dealing with the other side of the equation, the reclamation and discussion of past and *present* third world literatures, were diverted into continually discussing the new literary theory.

From my point of view as a critic of contemporary Afro-American women's writing, this orientation is extremely problematic. In attempting to find the deep structures in the literary tradition, a major preoccupation of the new New Criticism, many of us have become obsessed with the nature of reading itself to the extent that we have stopped writing about literature being written today. Since I am slightly paranoid, it has begun to occur to me that the literature being produced *is* precisely one of the reasons why this new philosophical-literary-critical theory of relativity is so prominent. In other words, the literature of blacks, women of South America and Africa, etc., as overtly "political" literature was being preempted by a new Western concept which proclaimed that reality does not exist, that everything is relative, and that every text is silent about something – which indeed it must necessarily be.

There is, of course, much to be learned from exploring how we know what we know, how we read what we read, an exploration which, of necessity, can have no end. But there also has to be a "what," and that "what," when it is even mentioned by the new philosophers, are texts of the past, primarily Western male texts, whose norms are again being transferred onto third world, female texts as theories of reading proliferate. Inevitably a hierarchy has now developed between what is called theoretical criticism and practical criticism, as mind is deemed superior to matter. I have no quarrel with those who wish to philosophize about how we know what we know. But I do resent the fact that this particular orientation is so privileged and has diverted so many of us from doing the first readings of the literature being written today as well as of past works about which nothing has been written. I note, for example, that there is little work done on Gloria Naylor, that most of Alice Walker's works have not been commented on – despite the rage around *The Color Purple* – that there has yet to be an in-depth study of Frances Harper, the nineteenth-century abolitionist poet and novelist. If our emphasis on theoretical criticism continues, critics of the future may have to reclaim the writers we are now ignoring, that is, if they are even aware these artists exist.

I am particularly perturbed by the movement to exalt theory, as well,

because of my own adult history. I was an active member of the Black
Arts Movement of the sixties and know how dangerous theory can
become. Many today may not be aware of this, but the Black Arts
Movement tried to create Black Literary Theory and in doing so became
prescriptive. My fear is that when theory is not rooted in practice, it
becomes prescriptive, exclusive, élitish.

An example of this prescriptiveness is the approach the Black Arts
Movement took towards language. For it, blackness resided in the use
of black talk which they defined as hip urban language. So that when
Nikki Giovanni reviewed Paule Marshall's *Chosen Place, Timeless People*,
she criticized the novel on the grounds that it was not black for the
language was too elegant, too white. Blacks, she said, did not speak that
way. Having come from the West Indies where we do, some of the time,
speak that way, I was amazed by the narrowness of her vision. The
emphasis on *one way* to be black resulted in the works of Southern
writers being seen as non-black since the black talk of Georgia does not
sound like the black talk of Philadelphia. Because the ideologues, like
Baraka, come from the urban centers they tended to privilege their way
of speaking, thinking, writing, and to condemn other kinds of writing as
not being black enough. Whole areas of the canon were assessed
according to the dictum of the Black Arts Nationalist point of view, as
in Addison Gayle's *The Way of the New World*, while other works were
ignored because they did not fit the scheme of cultural nationalism.
Older writers like Ellison and [James] Baldwin were condemned because
they saw that the intersection of Western and African influences resulted
in a new Afro-American culture, a position with which many of the
Black Nationalist ideologues disagreed. Writers were told that writing
love poems was not being black. Further examples abound.

It is true that the Black Arts Movements resulted in a necessary and
important critique both of previous Afro-American literature and of the
white-established literary world. But in attempting to take over power,
it, as Ishmael Reed satirizes so well in *Mumbo Jumbo*, became much
like its opponent, monolithic and downright repressive. It is this tendency towards the monolithic, monotheistic, etc., which worries me about
the race for theory. Constructs like the *center* and the *periphery* reveal
that tendency to want to make the world less complex by organizing it
according to one principle, to fix it through an idea which is really an
ideal. Many of us are particularly sensitive to monolithism since one
major element of ideologies of dominance, such as sexism and racism, is

to dehumanize people by stereotyping them, by denying them their variousness and complexity. Inevitably, monolithism becomes a metasystem, in which there is a controlling ideal, especially in relation to pleasure. Language as one form of pleasure is immediately restricted, and becomes heavy, abstract, prescriptive, monotonous.

Variety, multiplicity, eroticism are difficult to control. And it may very well be that these are the reasons why writers are often seen as *persona non grata* by political states, whatever form they take, since writers/artists have a tendency to refuse to give up their way of seeing the world and of playing with possibilities; in fact, their very expression relies on that insistence. Perhaps that is why creative literature, even when written by politically reactionary people, can be so freeing, for in having to embody ideas and recreate the world, writers cannot merely produce "one way."

The characteristics of the Black Arts Movement are, I am afraid, being repeated again today, certainly in the other area to which I am especially tuned. In the race for theory, feminists, eager to enter the halls of power, have attempted their own prescriptions. So often I have read books on feminist literary theory that restrict the definition of what *feminist* means and overgeneralize about so much of the world that most women as well as men are excluded. Seldom do feminist theorists take into account the complexity of life – that women are of many races and ethnic backgrounds with different histories and cultures and that as a rule women belong to different classes that have different concerns. Seldom do they note these distinctions, because if they did they could not articulate a theory. Often as a way of clearing themselves they do acknowledge that women of color, for example, do exist, then go on to do what they were going to do anyway, which is to invent a theory that has little relevance for us.

That tendency towards monolithism is precisely how I see the French feminist theorists. They concentrate on the female body as the means to creating a female language, since language, they say, is male and necessarily conceives of woman as other. Clearly many of them have been irritated by the theories of Lacan for whom language is phallic. But suppose there are peoples in the world whose language was invented primarily in relation to women, who after all are the ones who relate to children and teach language. Some Native American languages, for example, use female pronouns when speaking about non-gender specific activity. Who knows who, according to gender, created languages?

Further, by positing the body as the source of everything French feminists return to the old myth that biology determines everything and ignore the fact that gender is a social rather than a biological construct.

I could go on critiquing the positions of French feminists who are themselves more various in their points of view than the label which is used to describe them, but that is not my point. What I am concerned about is the authority this school now has in feminist scholarship – the way it has become *authoritative discourse*, monologic, which occurs precisely because it does have access to the means of promulgating its ideas. The Black Arts Movement was able to do this for a time because of the political movements of the 1960s – so too with the French feminists who could not be inventing "theory" if a space had not been created by the Women's Movement. In both cases, both groups posited a theory that excluded many of the people who made that space possible. Hence one of the reasons for the surge of Afro-American women's writing during the 1970s and its emphasis on sexism in the black community is precisely that when the ideologues of the 1960s said *black*, they meant *black male*.

I and many of my sisters do not see the world as being so simple. And perhaps that is why we have not rushed to create abstract theories. For we know there are countless women of color, both in America and in the rest of the world, to whom our singular ideas would be applied. There is, therefore, a caution we feel about pronouncing black feminist theory that might be seen as a decisive statement about third world women. This is not to say we are not theorizing. Certainly our literature is an indication of the ways in which our theorizing, of necessity, is based on our multiplicity of experiences.

There is at least one other lesson I learned from the Black Arts Movement. One reason for its monolithic approach had to do with its desire to destroy the power which controlled black people, but it was a power which many of its ideologues wished to achieve. The nature of our context today is such that an approach which desires power singlemindedly must of necessity become like that which it wishes to destroy. Rather than wanting to change the whole model, many of us want to be at the center. It is this point of view that writers like June Jordan and Audre Lorde continually critique even as they call for empowerment, as they emphasize the fear of difference among us and our need for leaders rather than a reliance on ourselves.

For one must distinguish the desire for power from the need to become empowered – that is, seeing oneself as capable of and having the right to determine one's life. Such empowerment is partially derived from a knowledge of history. The Black Arts Movement did result in the creation of Afro-American Studies as a concept, thus giving it a place in the university where one might engage in the reclamation of Afro-American history and culture and pass it on to others. I am particularly concerned that institutions such as Black Studies and Women's Studies, fought for with such vigor and at some sacrifice, are not often seen as important by many of our black or women scholars precisely because the old hierarchy of traditional departments is seen as superior to these "marginal" groups. Yet it is in this context that many others of us are discovering the extent of our complexity, the interrelationships of different areas of knowledge in relation to a distinctly Afro-American or female experience. Rather than having to view our world as subordinate to others, or rather than having to work as if we were hybrids, we can pursue ourselves as subjects.

My major objection to the race for theory, as some readers have probably guessed by now, really hinges on the question, "for whom are we doing what we are doing when we do literary criticism?" It is, I think, the central question today especially for the few of us who have infiltrated the academy enough to be wooed by it. The answer to that question determines what orientation we take in our work, the language we use, the purposes for which it is intended.

I can only speak for myself. But what I write and how I write is done in order to save my own life. And I mean that literally. For me literature is a way of knowing that I am not hallucinating, that whatever I feel/know *is*. It is an affirmation that sensuality is intelligence, that sensual language is language that makes sense. My response, then, is directed to those who write what I read and to those who read what I read – put concretely – to Toni Morrison and to people who read Toni Morrison (among whom I would count few academics). That number is increasing, as is the readership of Walker and Marshall. But in no way is the literature Morrison, Marshall, or Walker create supported by the academic world. Nor, given the political context of our society, do I expect that to change soon. For there is no reason, given who controls these institutions, for them to be anything other than threatened by these writers.

My readings do presuppose a need, a desire among folk who like me also want to save their own lives. My concern, then, is a passionate one, for the literature of people who are not in power has always been in danger of extinction or of cooptation, not because we do not theorize, but because what we can even imagine, far less who we can reach, is constantly limited by societal structures. For me, literary criticism is promotion as well as understanding, a response to the writer to whom there is often no response, to folk who need the writing as much as they need anything. I know, from literary history, that writing disappears unless there is a response to it. Because I write about writers who are now writing, I hope to help ensure that their tradition has continuity and survives.

So my "method," to use a new "lit. crit" word, is not fixed but relates to what I read and to the historical context of the writers I read *and* to the many critical activities in which I am engaged, which may or may not involve writing. It is a learning from the language of creative writers, which is one of surprise, so that I might discover what language I might use. For my language is very much based on what I read and how it affects me, that is, on the surprise that comes from reading something that compels you to read differently, as I believe literature does. I, therefore, have no set method, another prerequisite of the new theory, since for me every work suggests a new approach. As risky as that might seem, it is, I believe, what intelligence means – a tuned sensitivity to that which is alive and therefore cannot be known until it is known. Audre Lorde puts it in a far more succinct and sensual way in her essay "Poetry is not a Luxury":

As they become known to and accepted by us, our feelings and the honest exploration of them become sanctuaries and spawning grounds for the most radical and daring of ideas. They become a safe-house for that difference so necessary to change and the conceptualization of any mean-ingful action. Right now, I could name at least ten ideas I would have found intolerable or incomprehensible and frightening, except as they came after dreams and poems. This is not idle fantasy, but a disciplined attention to the true meaning of "it feels right to me." We can train ourselves to respect our feelings and to transpose them into a language so they can be shared. And where that language does not yet exist, it is our poetry which helps to fashion it. Poetry is not only dream and vision; it is the skeleton architecture of our lives. It lays the foundations for a future of change, a bridge across our fears of what has never been before.[1]

Note

1 Audre Lorde, *Sister Outsider: Essays and Speeches* (Trumansburg, NY: The Crossing Press, 1984), 37.

TWO

···

Unspeakable Things Unspoken: The Afro-American Presence in American Literature

Toni Morrison

I

I planned to call this paper "Canon Fodder," because the terms put me in mind of a kind of trained muscular response that appears to be on display in some areas of the recent canon debate.* But I changed my mind (so many have used the phrase) and hope to make clear the appropriateness of the title I settled on.

My purpose here is to observe the panoply of this most recent and most anxious series of questions concerning what should or does constitute a literary canon in order to suggest ways of addressing the Afro-American presence in American literature that require neither slaughter nor reification – views that may spring the whole literature of an entire nation from the solitude into which it has been locked. There is something called American literature, that according to conventional wisdom, is certainly not Chicano literature, or Afro-American literature, or Asian-American, or Native American, or . . . It is somehow separate from them and they from it, and in spite of the efforts of recent literary histories, restructured curricula and anthologies, this separate confinement, be it breached or endorsed, is the subject of a large part of these debates. Although the terms used, like the vocabulary of earlier canon debates, refer to literary and/or humanistic value, aesthetic criteria, value-free or socially anchored readings, the contemporary battle plain

* This paper was originally presented as the Tanner Lecture on Human Values at the University of Michigan, October 7, 1988.

is most often understood to be the claims of others against the whitemale origins and definitions of those values; whether those definitions reflect an eternal, universal and transcending paradigm or whether they constitute a disguise for a temporal, political and culturally specific program.

Part of the history of this particular debate is located in the successful assault that the feminist scholarship of men and women (black and white) made and continues to make on traditional literary discourse. The male part of the whitemale equation is already deeply engaged, and no one believes the body of literature and its criticism will ever again be what it was in 1965: the protected preserve of the thoughts and works and analytical strategies of whitemen.

It is, however, the "white" part of the question that this paper focuses on, and it is to my great relief that such terms as "white" and "race" can enter serious discussion of literature. Although still a swift and swiftly obeyed call to arms, their use is no longer forbidden.[1] It may appear churlish to doubt the sincerity, or question the proclaimed well-intentioned selflessness of a 900-year-old academy struggling through decades of chaos to "maintain standards." Yet of what use is it to go on about "quality" being the only criterion for greatness knowing that the definition of quality is itself the subject of much rage and is seldom universally agreed upon by everyone at all times? Is it to appropriate the term for reasons of state; to be in the position to distribute greatness or withhold it? Or to actively pursue the ways and places in which quality surfaces and stuns us into silence or into language worthy enough to describe it? What is possible is to try to recognize, identify and applaud the fight for and triumph of quality when it is revealed to us and to let go the notion that only the dominant culture or gender can make those judgments, identify that quality or produce it.

Those who claim the superiority of Western culture are entitled to that claim only when Western civilization is measured thoroughly against other civilizations and not found wanting, and when Western civilization owns up to its own sources in the cultures that preceded it.

A large part of the satisfaction I have always received from reading Greek tragedy, for example, is in its similarity to Afro-American communal structures (the function of song and chorus, the heroic struggle between the claims of community and individual hubris) and African religion and philosophy. In other words, that is part of the reason it has quality for me – I feel intellectually at home there. But that could hardly be so for those unfamiliar with my "home," and hardly a requisite for the pleasure they take. The point is, the form (Greek tragedy) makes available these varieties of provocative love because it is masterly – not because the civilization that is its referent was flawless or superior to all others.

One has the feeling that nights are becoming sleepless in some quarters, and it seems to me obvious that the recoil of traditional "humanists" and some post-modern theorists to this particular aspect of the debate, the "race" aspect, is as severe as it is because the claims for attention come from that segment of scholarly and artistic labor in which the mention of "race" is either inevitable or elaborately, painstakingly masked; and if all of the ramifications that the term demands are taken seriously, the bases of Western civilization will require re-thinking. Thus, in spite of its implicit and explicit acknowledgement, "race" is still a virtually unspeakable thing, as can be seen in the apologies, notes of "special use" and circumscribed definitions that accompany it[2] – not least of which is my own deference in surrounding it with quotation marks. Suddenly (for our purposes, suddenly) "race" does not exist. For three hundred years black Americans insisted that "race" was no usefully distinguishing factor in human relationships. During those same three centuries every academic discipline, including theology, history, and natural science, insisted "race" was the determining factor in human development. When blacks discovered they had shaped or become a culturally formed race, and that it had specific and revered difference, suddenly they were told there is no such thing as "race," biological or cultural, that matters and that genuinely intellectual exchange cannot accommodate it.[3] In trying to come to some terms about "race" and writing, I am tempted to throw my hands up. It always seemed to me that the people who invented the hierarchy of "race" when it was convenient for them ought not to be the ones to explain it away, now that it does not suit their purposes for it to exist. But there *is* culture and both gender and "race" inform and are informed by it. Afro-American culture exists and though it is clear (and becoming clearer) how it has responded to Western culture, the instances where and means by which it has shaped Western culture are poorly recognized or understood.

I want to address ways in which the presence of Afro-American literature and the awareness of its culture both resuscitate the study of literature in the United States and raise that study's standards. In pursuit of that goal, it will suit my purposes to contextualize the route canon debates have taken in Western literary criticism.

I do not believe this current anxiety can be attributed solely to the routine, even cyclical arguments within literary communities reflecting unpredictable yet inevitable shifts in taste, relevance or perception. Shifts in which an enthusiasm for and official endorsement of William Dean Howells, for example, withered; or in which the legalization of Mark Twain in critical court rose and fell like the fathoming of a sounding line (for which he may or may not have named himself); or even the slow, delayed but steady swell of attention and devotion on which Emily Dickinson soared to what is now, surely, a permanent crest of respect. No. Those were discoveries, reappraisals of individual artists. Serious but not destabilizing. Such accommodations were simple because the questions they posed were simple: Are there one hundred sterling examples of high literary art in American literature and no more? One hundred and six? If one or two fall into disrepute, is there space, then, for one or two others in the vestibule, waiting like girls for bells chimed by future husbands who alone can promise them security, legitimacy – and in whose hands alone rests the gift of critical longevity? Interesting questions, but, as I say, not endangering.

Nor is this detectable academic sleeplessness the consequence of a much more radical shift, such as the mid-nineteenth century one heralding the authenticity of American literature itself. Or an even earlier upheaval – receding now into the distant past – in which theology, and thereby Latin, was displaced for the equally rigorous study of the classics and Greek to be followed by what was considered a strangely arrogant and upstart proposal: that English literature was a suitable course of study for an aristocratic education, and not simply morally instructive fodder designed for the working classes. (The Chaucer Society was founded in 1848, four hundred years after Chaucer died.) No. This exchange seems unusual somehow, keener. It has a more strenuously argued (and felt) defense and a more vigorously insistent attack. And both defenses and attacks have spilled out of the academy into the popular press. Why? Resistance to displacement within or expansion of a canon is not, after all, surprising or unwarranted. That's what canonization is for. (And the question of whether there should be a canon or not seems disingenuous to me – there always is one whether there should be or not – for it is in the interests of the professional critical community to have one.) Certainly a sharp alertness as to why a work is or is not worthy of study is the legitimate occupation of the critic, the pedagogue and the artist. What is astonishing in the contemporary debate is not the resistance to displacement of works or to the expansion of genre within it, but the virulent passion that accompanies this resistance and, more importantly, the quality of its defense weaponry. The guns are very big; the trigger-fingers quick. But I am convinced the mechanism of the defenders of the flame is faulty. Not only may the hands of the gun-slinging cowboy-scholars be blown off, not only may the target be missed, but the subject of the conflagration (the sacred texts) is sacrificed, disfigured in the battle. This canon fodder may kill the canon. And I, at least, do not intend to live without Aeschylus or William Shakespeare, or James or Twain or Hawthorne, or Melville, etc., etc., etc. There must be some way to enhance canon readings without enshrining them.

When Milan Kundera, in *The Art of the Novel*, identified the historical territory of the novel by saying "The novel is Europe's creation" and that "The only context for grasping a novel's worth is the history of the European novel," the *New Yorker* reviewer stiffened. Kundera's "personal 'idea of the novel,'" he wrote,

> is so profoundly Eurocentric that it's likely to seem exotic, even perverse to American readers . . . *The Art of the Novel* gives off the occasional (but pungent) whiff of cultural arrogance, and we may feel that Kundera's discourse . . . reveals an aspect of his character that we'd rather not have known about . . . In order to become the artist he now is, the Czech novelist had to discover himself a second time as a European. But what if that second, grander possibility hadn't been there to be discovered? What if Broch, Kafka, Musil – all that reading – had never been a part of his education, or had entered it only as exotic, alien presence? Kundera's polemical fervor in *The Art of the Novel* annoys us, as American readers, because we feel defensive, excluded from the transcendent "idea of the novel" that for him seems simply to have been there for the taking. (If only he had cited in his redeeming version of the novel's history, a few more heroes from the New World's culture.) Our novelists don't discover cultural values within themselves; they invent them.[4]

Kundera's views, obliterating American writers (with the exception of William Faulkner) from his own canon, are relegated to a "smugness" that Terrence Rafferty disassociates from Kundera's imaginative work and applies to the "sublime confidence" of his critical prose. The confidence of an exile who has the sentimental education of, and the choice to become, a European.

I was refreshed by Rafferty's comments. With the substitution of certain phrases, his observations and the justifiable umbrage he takes can be appropriated entirely by Afro-American writers regarding their own exclusion from the "transcendent 'idea of the novel.'"

For the present turbulence seems not to be about the flexibility of a canon, its range among and between Western countries, but about its miscegenation. The word is informative here and I do mean its use. A powerful ingredient in this debate concerns the incursion of third world or so-called minority literature into a Eurocentric stronghold. When the topic of third world culture is raised, unlike the topic of Scandinavian culture, for example, a possible threat to and implicit criticism of the reigning equilibrium is seen to be raised as well. From the seventeenth century to the twentieth, the arguments resisting that incursion have marched in predictable sequence: 1) there is no Afro-American (or third world) art; 2) it exists but is inferior; 3) it exists and is superior when it measures up to the "universal" criteria of Western art; 4) it is not so much "art" as ore – rich ore – that requires a Western or Eurocentric smith to refine it from its "natural" state into an aesthetically complex form.

A few comments on a larger, older, but no less telling academic struggle – an extremely successful one – may be helpful here. It is telling because it sheds light on certain aspects of this current debate and may locate its sources. I made reference above to the radical upheaval in canon-building that took place at the inauguration of classical studies and Greek. This canonical re-routing from scholasticism to humanism was not merely radical, it must have been (may I say it?) savage. And it took some seventy years to accomplish. Seventy years to eliminate Egypt as the cradle of civilization *and* its model and replace it with Greece. The triumph of that process was that Greece lost its own origins and became itself original. A number of scholars in various disciplines (history, anthropology, ethnobotany, etc.) have put forward their research into cross-cultural and inter-cultural transmissions with varying degrees of success in the reception of their work. I am reminded of the curious publishing history of Ivan van Sertima's work, *They Came Before Columbus*, which researches the African presence in Ancient America. I am reminded of Edward Said's *Orientalism*, and especially the work of Martin Bernal, a linguist, trained in Chinese history, who has defined himself as an interloper in the field of classical civilization but who has offered, in *Black Athena*, a stunning investigation of the field. According to Bernal, there are two "models" of Greek history: one views Greece as Aryan or European (the Aryan Model); the other sees it as Levantine – absorbed by Egyptian and Semitic culture (the Ancient Model). "If I am right," writes Professor Bernal,

> in urging the overthrow of the Aryan Model and its replacement by the Revised Ancient one, it will be necessary not only to rethink the fundamental bases of "Western Civilization" but also to recognize the penetration of racism and "continental chauvinism" into all our historiography, or philosophy of writing history. The Ancient Model had no major "internal" deficiencies or weaknesses in explanatory power. It was overthrown for external reasons. For eighteenth and nineteenth century Romantics and racists it was simply intolerable for Greece, which was seen not merely as the epitome of Europe but also as its pure childhood, to have been the result of the mixture of native Europeans and *colonizing* Africans and Semites. Therefore the Ancient Model had to be overthrown and replaced by something more acceptable.[5]

It is difficult not to be persuaded by the weight of documentation Martin Bernal brings to his task and his rather dazzling analytical insights. What struck me in his analysis were the *process* of the fabrication of Ancient Greece and the *motives* for the fabrication. The latter (motive) involved the concept of purity, of progress. The former (process) required misreading, pre-determined selectivity of authentic sources, and – silence. From the Christian theological appropriation of Israel (the Levant), to the early nineteenth-century work of the prodigious Karl Müller, work that effectively dismissed the Greeks' own record of their influences and origins as their "Egyptomania," their tendency to be "wonderstruck" by Egyptian culture, a tendency "manifested in the 'delusion' that Egyptians and other non-European 'barbarians' had possessed superior cultures, from which the Greeks had borrowed massively,"[6] on through the Romantic response to the Enlightenment, and the decline into disfavor of the Phoenicians, "the essential force behind the rejection of the tradition of massive Phoenician influence on early Greece was the rise of racial – as opposed to religious – anti-Semitism. This was because the Phoenicians were correctly perceived to have been culturally very close to the Jews."[7]
I have quoted at perhaps too great a length from Bernal's text because *motive*, so seldom an element brought to bear on the history of history,

is located, delineated and confronted in Bernal's research, and has helped my own thinking about the process and motives of scholarly attention to and an appraisal of Afro-American presence in the literature of the United States.

Canon building is empire building. Canon defense is national defense. Canon debate, whatever the terrain, nature and range (of criticism, of history, of the history of knowledge, of the definition of language, the universality of aesthetic principles, the sociology of art, the humanistic imagination), is the clash of cultures. And all of the interests are vested.

In such a melee as this one – a provocative, healthy, explosive melee – extraordinarily profound work is being done. Some of the controversy, however, has degenerated into *ad hominem* and unwarranted speculation on the personal habits of artists, specious and silly arguments about politics (the destabilizing forces are dismissed as merely political; the status quo sees itself as not – as though the term "*a*political" were only its prefix and not the most obviously political stance imaginable since one of the functions of political ideology is to pass itself off as immutable, natural and "innocent"), and covert expressions of critical inquiry designed to neutralize and disguise the political interests of the discourse. Yet much of the research and analysis has rendered speakable what was formerly unspoken and has made humanistic studies once again the place where one has to go to find out what's going on. Cultures whether silenced or monologistic, whether repressed or repressing, seek meaning in the language and images available to them.

Silences are being broken, lost things have been found and at least two generations of scholars are disentangling received knowledge from the apparatus of control, most notably those who are engaged in investigations of French and British Colonialist Literature, American slave narratives, and the delineation of the Afro-American literary tradition.

Now that Afro-American artistic presence has been "discovered" actually to exist, now that serious scholarship has moved from silencing the witnesses and erasing their meaningful place in and contribution to American culture, it is no longer acceptable merely to imagine us and imagine for us. We have always been imagining ourselves. We are not Isak Dinesen's "aspects of nature," nor [Joseph] Conrad's unspeaking. We are the subjects of our own narrative, witnesses to and participants in our own experience, and, in no way coincidentally, in the experience of those with whom we have come in contact. We are not, in fact,

"other." We are choices. And to read imaginative literature by and
about us is to choose to examine centers of the self and to have the
opportunity to compare these centers with the "raceless" one with which
we are, all of us, most familiar.

II

Recent approaches to the reading of Afro-American literature have come
some distance; have addressed those arguments, mentioned earlier
(which are not arguments, but attitudes), that have, since the seventeenth
century, effectively silenced the autonomy of that literature. As for the
charge that "there is no Afro-American art," contemporary critical
analysis of the literature and the recent surge of reprints and re-
discoveries have buried it, and are pressing on to expand the traditional
canon to include classic Afro-American works where generically and
chronologically appropriate, and to devise strategies for reading and
thinking about these texts.

As to the second silencing charge, "Afro-American art exists, but it is
inferior," again, close readings and careful research into the culture out
of which the art is born have addressed and still address the labels that
once passed for stringent analysis but can no more: that it is imitative,
excessive, sensational, mimetic (merely), and unintellectual, though very
often "moving," "passionate," "naturalistic," realistic" or sociologically
"revealing." These labels may be construed as compliments or pejora-
tives and if valid, and shown as such, so much the better. More often
than not, however, they are the lazy, easy brand-name applications when
the hard work of analysis is deemed too hard, or when the critic does
not have access to the scope the work demands. Strategies designed to
counter this lazy labeling include the application of recent literary
theories to Afro-American literature so that non-canonical texts can be
incorporated into existing and forming critical discourse.

The third charge, that "Afro-American art exists, but is superior only
when it measures up to the 'universal' criteria of Western art," produces
the most seductive form of analysis, for both writer and critic, because
comparisons are a major form of knowledge and flattery. The risks,
nevertheless, are twofold: 1) The gathering of a culture's difference into
the skirts of the Queen is a neutralization designed and constituted to
elevate and maintain hegemony. 2) Circumscribing and limiting the

literature to a mere reaction to or denial of the Queen, judging the work solely in terms of its referents to Eurocentric criteria, or its sociological accuracy, political correctness or its pretense of having no politics at all, cripple the literature and infantilize the serious work of imaginative writing. This response-oriented concept of Afro-American literature contains the seeds of the next (fourth) charge: that when Afro-American art is worthy, it is because it is "raw" and "rich," like ore, and like ore needs refining by Western intelligences. Finding or imposing Western influences in/on Afro-American literature has value, but when its sole purpose is to *place* value only where that influence is located it is pernicious.

My unease stems from the possible, probable, consequences these approaches may have upon the work itself. They can lead to an incipient orphanization of the work in order to issue its adoption papers. They can confine the discourse to the advocacy of diversification within the canon and/or a kind of benign co-existence near or within reach of the already sacred texts. Either of these two positions can quickly become another kind of silencing if permitted to ignore the indigenous created qualities of the writing. So many questions surface and irritate. What have these critiques made of the work's own canvas? Its paint, its frame, its framelessness, its spaces? Another list of approved subjects? Of approved treatments? More self-censoring, more exclusion of the specificity of the culture, the gender, the language? Is there perhaps an alternative utility in these studies? To advance power or locate its fissure? To oppose elitist interests in order to enthrone egalitarian effacement? Or is it merely to rank and grade the readable product as distinct from the writeable production? Can this criticism reveal ways in which the author combats and confronts received prejudices and even creates *other terms* in which to rethink one's attachment to or intolerance of the material of these works? What is important in all of this is that the critic not be engaged in laying claim on behalf of the text to his or her own dominance and power. Nor to exchange his or her professional anxieties for the imagined turbulence of the text. "The text should become a problem of passion, not a pretext for it."

There are at least three focuses that seem to me to be neither reactionary nor simple pluralism, nor the even simpler methods by which the study of Afro-American literature remains the helpful doorman into the halls of sociology. Each of them, however, requires wakefulness.

One is the development of a theory of literature that truly accommodates Afro-American literature: one that is based on its culture, its history, and the artistic strategies the works employ to negotiate the world it inhabits.

Another is the examination and reinterpretation of the American canon, the founding nineteenth-century works, for the "unspeakable things unspoken"; for the ways in which the presence of Afro-Americans has shaped the choices, the language, the structure – the meaning of so much American literature. A search, in other words, for the ghost in the machine.

A third is the examination of contemporary and/or non-canonical literature for this presence, regardless of its category as mainstream, minority, or what you will. I am always amazed by the resonances, the structural gear-shifts, and the *uses* to which Afro-American narrative, persona and idiom are put in contemporary "white" literature. And in Afro-American literature itself the question of difference, of essence, is critical. What makes a work "Black"? The most valuable point of entry into the question of cultural (or racial) distinction, the one most fraught, is its language – its unpoliced, seditious, confrontational, manipulative, inventive, disruptive, masked and unmasking language. Such a penetration will entail the most careful study, one in which the impact of Afro-American presence on modernity becomes clear and is no longer a well-kept secret.

I would like to touch, for just a moment, on focuses two and three.

We can agree, I think, that invisible things are not necessarily "not-there"; that a void may be empty, but is not a vacuum. In addition, certain absences are so stressed, so ornate, so planned, they call attention to themselves; arrest us with intentionality and purpose, like neighborhoods that are defined by the population held away from them. Looking at the scope of American literature, I can't help thinking that the question should never have been "Why am I, an Afro-American, absent from it?" It is not a particularly interesting query anyway. The spectacularly interesting question is "What intellectual feats had to be performed by the author or his critic to erase me from a society seething with my presence, and what effect has that performance had on the work?" What are the strategies of escape from knowledge? Of willful oblivion? I am not recommending an inquiry into the obvious impulse that overtakes a soldier sitting in a World War I trench to think of salmon fishing. That kind of pointed "turning from," deliberate escapism or transcendence may be life-saving in a circumstance of immediate duress. The exploration I am suggesting is, how does one sit in the audience observing, watching the performance of Young America, say, in the nineteenth century, say, and reconstruct the play, its director, its plot and its cast in such a manner that its very point never surfaces? Not why. How? Ten years after [Alexis de] Tocqueville's prediction in 1840 that " 'Finding no stuff for the ideal in what is real and true, poets would flee to imaginary regions . . .' in 1850 at the height of slavery and burgeoning abolitionism, American writers chose romance."[8] Where, I wonder, in these romances is the shadow of the presence from which the text has fled? Where does it heighten, where does it dislocate, where does it necessitate novelistic invention; what does it release, what does it hobble?

The device (or arsenal) that serves the purpose of flight can be Romanticism versus verisimilitude; new criticism versus shabbily disguised and questionably sanctioned "moral uplift"; the "complex series of evasions," that is sometimes believed to be the essence of modernism, the perception of the evolution of art; the cultivation of irony, parody, the nostalgia for "literary language"; the rhetorically unconstrained textuality versus socially anchored textuality, and the undoing of textuality altogether. These critical strategies can (but need not) be put into service to reconstruct the historical world to suit specific cultural and political purposes. Many of these strategies have produced powerfully creative work. Whatever *uses* to which Romanticism is put, however suspicious its origins, it has produced an incontestably wonderful body of work. In other instances these strategies have succeeded in paralyzing both the work and its criticism. In still others they have led to a virtual infantilization of the writer's intellect, his sensibility, his craft. They have reduced the meditations on theory into a "power struggle among sects" reading unauthored and unauthorable material, rather than an outcome of reading *with* the author the text both construct.

In other words, the critical process has made wonderful work of some wonderful work, and recently the means of access to the old debates have altered. The problem now is putting the question. Is the nineteenth century flight from blackness, for example, successful in mainstream American literature? Beautiful? Artistically problematic? Is the text sabotaged by its own proclamations of "universality"? Are there ghosts in the machine? Active but unsummoned presences that can distort the workings of the machine and can also *make* it work? These kinds of

questions have been consistently put by critics of Colonial Literature vis-
à-vis Africa and India and other third world countries. American literature would benefit from similar critiques. I am made melancholy when I
consider that the act of defending the Eurocentric Western posture in
literature as not only "universal" but also "race-free" may have resulted
in lobotomizing that literature, and in diminishing both the art and the
artist. Like the surgical removal of legs so that the body can remain
enthroned, immobile, static – under house arrest, so to speak. It may be,
of course, that contemporary writers deliberately exclude from their
conscious writerly world the subjective appraisal of groups perceived as
"other," and whitemale writers frequently abjure and deny the excite-
ment of framing or locating their literature in the political world.
Nineteenth-century writers, however, would never have given it a
thought. Mainstream writers in Young America understood their competition to be national, cultural, but only in relationship to the Old
World, certainly not vis-à-vis an ancient race (whether Native American
or African) that was stripped of articulateness and intellectual thought,
rendered, in D. H. Lawrence's term, "uncreate." For these early American writers, how could there be competition with nations or peoples
who were presumed unable to handle or uninterested in handling the
written word? One could write about them, but there was never the
danger of their "writing back." Just as one could speak to them without
fear of their "talking back." One could even observe them, hold them in
prolonged gaze, without encountering the risk of being observed,
viewed, or judged in return. And if, on occasion, they were themselves
viewed and judged, it was out of a political necessity and, for the
purposes of art, could not matter. Or so thought Young America. It
could never have occurred to Edgar Allan Poe in 1848 that I, for
example, might read *The Gold Bug* and watch his efforts to render my
grandfather's speech to something as close to braying as possible, an
effort so intense you can see the perspiration – and the stupidity – when
Jupiter says "I knows," and Mr. Poe spells the verb "nose."*

Yet in spite or because of this monologism there is a great ornamental

---

* Author's note: Older America is not always distinguishable from its infancy. We may
pardon Edgar Allan Poe in 1848, but it should have occurred to Kenneth Lynn in 1986
that some young Native American might read his Hemingway biography and see herself
described as "squaw" by this respected scholar, and that some young men might shudder
reading the words "buck" and "half-breed" so casually included in his scholarly
speculations.

prescribed absence in early American literature and, I submit, it is instructive. It only seems that the canon of American literature is "naturally" or "inevitably" "white." In fact it is studiously so. In fact these absences of vital presences in Young American literature may be the insistent fruit of the scholarship rather than the text. Perhaps some of these writers, although under current house arrest, have much more to say than has been realized. Perhaps some were not so much transcending politics, or escaping blackness, as they were transforming it into intelligible, accessible, yet artistic modes of discourse. To ignore this possibility by never questioning the strategies of transformation is to disenfranchise the writer, diminish the text and render the bulk of the literature aesthetically and historically incoherent – an exorbitant price for cultural (whitemale) purity, and, I believe, a spendthrift one. The reexamination of founding literature of the United States for the unspeakable unspoken may reveal those texts to have deeper and other meanings, deeper and other power, deeper and other significances.

One such writer, in particular, it has been almost impossible to keep under lock and key is Herman Melville.

Among several astute scholars, Michael Rogin has done one of the most exhaustive studies of how deeply Melville's social thought is woven into his writing. He calls our attention to the connection Melville made between American slavery and American freedom, how heightened the one rendered the other. And he has provided evidence of the impact on the work of Melville's family, milieu, and, most importantly, the raging, all-encompassing conflict of the time: slavery. He has reminded us that it was Melville's father-in-law who had, as judge, decided the case that made the Fugitive Slave Law law, and that

> other evidence in *Moby Dick* also suggests the impact of Shaw's ruling on the climax of Melville's tale. Melville conceived the final confrontation between Ahab and the white whale some time in the first half of 1851. He may well have written his last chapters only after returning from a trip to New York in June. [Judge Shaw's decision was handed down in April, 1851.] When New York anti-slavery leaders William Seward and John van Buren wrote public letters protesting the *Sims* ruling, the New York *Herald* responded. Its attack on "The Anti-Slavery Agitators" began: "Did you ever see a whale? Did you ever see a mighty whale struggling?"[9]

Rogin also traces the chronology of the whale from its "birth in a state of nature" to its final end as commodity.[10] Central to his argument is that Melville in *Moby Dick* was being allegorically and insistently political in his choice of the whale. But within his chronology, one singular whale transcends all others, goes beyond nature, adventure, politics and commodity to an abstraction. What is this abstraction? This "wicked idea"? Interpretation has been varied. It has been viewed as an allegory of the state in which Ahab is Calhoun, or Daniel Webster; an allegory of capitalism and corruption, God and man, the individual and fate, and most commonly, the single allegorical meaning of the white whale is understood to be brute, indifferent Nature, and Ahab the madman who challenges that Nature.

But let us consider, again, the principal actor, Ahab, created by an author who calls himself Typee, signed himself Tawney, identified himself as Ishmael, and who had written several books before *Moby Dick* criticizing missionary forays into various paradises.

Ahab loses sight of the commercial value of his ship's voyage, its point, and pursues an idea in order to destroy it. His intention, revenge, "an audacious, immitigable and supernatural revenge," develops stature – maturity – when we realize that he is not a man mourning his lost leg or a scar on his face. However intense and dislocating his fever and recovery had been after his encounter with the white whale, however satisfactorily "male" this vengeance is read, the vanity of it is almost adolescent. But if the whale is more than blind, indifferent Nature insubduable by masculine aggression, if it is as much its adjective as it is its noun, we can consider the possibility that Melville's "truth" was his recognition of the moment in America when whiteness became ideology. And if the white whale is the ideology of race, what Ahab has lost to it is personal dismemberment and family and society and his own place as a human in the world. The trauma of racism is, for the racist and the victim, the severe fragmentation of the self, and has always seemed to me a cause (not a symptom) of psychosis – strangely of no interest to psychiatry. Ahab, then, is navigating between an idea of civilization that he renounces and an idea of savagery he must annihilate, because the two cannot co-exist. The former is based on the latter. What is terrible in its complexity is that the idea of savagery is not the missionary one: it is white racial ideology that is savage and if, indeed, a white, nineteenth-century, American male took on not abolition, not the amelioration of racist institutions or their laws, but the very concept of whiteness as an inhuman idea, he would be very alone, very desperate, and very doomed. Madness would be the only appropriate description of such audacity, and "he heaves me," the most succinct and appropriate description of that obsession.

I would not like to be understood to argue that Melville was engaged in some simple and simple-minded black/white didacticism, or that he was satanizing white people. Nothing like that. What I am suggesting is that he was overwhelmed by the philosophical and metaphysical inconsistencies of an extraordinary and unprecedented idea that had its fullest manifestation in his own time in his own country, and that that idea was the successful assertion of whiteness as ideology.

On the *Pequod* the multiracial, mainly foreign, proletariat is at work to produce a commodity, but it is diverted and converted from that labor to Ahab's more significant intellectual quest. We leave whale as commerce and confront whale as metaphor. With that interpretation in place, two of the most famous chapters of the book become luminous in a completely new way. One is Chapter 9, "The Sermon." In Father Mapple's thrilling rendition of Jonah's trials, emphasis is given to the purpose of Jonah's salvation. He is saved from the fish's belly for one single purpose, "To preach the Truth to the face of Falsehood! That was it!" Only then the reward "Delight" – which strongly calls to mind Ahab's lonely necessity. "Delight is to him . . . who against the proud gods and commodores of this earth, ever stand forth his own inexorable self. . . . Delight is to him whose strong arms yet support him, when the ship of this base treacherous World has gone down beneath him. Delight is to him who gives no quarter in the truth and kills, burns, and destroys all *sin* though he pluck it out from under the robes of Senators and judges. Delight – top-gallant delight is to him who acknowledges no law or lord, but the Lord his God, and is only a *patriot* to heaven" [italics mine]. No one, I think, has denied that the sermon is designed to be prophetic, but it seems unremarked what the nature of the sin is – the sin that must be destroyed, regardless. Nature? A sin? The terms do not apply. Capitalism? Perhaps. Capitalism fed greed, lent itself inexorably to corruption, but probably was not in and of itself sinful to Melville. Sin suggests a moral outrage within the bounds of man to repair. The concept of racial superiority would fit seamlessly. It is difficult to read those words ("destruction of sin," "patriot to heaven") and not hear in them the description of a different Ahab. Not an adolescent male in adult clothing, a maniacal egocentric, or the "exotic plant" that V. S. Parrington thought Melville was. Not even a morally fine liberal voice adjusting, balancing, compromising with racial institutions. But another

Ahab: the only white male American heroic enough to try to slay the monster that was devouring the world as he knew it.

Another chapter that seems freshly lit by this reading is Chapter 42, "The Whiteness of the Whale." Melville points to the do-or-die significance of his effort to say something unsayable in this chapter. "I almost despair," he writes, "of putting it in a comprehensive form. It was the whiteness of the whale that above all things appalled me. But how can I hope to explain myself here; and yet in some dim, random way, explain myself I must, *else all these chapters might be naught*" [italics mine]. The language of this chapter ranges between benevolent, beautiful images of whiteness and whiteness as sinister and shocking. After dissecting the ineffable, he concludes: "Therefore . . . symbolize whatever grand or gracious he will by whiteness, no man can deny that in its profoundest *idealized significance* it calls up a peculiar apparition to the soul." I stress "idealized significance" to emphasize and make clear (if such clarity needs stating) that Melville is not exploring white people, but whiteness idealized. Then, after informing the reader of his "hope to light upon some chance clue to conduct us to the hidden course we seek," he tries to nail it. To provide the key to the "hidden course." His struggle to do so is gigantic. He cannot. Nor can we. But in nonfigurative language, he identifies the imaginative tools needed to solve the problem: "subtlety appeals to subtlety, and without imagination no man can follow another into these halls." And his final observation reverberates with personal trauma. "This visible [colored] world seems formed in love, the invisible [white] spheres were formed in fright." The necessity for whiteness as privileged "natural" state, the invention of it, was indeed formed in fright.

"Slavery," writes Rogin, "confirmed Melville's isolation, decisively established in *Moby Dick*, from the dominant consciousness of his time." I differ on this point and submit that Melville's hostility and repugnance for slavery would have found company. There were many white Americans of his acquaintance who felt repelled by slavery, wrote journalism about it, spoke about it, legislated on it and were active in abolishing it. His attitude to slavery alone would not have condemned him to the almost autistic separation visited upon him. And if he felt convinced that blacks were worthy of being treated like whites, or that capitalism was dangerous – he had company or could have found it. But to question the very notion of white progress, the very idea of racial superiority, of whiteness as privileged place in the evolutionary ladder of humankind, and to meditate on the fraudulent, self-destroying philosophy of that superiority, to "pluck it out from under the robes of Senators and Judges," to drag the "judge himself to the bar," – that was dangerous, solitary, radical work. Especially then. Especially now. To be "only a patriot to heaven" is no mean aspiration in Young America for a writer – or the captain of a whaling ship.

A complex, heaving, disorderly, profound text is *Moby Dick*, and among its several meanings it seems to me this "unspeakable" one has remained the "hidden course," the "truth in the Face of Falsehood." To this day no novelist has so wrestled with its subject. To this day literary analyses of canonical texts have shied away from that perspective: the informing and determining Afro-American presence in traditional American literature. The chapters I have made reference to are only a fraction of the instances where the text surrenders such insights, and points a helpful finger toward the ways in which the ghost drives the machine.

Melville is not the only author whose works double their fascination and their power when scoured for this presence and the writerly strategies taken to address or deny it. Edgar Allan Poe will sustain such a reading. So will Nathaniel Hawthorne and Mark Twain, and in the twentieth century, Willa Cather, Ernest Hemingway, F. Scott Fitzgerald, and William Faulkner, to name a few. Canonical American literature is begging for such attention.

It seems to me a more than fruitful project to produce some cogent analysis showing instances where early American literature identifies itself, risks itself, to assert its antithesis to blackness. How its linguistic gestures prove the intimate relationship to what is being nulled by implying a full descriptive apparatus (identity) to a presence-that-is-assumed-not-to-exist. Afro-American critical inquiry can do this work.

I mentioned earlier that finding or imposing Western influences in/on Afro-American literature had value provided the valued process does not become self-anointing. There is an adjacent project to be undertaken – the third focus in my list: the examination of contemporary literature (both the sacred and the profane) for the impact Afro-American presence has had on the structure of the work, the linguistic practice, and fictional enterprise in which it is engaged. Like focus two, this critical process must also eschew the pernicious goal of equating the fact of that presence with the achievement of the work. A work does not get better because it is responsive to another culture; nor does it become automatically flawed because of that responsiveness. The point is to clarify, not to enlist. And it does not "go without saying" that a work written by an Afro-American is automatically subsumed by an enforcing Afro-American presence. There is a clear flight from blackness in a great deal of Afro-American literature. In others there is the duel with blackness, and in some cases, as they say, "You'd never know."

III

It is on this area, the impact of Afro-American culture on contemporary American literature, that I now wish to comment. I have already said that works by Afro-Americans can respond to this presence (just as non-black works do) in a number of ways. The question of what constitutes the art of a black writer, for whom that modifier is more search than fact, has some urgency. In other words, other than melanin and subject matter, what, in fact, may make me a black writer? Other than my own ethnicity – what is going on in my work that makes me believe it is demonstrably inseparable from a cultural specificity that is Afro-American?

Please forgive the use of my own work in these observations. I use it not because it provides the best example, but because I know it best, know what I did and why, and know how central these queries are to me. Writing is, *after* all, an act of language, its practice. But *first* of all it is an effort of the will to discover.

Let me suggest some of the ways in which I activate language and ways in which that language activates me. I will limit this perusal by calling attention only to the first sentences of the books I've written, and hope that in exploring the choices I made, prior points are illuminated.

The Bluest Eye begins "Quiet as it's kept, there were no marigolds in the fall of 1941." That sentence, like the ones that open each succeeding book, is simple, uncomplicated. Of all the sentences that begin all the books, only two of them have dependent clauses, the other three are simple sentences and two are stripped down to virtually subject, verb, modifier. Nothing fancy here. No words need looking up; they are ordinary, everyday words. Yet I hoped the simplicity was not simple-minded, but devious, even loaded. And that the process of selecting each word, for itself and its relationship to the others in the sentence, along with the rejection of others for their echoes, for what is determined and what is not determined, what is almost there and what must be gleaned, would not theatricalize itself, would not erect a proscenium – at least not a noticeable one. So important to me was this unstaging, that in this first novel I summarized the whole of the book on the first page. (In the first edition, it was printed in its entirety on the jacket.)

The opening phrase of this sentence, "Quiet as it's kept," had several attractions for me. First, it was a familiar phrase familiar to me as a child listening to adults; to black women conversing with one another; telling a story, an anecdote, gossip about someone or event within the circle, the family, the neighborhood. The words are conspiratorial. "Shh, don't tell anyone else," and "No one is allowed to know this." It is a secret between us and a secret that is being kept from us. The conspiracy is both held and withheld, exposed and sustained. In some sense it was precisely what the act of writing the book was: the public exposure of a private confidence. In order fully to comprehend the duality of that position, one needs to think of the immediate political climate in which the writing took place, 1965–1969, during great social upheaval in the life of black people. The publication (as opposed to the writing) involved the exposure; the writing was the disclosure of secrets, secrets "we" shared and those withheld from us by ourselves and by the world outside the community.

"Quiet as it's kept," is also a figure of speech that is written, in this instance, but clearly chosen for how speakerly it is, how it speaks and bespeaks a particular world and its ambience. Further, in addition to its "back fence" connotation, its suggestion of illicit gossip, of thrilling revelation, there is also, in the "whisper," the assumption (on the part of the reader) that the teller is on the inside, knows something others do not, and is going to be generous with this privileged information. The intimacy I was aiming for, the intimacy between the reader and the page, could start up immediately because the secret is being shared, at best, and eavesdropped upon, at the least. Sudden familiarity or instant intimacy seemed crucial to me then, writing my first novel. I did not want the reader to have time to wonder "What do I have to do, to give up, in order to read this? What defense do I need, what distance maintain?" Because I know (and the reader does not – he or she has to wait for the second sentence) that this is a terrible story about things one would rather not know anything about.

What, then, is the Big Secret about to be shared? The thing we (reader and I) are "in" on? A botanical aberration. Pollution, perhaps. A skip, perhaps, in the natural order of things: a September, an autumn, a fall without marigolds. Bright common, strong and sturdy marigolds. When? In 1941, and since that is a momentous year (the beginning of World War II for the United States), the "fall" of 1941, just before the declaration of war, has a "closet" innuendo. In the temperate zone where there is a season known as "fall" during which one expects marigolds to be at their peak, in the months before the beginning of US participation in World War II, something grim is about to be divulged. The next sentence will make it clear that the saver, the one who knows, is a child speaking, mimicking the adult black women on the porch or in the backyard. The opening phrase is an effort to be grown-up about this shocking information. The point of view of a child alters the priority an adult would assign the information. "We thought it was because Pecola was having her father's baby that the marigolds did not grow" foregrounds the flowers, backgrounds illicit, traumatic, incomprehensible sex coming to its dreamed fruition. This foregrounding of "trivial" information and backgrounding of shocking knowledge secures the point of view but gives the reader pause about whether the voice of children can be trusted at all or is more trustworthy than an adult's. The reader is thereby protected from a confrontation too soon with the painful details, while simultaneously provoked into a desire to know them. The novelty, I thought, would be in having this story of female violation revealed from the vantage point of the victims or could-be victims of rape – the persons no one inquired of (certainly not in 1965) – the girls themselves. And since the victim does not have the vocabulary to understand the violence or its context, gullible, vulnerable girl friends, looking back as the knowing adults they pretended to be in the beginning, would have to do that for her, and would have to fill those silences with their own reflective lives. Thus, the opening provides the stroke that announces something more than a secret shared, but a silence broken, a void filled, an unspeakable thing spoken at last. And they draw the connection between a minor destabilization in seasonal flora with the insignificant destruction of a black girl. Of course "minor" and "insignificant" represent the outside world's view – for the girls both phenomena are earthshaking depositories of information they spend that whole year of childhood (and afterwards) trying to fathom, and cannot. If they have any success, it will be in transferring the problem of fathoming to the presumably adult reader, to the inner circle of listeners. At the least they have distributed the weight of these problematical questions to a larger constituency, and justified the public exposure of a privacy. If the conspiracy that the opening words announce is entered into by the reader, then the book can be seen to open with its close: a speculation on the disruption of "nature," as being a social disruption with tragic individual consequences in which the reader, as part of the population of the text, is implicated.

However a problem, unsolved, lies in the central chamber of the novel. The shattered world I built (to complement what is happening to Pecola), its pieces held together by seasons in childtime and commenting at every turn on the incompatible and barren white family primer, does not in its present form handle effectively the silence at its center. The void that is Pecola's "unbeing." It should have had a shape – like the emptiness left by a boom or a cry. It required a sophistication unavailable to me, and some deft manipulation of the voices around her. She is not *seen* by herself until she hallucinates a self. And the fact of her hallucination becomes a point of outside-the-book conversation, but does not work in the reading process.

Also, although I was pressing for a female expressiveness (a challenge that re-surfaced in *Sula*), it eluded me for the most part, and I had to content myself with female personae because I was not able to secure throughout the work the feminine subtext that is present in the opening sentence (the women gossiping, eager and aghast in "Quiet as it's kept"). The shambles this struggle became is most evident in the section on Pauline Breedlove where I resorted to two voices, hers and the urging narrator's, both of which are extremely unsatisfactory to me. It is interesting to me now that where I thought I would have the most difficulty subverting the language to a feminine mode, I had the least: connecting Cholly's "rape" by the whitemen to his own of his daughter. This most masculine act of aggression becomes feminized in my language, "passive," and, I think, more accurately repellent when deprived of the male "glamour of shame" rape is (or once was) routinely given.

The points I have tried to illustrate are that my choices of language (speakerly, aural, colloquial), my reliance for full comprehension on codes embedded in black culture, my effort to effect immediate co-conspiracy and intimacy (without any distancing, explanatory fabric), as well as my (failed) attempt to shape a silence while breaking it are attempts (many unsatisfactory) to transfigure the complexity and wealth of Afro-American culture into a language worthy of the culture.

In *Sula*, it's necessary to concentrate on the *two* first sentences because what survives in print is not the one I had intended to be the first. Originally the book opened with "Except for World War II nothing ever interfered with National Suicide Day." With some encouragement, I recognized that it was a false beginning. "*In medias res*" with a vengeance, because there was no *res* to be in the middle of – no implied world in which to locate the specificity and the resonances in the sentence. More to the point, I knew I was writing a second novel, and that it too would be about people in a black community not just foregrounded but totally dominant; and that it was about black women – also foregrounded and dominant. In 1988, certainly, I would not need (or feel the need for) the sentence – the short section – that now opens *Sula*. The threshold between the reader and the black-topic text need not be the safe, welcoming lobby I persuaded myself it needed at that time. My preference was the demolition of the lobby altogether. As can be seen from *The Bluest Eye*, and in every other book I have written, only *Sula* has this "entrance." The others refuse the "presentation"; refuse the seductive safe harbor; the line of demarcation between the sacred and the obscene, public and private, them and us. Refuse, in effect, to cater to the diminished expectations of the reader, or his or her alarm heightened by the emotional luggage one carries into the black-topic text. (I should remind you that *Sula* was begun in 1969, while my first book was in proof, in a period of extraordinary political activity.)

Since I had become convinced that the effectiveness of the original beginning was only in my head, the job at hand became how to construct an alternate beginning that would not force the work to genuflect and would complement the outlaw quality in it. The problem presented itself this way: to fashion a door. Instead of having the text open wide the moment the cover is opened (or, as in *The Bluest Eye*, to have the book stand exposed before the cover is even touched, much less opened, by placing the complete "plot" on the first page – and finally on the cover of the first edition), here I was to posit a door, turn its knob and beckon for some four or five pages. I had determined not to mention any characters in those pages, there would be no people in the lobby – but I did, rather heavy-handedly in my view, end the welcome aboard with the mention of Shadrack and Sula. It was a craven (to me, still) surrender to a worn-out technique of novel writing: the overt announcement to the reader whom to pay attention to. Yet the bulk of the opening I finally wrote is about the community, a view of it, and the view is not from within (this is a door, after all) but from the point of view of a stranger – the "valley man" who might happen to be there on some errand, but who obviously does not live there and to and for whom all this is mightily strange, even exotic. You can see why I despise much of this beginning. Yet I tried to place in the opening sentence the signature terms of loss: "There used to be a neighborhood here; not any more." That may not be the world's worst sentence, but it doesn't "play," as they say in the theater.

My new first sentence became "In that place, where they tore the nightshade and blackberry patches from their roots to make room for the Medallion City Golf Course, there was once a neighborhood." Instead of my original plan, here I am introducing an outside-the-circle reader into the circle. I am translating the anonymous into the specific, a "place" into a "neighborhood," and letting a stranger in through whose eyes it can be viewed. In between "place" and "neighborhood" I now have to squeeze the specificity and the *difference*; the nostalgia, the history, and the nostalgia for the history; the violence done to it and the consequences of that violence. (It took three months, those four pages, a whole summer of nights.) The nostalgia is sounded by "once"; the history and a longing for it is implied in the connotation of "neighborhood." The violence lurks in having something torn out by its roots – it will not, cannot grow again. Its consequences are that what has been destroyed is considered weeds, refuse necessarily removed in urban "development" by the unspecified but no less known "they" who do not, cannot, afford to differentiate what is displaced, and would not care that this is "refuse" of a certain kind. Both plants have darkness in them: "black" and "night." One is unusual (nightshade) and has two darkness words: "night" and "shade." The other (blackberry) is common. A familiar plant and an exotic one. A harmless one and a dangerous one. One produces a nourishing berry: one delivers toxic ones. But they both thrived there together, *in that place when it was a neighborhood*. Both are gone now, and the description that follows is of the other specific things, in this black community, destroyed in the wake of the golf course. Golf conveys what it is not, in this context: not houses, or factories, or even a public park, and certainly not residents.

It is a manicured place where the likelihood of the former residents showing up is almost nil.

I want to get back to those berries for a moment (to explain, perhaps, the length of time it took for the language of that section to arrive). I always thought of Sula as quintessentially black, metaphysically black, if you will, which is not melanin and certainly not unquestioning fidelity to the tribe. She is new world black and new world woman extracting choice from choicelessness, responding inventively to found things. Improvisational. Daring, disruptive, imaginative, modern, out-of-the-house, outlawed, unpolicing, uncontained and uncontainable. And dangerously female. In her final conversation with Nel she refers to herself as a special kind of black person woman, one with choices. Like a redwood, she says. (With all due respect to the dream landscape of Freud, trees have always seemed feminine to me.) In any case, my perception of Sula's double-dose of *chosen* blackness and *biological* blackness is in the presence of those two words of darkness in "nightshade" as well as in the uncommon quality of the vine itself. One variety is called "enchanter," and the other "bittersweet" because the berries taste bitter at first and then sweet. Also nightshade was thought to counteract witchcraft. All of this seemed a wonderful constellation of signs for Sula. And "blackberry patch" seemed equally appropriate for Nel: nourishing, never needing to be tended or cultivated, once rooted and bearing. Reliably sweet but thorn-bound. Her process of becoming, heralded by the explosive dissolving of her fragilely-held-together ball of string and fur (when the thorns of her self-protection are removed by Eva), puts her back in touch with the complex, contradictory, evasive, independent, liquid modernity Sula insisted upon. A modernity which overturns pre-war definitions, ushers in the Jazz Age (an age *defined* by Afro-American art and culture), and requires new kinds of intelligences to define oneself.

The stage-setting of the first four pages is embarrassing to me now, but the pains I have taken to explain it may be helpful in identifying the strategies one can be forced to resort to in trying to accommodate the mere fact of writing about, for and out of black culture while accommodating and responding to mainstream "white" culture. The "valley man's" guidance into the territory was my compromise. Perhaps it "worked," but it was not the work I wanted to do.

Had I begun with Shadrack, I would have ignored the smiling welcome and put the reader into immediate confrontation with his wound and his scar. The difference my preferred (original) beginning would have made would be calling greater attention to the traumatic displacement this most wasteful capitalist war had on black people in particular, and throwing into relief the creative, if outlawed, determination to survive it whole. Sula as (feminine) solubility and Shadrack's (male) fixative are two extreme ways of dealing with displacement – a prevalent theme in the narrative of black people. In the final opening I replicated the demiurge of discriminatory, prosecutorial racial oppression in the loss to commercial "progress" of the village, but the references to the community's stability and creativeness (music, dancing, craft, religion, irony, wit all referred to in the "valley man's" presence) refract and subsume their pain while they are in the thick of it. It is a softer embrace than Shadrack's organized, public madness – his disruptive remembering presence which helps (for a while) to cement the community, until Sula challenges them.

"The North Carolina Mutual Life Insurance agent promised to fly from Mercy to the other side of Lake Superior at 3:00."

This declarative sentence is designed to mock a journalistic style; with a minor alteration it could be the opening of an item in a small town newspaper. It has the tone of an everyday event of minimal local interest. Yet I wanted it to contain (as does the scene that takes place when the agent fulfills his promise) the information that *Song of Solomon* both centers on and radiates from.

The name of the insurance company is real, a well known black-owned company dependent on black clients, and in its corporate name are "life" and "mutual;" *agent* being the necessary ingredient of what enables the relationship between them. The sentence also moves from North Carolina to Lake Superior – geographical locations, but with a sly implication that the move from North Carolina (the south) to Lake Superior (the north) might not actually involve progress to some "superior state" – which, of course it does not. The two other significant words are "fly," upon which the novel centers and "Mercy," the name of the place from which he is to fly. Both constitute the heartbeat of the narrative. Where is the insurance man flying to? The other side of Lake Superior is Canada, of course, the historic terminus of the escape route for black people looking for asylum. "Mercy," the other significant term, is the grace note; the earnest though, with one exception, unspoken wish of the narrative's population. Some grant it; some never find it, one, at least, makes it the text and cry of her extemporaneous sermon upon the death of her granddaughter. It touches, turns and returns to Guitar at the end of the book – he who is least deserving of it – and moves him to make it his own final gift. It is what one wishes for Hagar; what is unavailable to and unsought by Macon Dead, senior; what his wife learns to demand from him, and what can never come from the white world as is signified by the inversion of the name of the hospital from Mercy to "no-Mercy." It is only available from within. The center of the narrative is flight; the springboard is mercy.

But the sentence turns, as all sentences do, on the verb: promised. The insurance agent does not declare, announce, or threaten his act. He promises, as though a contract is being executed – faithfully – between himself and others. Promises broken, or kept; the difficulty of ferreting out loyalties and ties that bind or bruise wend their way throughout the action and the shifting relationships. So the agent's flight, like that of the Solomon in the title, although toward asylum (Canada, or freedom, or home, or the company of the welcoming dead), and although it carries the possibility of failure and the certainty of danger, is toward change, an alternative way, a cessation of things-as-they-are. It should not be understood as a simple desperate act, the end of a fruitless life, a life without gesture, without examination, but as obedience to a deeper contract with his people. It is his commitment to them, regardless of whether, in all its details, they understand it. There is, however, in their response to his action, a tenderness, some contrition, and mounting respect ("They didn't know he had it in him.") and an awareness that the gesture enclosed rather than repudiated themselves. The note he leaves asks for forgiveness. It is tacked on his door as a mild invitation to whomever might pass by, but it is not an advertisement. It is an almost Christian declaration of love as well as humility of one who was not to do more.

There are several other flights in the work and they are motivationally different. Solomon's the most magical, the most theatrical and, for Milkman, the most satisfying. It is also the most problematic – to those left behind. Milkman's flight binds these two elements of loyalty (Mr. Smith's) and abandon and self-interest (Solomon's) into a third thing: a merging of fealty and risk that suggests the "agency" for "mutual" "life," which he offers at the end and which is echoed in the hills behind him, and is the marriage of surrender and domination, acceptance and rule, commitment to a group *through* ultimate isolation. Guitar recognizes this marriage and recalls enough of how lost he himself is to put his weapon down.

The journalistic style at the beginning, its rhythm of a familiar, hand-me-down dignity is pulled along by an accretion of detail displayed in a meandering unremarkableness. Simple words, uncomplex sentence structures, persistent understatement, highly aural syntax – but the ordinariness of the language, its colloquial vernacular, humorous and, upon occasion, parabolic quality sabotage expectations and mask judgments when it can no longer defer them. The composition of red, white and blue in the opening scene provides the national canvas/flag upon which the narrative works and against which the lives of these black people must be seen, but which must not overwhelm the enterprise the novel is engaged in. It is a composition of color that heralds Milkman's birth, protects his youth, hides its purpose and though which he must burst (through blue Buicks, red tulips in his waking dream, and his sisters' white stockings, ribbons and gloves) before discovering that the gold of his search is really Pilate's yellow orange and the glittering metal of the box in her ear.

These spaces, which I am filling in, and can fill in because they were planned, can conceivably be filled in with other significances. That is planned as well. The point is that into these spaces should fall the ruminations of the reader and his or her invented or recollected or misunderstood knowingness. The reader as narrator asks the questions the community asks, and both reader and "voice" stand among the crowd, within it, with privileged intimacy and contact, but without any more privileged information than the crowd has. That egalitarianism which places us all (reader, the novel's population, the narrator's voice) on the same footing reflected for me the force of flight and mercy, and the precious, imaginative yet realistic gaze of black people who (at one time, anyway) did not mythologize what or whom it mythologized. The "song" itself contains this unblinking evaluation of the miraculous and heroic flight of the legendary Solomon, an unblinking gaze which is lurking in the tender but amused choral-community response to the agent's flight. Sotto (but not completely) is my own giggle (in Afro-American terms) of the proto-myth of the journey to manhood. Whenever characters are cloaked in Western fable, they are in deep trouble, but the African myth is also contaminated. Unprogressive, unreconstructed, self-born Pilate is unimpressed by Solomon's flight and knocks Milkman down when, made new by his appropriation of his own family's fable, he returns to educate her with it. Upon hearing all he has to say, her only interest is filial. "Papa? . . . I've been carryin' Papa?" And her longing to hear the song, finally, is a longing for balm to die by, not a submissive obedience to history – anybody's.

The opening sentence of *Tar Baby*, "He believed he was safe," is the second version of itself. The first, "He thought he was safe," was discarded because "thought" did not contain the doubt I wanted to plant in the reader's mind about whether or not he really was – safe. "Thought" came to me at once because it was the verb my parents and grandparents used when describing what they had dreamed the night before. Not "I dreamt," or "It seemed" or even "I saw or did" this or that – but "I thought." It gave the dream narrative distance (a dream is not "real") and power (the control implied in thinking rather than dreaming). But to use "thought" seemed to undercut the faith of the character and the distrust I wanted to suggest to the reader. "Believe" was chosen to do the work properly. And the person who does the believing is, in a way, about to enter a dream world, and convinces himself, eventually, that he is in control of it. He believed; was convinced. And although the word suggests his conviction, it does not reassure the reader. If I had wanted the reader to trust this person's point of view I would have written "He was safe." Or, "Finally, he was safe." The unease about this view of safety is important because safety itself is the desire of each person in the novel. Locating it, creating it, losing it.

You may recall that I was interested in working out the mystery of a piece of lore, a folk tale, which is also about safety and danger and the skills needed to secure the one and recognize and avoid the other. I was not, of course, interested in re-telling the tale; I suppose that is an idea to pursue, but it is certainly not interesting enough to engage me for four years. I have said, elsewhere, that the exploration of the Tar Baby tale was like stroking a pet to see what the anatomy was like but not to disturb or distort its mystery. Folk lore may have begun as allegory for natural or social phenomena; it may have been employed as a retreat from contemporary issues in art, but folk lore can also contain myths that re-activate themselves endlessly through providers – the people who repeat, reshape, reconstitute and reinterpret them. The Tar Baby tale seemed to me to be about masks. Not masks as covering what is to be hidden, but how masks come to life, take life over, exercise the tensions between itself and what it covers. For Son, the most effective mask is none. For the others the construction is careful and delicately borne, but the masks they make have a life of their own and collide with those they come in contact with. The texture of the novel seemed to want leanness, architecture that was worn and ancient like a piece of mask sculpture: exaggerated, breathing, just athwart the representational life it displaced. Thus, the first and last sentences had to match, as the exterior planes match the interior, concave ones inside the mask. Therefore "He believed he was safe" would be the twin of "Lickety split, rickety split, rickety rickety split." This close is 1) the last sentence of the folk tale. 2) the action of the character. 3) the indeterminate ending that follows from the untrustworthy beginning. 4) the complimentary meter of its twin sister [u u / u u / with u u u / u u u /] and 5) the wide and marvelous space between the contradiction of those two images: from a dream of safety to the sound of running feet. The whole mediated world in between. This masked and unmasked; enchanted, disenchanted; wounded and wounding world is played out on and by the varieties of interpretation (Western and Afro-American) the Tar Baby myth has been (and continues to be) subjected to. Winging one's way through the vise and expulsion of history becomes possible in creative encounters with that history. Nothing, in those encounters, is safe, or should be. Safety is the foetus of power as well as protection from it, as the uses to which masks and myths are put in Afro-American culture remind us.

"124 was spiteful. Full of a baby's venom."

Beginning *Beloved* with numerals rather than spelled out numbers, it was my intention to give the house an identify separate from the street or even the city; to name it the way "Sweet Home" was named; the way plantations were named, but not with nouns or "proper" names – with numbers instead because numbers have no adjectives, no posture of coziness or grandeur or the haughty yearning of arrivistes and estate builders for the parallel beautifications of the nation they left behind, laying claim to instant history and legend. Numbers here constitute an address, a thrilling enough prospect for slaves who had owned nothing, least of all an address. And although the numbers, unlike words, can have no modifiers, I give these an adjective – spiteful (There are three others). The address is therefore personalized, but personalized by its own activity, not the pasted on desire for personality.

Also there is something about numerals that makes them spoken, heard, in this context, because one expects words to read in a book, not numbers to say, or hear. And the sound of the novel, sometimes cacophonous, sometimes harmonious, must be an inner ear sound or a sound just beyond hearing, infusing the text with a musical emphasis that words can do sometimes even better than music can. Thus the second sentence is not one: it is a phrase that properly, grammatically, belongs as a dependent clause with the first. Had I done that, however (124 was spiteful, comma, full of a baby's venom, or 124 was full of a baby's venom), I could not have had the accent on *full* [/ u u / u / u pause / u u u u / u].

Whatever the risks of confronting the reader with what must be immediately incomprehensible in that simple, declarative authoritative sentence, the risk of unsettling him or her, I determined to take. Because the *in medias res* opening that I am so committed to is here excessively demanding. It is abrupt, and should appear so. No native informant here. The reader is snatched, yanked, thrown into an environment completely foreign, and I want it as the first stroke of the shared experience that might be possible between the reader and the novel's population. Snatched just as the slaves were from one place to another, from any place to another, without preparation and without defense. No lobby, no door, no entrance – a gangplank, perhaps (but a very short one). And the house into which this snatching – this kidnapping – propels one, changes from spiteful to loud to quiet, as the sounds in the body of the ship itself may have changed. A few words have to be read before it is clear that 124 refers to the house (in most of the early drafts "The women *in the house* knew it" was simply "The women knew it." "House" was not mentioned for seventeen lines), and a few more have to be read to discover why it is spiteful, or rather the source of the spite. By then it is clear, if not at once, that something is beyond control, but is not beyond understanding since it is not beyond accommodation by both the "women" and the "children." The fully realized presence of the haunting is both a major incumbent of the narrative and sleight of hand. One of its purposes is to keep the reader preoccupied with the nature of the incredible spirit world while being supplied a controlled diet of the incredible political world.

The subliminal, the underground life of a novel is the area most likely to link arms with the reader and facilitate making it one's own. Because one must, to get from the first sentence to the next and the next and the next. The friendly observation post I was content to build and man in

Sula (with the stranger in the midst), or the down-home journalism of *Song of Solomon* or the calculated mistrust of the point of view in *Tar Baby* would not serve here. Here I wanted the compelling confusion of being there as they (the characters) are; suddenly, without comfort or succor from the "author," with only imagination, intelligence, and necessity available for the journey. The painterly language of *Song of Solomon* was not useful to me in *Beloved*. There is practically no color whatsoever in its pages, and when there is, it is so stark and remarked upon, it is virtually raw. Color seen for the first time, without its history. No built architecture as in *Tar Baby*, no play with Western chronology as in *Sula*; no exchange between book life and "real" life discourse – with printed text units rubbing up against seasonal black childtime units as in *The Bluest Eye*. No compound of houses, no neighborhood, no sculpture, no paint, no time, especially no time because memory, pre-historic memory, has no time. There is just a little music, each other and the urgency of what is at stake. Which is all they had. For that work, the work of language is to get out of the way.

I hope you understand that in this explication of how I practice language is a search for and deliberate posture of vulnerability to those aspects of Afro-American culture that can inform and position my work. I sometimes know when the work works, when *nommo* has effectively summoned, by reading and listening to those who have entered the text. I learn nothing from those who resist it, except, of course, the sometimes fascinating display of their struggle. My expectations of and my grati-tude to those critics who enter, are great. To those who talk about how as well as what; who identify the workings as well as the work; for whom the study of Afro-American literature is neither a crash course in neighborliness and tolerance, nor an infant to be carried, instructed or chastised or even whipped like a child, but the serious study of art forms that have much work to do, but are already legitimatized by their own cultural sources and predecessors – in or out of the canon I owe much.

For an author, regarding canons, it is very simple: in fifty, a hundred or more years his or her work may be relished for its beauty or its insight or it may be condemned for its vacuousness and pretension – and junked. Or in fifty or a hundred years the critic (as canon builder) may be applauded for his or her intelligent scholarship and powers of critical inquiry. Or laughed at for ignorance and shabbily disguised assertions of power – and junked. It's possible that the reputations of both will thrive, or that both will decay. In any case, as far as the future is concerned, when one writes, as critic or as author, all necks are on the line.

Notes

1   See *"Race," Writing, and Difference*, ed. Henry Louis Gates (Chicago: University of Chicago Press, 1986).

2   Among many examples, Ivan van Sertima, *They Came Before Columbus: The African Presence in Ancient America* (New York: Random House, 1976), xvi–xvii.

3   Tzvetan Todorov, "'Race,'Writing, and Culture," trans. Loulou Mack, in Gates, *"Race," Writing and Difference*, 370–80.

4   Terrence Rafferty, "Articles of Faith," *The New Yorker* (16 May 1988), 110–18.

5   Martin Bernal, *Black Athena*: *The Afroasiatic Roots of Classical Civilization*, volume 1: *The Fabrication of Ancient Greece 1785–1985* (New Brunswick: Rutgers University Press, 1987), 2.

6   Ibid., 310.

7   Ibid., 337.

8   See Michael Paul Rogin, *Subversive Genealogy: The Politics and Art of Herman Melville* (Berkeley and Los Angeles: University of California Press, 1985), 15.

9   Ibid., 107 and 142.

10   Ibid., 112.

THREE

Mama's Baby, Papa's Maybe: An American Grammar Book

Hortense J. Spillers

I

Let's face it. I am a marked woman, but not everybody knows my name. "Peaches" and "Brown Sugar," "Sapphire" and "Earth Mother," "Aunty," "Granny," God's "Holy Fool," a "Miss Ebony First," or "Black Woman at the Podium": I describe a locus of confounded identities, a meeting ground of investments and privations in the national treasury of rhetorical wealth. My country needs me, and if I were not here, I would have to be invented.

W. E. B. Du Bois predicted as early as 1903 that the twentieth century would be the century of the "color line." We could add to this spatiotemporal configuration another thematic of analogously terrible weight: if the "black woman" can be seen as a particular figuration of the split subject that psychoanalytic theory posits, then this century marks the site of "its" profoundest revelation. The problem before us is deceptively simple: the terms enclosed in quotation marks in the preceding paragraph isolate overdetermined nominative properties. Embedded in bizarre axiological ground, they demonstrate a sort of telegraphic coding; they are markers so loaded with mythical prepossession that there is no easy way for the agents buried beneath them to come clean. In that regard, the names by which I am called in the public place render an example of signifying property *plus*. In order for me to speak a truer word concerning myself, I must strip down through layers of attenuated meanings, made an excess in time, over time, assigned by a particular historical order, and there await whatever marvels of my own inventiveness. The personal pronouns are offered in the service of a collective function.

In certain human societies, a child's identity is determined through the line of the Mother, but the United States, from at least one author's point of view, is not one of them: "In essence, the Negro community has been forced into a matriarchal structure which, because it is so far out of line with the *rest of American society*, seriously retards the progress of the group as a whole, and imposes a crushing burden on the Negro male and, in consequence, on a great many Negro women as well" (Moynihan 75; emphasis mine).

The notorious bastard, from Vico's banished Roman mothers of such sons, to Caliban, to Heathcliff, and Joe Christmas, has no official female equivalent. Because the traditional rites and laws of inheritance rarely pertain to the female child, bastard status signals to those who need to know which son of the Father's is the legitimate heir and which one the impostor. For that reason, property seems wholly the business of the male. A "she" cannot, therefore, qualify for bastard, or "natural son" status, and that she cannot provides further insight into the coils and recoils of patriarchal wealth and fortune. According to Daniel Patrick Moynihan's celebrated "Report" of the late sixties, the "Negro Family" has no Father to speak of – his Name, his Law, his Symbolic function mark the impressive missing agencies in the essential life of the black community, the "Report" maintains, and it is, surprisingly, the fault of the Daughter, or the female line. This stunning reversal of the castration thematic, displacing the Name and the Law of the Father to the territory of the Mother and Daughter, becomes an aspect of the African-American female's misnaming. We attempt to undo this misnaming in order to reclaim the relationship between Fathers and Daughters within this social matrix for a quite different structure of cultural fictions. For Daughters and Fathers are here made to manifest the very same rhetorical symptoms of absence and denial, to embody the double and contrastive agencies of a *prescribed* internecine degradation. "Sapphire" enacts her "Old Man" in drag, just as her "Old Man" becomes "Sapphire" in outrageous caricature.

In other words, in the historic outline of dominance, the respective subject-positions of "female" and "male" adhere to no symbolic integrity. At a time when current critical discourses appear to compel us more and more decidedly toward gender "undecidability," it would appear reactionary, if not dumb, to insist on the integrity of female/male gender. But undressing these conflations of meaning, as they appear under the rule of dominance, would restore, as figurative possibility, not only Power to the Female (for Maternity), but also Power to the Male (for Paternity). We would gain, in short, the *potential* for gender differentiation as it might express itself along a range of stress points, including human biology in its intersection with the project of culture.

Though among the most readily available "whipping boys" of fairly recent public discourse concerning African-Americans and national policy, "The Moynihan Report" is by no means unprecedented in its conclusions; it belongs, rather, to a class of symbolic paradigms that 1) inscribe "ethnicity" as a scene of negation and 2) confirm the human body as a metonymic figure for an entire repertoire of human and social arrangements. In that regard, the "Report" pursues a behavioral rule of public documentary. Under the Moynihan rule, "ethnicity" itself identifies a total objectification of human and cultural motives – the "white" family, by implication, and the "Negro Family," by outright assertion, in a constant opposition of binary meanings. Apparently spontaneous, these "actants" are *wholly* generated, with neither past nor future, as tribal currents moving out of time. Moynihan's "Families" are pure present and always tense. "Ethnicity" in this case freezes in meaning, takes on constancy, assumes the look and the affects of the Eternal. We could say, then, that in its powerful stillness, "ethnicity," from the point of view of the "Report," embodies nothing more than a mode of memorial time, as Roland Barthes outlines the dynamics of myth (see "Myth Today," 109–59; esp. 122–3). As a signifier that has no movement in the field of signification, the use of "ethnicity" for the living becomes purely appreciative, although one would be unwise not to concede its dangerous and fatal effects.

"Ethnicity" perceived as mythical time enables a writer to perform a variety of conceptual moves all at once. Under its hegemony, the human body becomes a defenseless target for rape and veneration, and the body, in its material and abstract phase, a resource for metaphor. For example, Moynihan's "tangle of pathology" provides the descriptive strategy for the work's fourth chapter, which suggests that "underachievement" in black males of the lower classes is primarily the fault of black females, who achieve out of all proportion, both to their numbers in the community and to the paradigmatic example before the nation: "Ours is a society which presumes male leadership in private and public affairs ... A subculture, such as that of the Negro American, in which this is not the pattern, is placed at a distinct disadvantage" (75). Between charts and diagrams, we are asked to consider the impact of qualitative measure on the black male's performance on standardized examinations, matriculation in schools of higher and professional training, etc. Even though Moynihan sounds a critique on his own argument here, he quickly withdraws from its possibilities, suggesting that black males should reign because that is the way the majority culture carries things out: "It is clearly a disadvantage for a minority group to be operating under one principle, while the great majority of the population . . . is operating on another" (75). Those persons living according to the perceived "matriarchal" pattern are, therefore, caught in a state of social "pathology."

Even though Daughters have their own agenda with reference to this order of Fathers (imagining for the moment that Moynihan's fiction – and others like it – does not represent an adequate one and that there is, once we dis-cover him, a Father here), my contention that these social and cultural subjects make doubles, unstable in their respective identities, in effect transports us to a common historical ground, the socio-political order of the New World. That order, with its human sequence written in blood, *represents* for its African and indigenous peoples a scene of actual mutilation, dismemberment, and exile. First of all, their New-World, diasporic plight marked a *theft of the body* – a willful and violent (and unimaginable from this distance) severing of the captive body from its motive will, its active desire. Under these conditions, we lose at least *gender* difference *in the outcome*, and the female body and the male body become a territory of cultural and political maneuver, not at all gender-related, gender-specific. But this body, at least from the point of view of the captive community, focuses a private and particular space, at which point of convergence biological, sexual, social, cultural, linguistic, ritualistic, and psychological fortunes join. This profound intimacy of interlocking detail is disrupted, however, by externally imposed meanings and uses: 1) the captive body becomes the source of an irresistible, destructive sensuality; 2) at the same time – in stunning contradiction – the captive body reduces to a thing, becoming *being for* the captor; 3) in this absence *from* a subject position, the captured sexualities provide a physical and biological expression of "otherness"; 4) as a category of "otherness," the captive body translates into a potential for pornotroping and embodies sheer physical powerlessness that slides into a more general "powerlessness," resonating through various centers of human and social meaning.

But I would make a distinction in this case between "body" and "flesh" and impose that distinction as the central one between captive and liberated subject-positions. In that sense, before the "body" there is the "flesh," that zero degree of social conceptualization that does not escape concealment under the brush of discourse, or the reflexes of iconography. Even though the European hegemonies stole bodies – some of them female – out of West African communities in concert with the African "middleman," we regard this human and social irreparability as high crimes against the *flesh*, as the person of African females and African males registered the wounding. If we think of the "flesh" as a primary narrative, then we mean its seared, divided, ripped-apartness, riveted to the ship's hole, fallen, or "escaped" overboard.

One of the most poignant aspects of William Goodell's contemporaneous study of the North American slave codes gives precise expression to the tortures and instruments of captivity. Reporting an instance of Jonathan Edwards's observations on the tortures of enslavement, Goodell narrates: "The smack of the whip is all day long in the ears of those who are on the plantation, or in the vicinity; and it is used with such dexterity and severity as not only to lacerate the skin, but to tear out small portions of the flesh at almost every stake" (221). The anatomical specifications of rupture, of altered human tissue, take on the objective description of laboratory prose – eyes beaten out, arms, backs, skulls branded, a left jaw, a right ankle, punctured; teeth missing, as the calculated work of iron, whips, chains, knives, the canine patrol, the bullet.

These undecipherable markings on the captive body render a kind of hieroglyphics of the flesh whose severe disjunctures come to be hidden to the cultural seeing by skin color. We might well ask if this phenomenon of marking and branding actually "transfers" from one generation to another, finding its various *symbolic substitutions* in an efficacy of meanings that repeat the initiating moments? As Elaine Scarry describes the mechanisms of torture (Scarry 27–59), these lacerations, woundings, fissures, tears, scars, openings, ruptures, lesions, rendings, punctures of the flesh create the distance between what I would designate a cultural *vestibularity* and the *culture*, whose state apparatus, including judges, attorneys, "owners," "soul drivers," "overseers," and "men of God," apparently colludes with a protocol of "search and destroy." This body whose flesh carries the female and the male to the frontiers of survival bears in person the marks of a cultural text whose inside has been turned outside.

The flesh is the concentration of "ethnicity" that contemporary critical discourses neither acknowledge nor discourse away. It is this "flesh and blood" entity, in the vestibule (or "pre-view") of a colonized North America, that is essentially ejected from "The Female Body in Western Culture" (see Suleiman, ed.) but it makes good theory or commemorative "herstory" to want to "forget," or to have failed to realize, that the African female subjected, under these historic conditions, is not only the target of rape – in one sense, an interiorized violation of body and mind – but also the topic of specifically *externalized* acts of torture and prostration that we imagine as the peculiar province of *male* brutality and torture inflicted by other males. A female body strung from a tree limb, or bleeding from the breast on any given day of field work because the "overseer," standing the length of a whip, has popped her flesh open, adds a lexical and living dimension to the narratives of women in culture and society (Davis 9). This materialized scene of unprotected female flesh – of female flesh "ungendered" – offers a praxis and a theory, a text for living and for dying, and a method for reading both through their diverse mediations.

Among the myriad uses to which the enslaved community was put, Goodell identifies its value for medical research: "Assortments of diseased, damaged, and disabled Negroes, deemed incurable and otherwise worthless are *bought up*, it seems ... by medical institutions, to be experimented and operated upon, for purposes of "medical education" and the interest of medical science" (86–7; Goodell's emphasis). From the *Charleston Mercury* for October 12, 1838, Goodell notes this advertisement:

"To planters and others. – Wanted, Fifty Negroes, any person, having sick Negroes, considered incurable by their respective physicians, and wishing to dispose of them, Dr. S. will *pay cash* for Negroes affected with scrofula, or king's evil, confirmed hypochondriasm, apoplexy, diseases of the liver, kidneys, spleen, stomach and intestines, bladder and its appendages, diarrhea, dysentery, etc. *The highest cash price will be paid*, on application as above." at No. 110 Church Street, Charleston. (87; Goodell's emphasis)

This profitable "atomizing" of the captive body provides another angle on the divided flesh: we lose any hint or suggestion of a dimension of ethics, of relatedness between human personality and its anatomical features, between one human personality and another, between human personality and cultural institutions. To that extent, the procedures adopted for the captive flesh demarcate a total objectification, as the entire captive community becomes a living laboratory.

The captive body, then, brings into focus a gathering of social realities as well as a metaphor for value so thoroughly interwoven in their literal and figurative emphases that distinctions between them are virtually useless. Even though the captive flesh/body has been "liberated" and no one need pretend that even the quotation marks do not *matter*, dominant symbolic activity, the ruling episteme that releases the dynamics of naming and valuation, remains grounded in the originating metaphors of captivity and mutilation so that it is as if neither time nor history, nor historiography and its topics, shows movement, as the human subject is "murdered" over and over again by the passions of a bloodless and anonymous archaism, showing itself in endless disguise. Faulkner's young Chick Mallison in *The Mansion* calls "it" by other names – "the ancient subterrene atavistic fear . . ." (227). And I would call it the Great Long National Shame. But people do not talk like that anymore – it is "embarrassing," just as the retrieval of mutilated female bodies will likely be "backward" for some people. Neither the shameface of the embarrassed, nor the not-looking-back of the self-assured is of much interest to us, and will not help at all if rigor is our dream. We might concede, at the very least, that sticks and bricks *might* break our bones, but words will most certainly *kill* us.

The symbolic order that I wish to trace in this writing, calling it an "American grammar," begins at the "beginning," which is really a rupture and a radically different kind of cultural continuation. The massive demographic shifts, the violent formation of a modern African consciousness, that take place on the subsaharan Continent during the initiative strikes which open the Atlantic Slave Trade in the fifteenth century of our Christ, interrupted hundreds of years of black African culture. We write and think, then, about an outcome of aspects of African-American life in the United States under the pressure of those events. I might as well add that the familiarity of this narrative does nothing to appease the hunger of recorded memory, nor does the persistence of the repeated rob these well-known, oft-told events of their power, even now, to startle. In a very real sense, every writing as revision makes the "discovery" all over again.

II

The narratives by African peoples and their descendants, though not as numerous from those early centuries of the "execrable trade" as the researcher would wish, suggest, in their rare occurrence, that the visual shock waves touched off when African and European "met" reverberated on both sides of the encounter. The narrative of the "Life of Olaudah Equiano, or Gustavus Vassa, the African. Written by Himself," first published in London in 1789, makes it quite clear that the first Europeans Equiano observed on what is now Nigerian soil *were* as unreal for him as he and others must have been for the European captors. The cruelty of "these white men with horrible looks, red faces, and long hair," of these "spirits," as the narrator would have it, occupies several pages of Equiano's attention, alongside a firsthand account of Nigerian interior life (27ff.). We are justified in regarding the outcome of Equiano's experience in the same light as he himself might have – as a "fall," as a veritable descent into the loss of communicative force.

If, as Todorov points out, the Mayan and Aztec peoples "lost control of communication" (61) in light of Spanish intervention, we could observe, similarly, that Vassa falls among men whose language is not only strange to him, but whose habits and practices strike him as "astonishing":

> [The sea, the slave ship] filled me with astonishment, which was soon converted into terror, when I was carried on board. I was immediately handled, and tossed up to see if I were sound, by some of the crew, and I was now persuaded that I had gotten into a world of bad spirits, and that they were going to kill me. Their complexions, too, differing so much from ours, their long hair, and the language they spoke (which was different from any I had ever heard), united to confirm me in this belief. (Equiano 27)

The captivating party does not only "earn" the right to dispose of the captive body as it sees fit, but gains, consequently, the right to name and "name" it: Equiano, for instance, identifies at least three different names that he is given in numerous passages between his Benin homeland and the Virginia colony, the latter and England – "Michael," "Jacob," "Gustavus Vassa" (35; 36).

The nicknames by which African-American women have been called, or regarded, or imagined on the New World scene – the opening lines of this essay provide examples – demonstrate the powers of distortion that the dominant community seizes as its unlawful prerogative. Moynihan's "Negro Family," then, borrows its narrative energies from the grid of associations, from the semantic and iconic folds buried deep in the collective past, that come to surround and signify the captive person. Though there is no absolute point of chronological initiation, we might repeat certain familiar impression points that lend shape to the business of dehumanized naming. Expecting to find direct and amplified reference to African women during the opening years of the Trade, the observer is disappointed time and again that this cultural subject is concealed beneath the mighty debris of the itemized account, between the lines of the massive logs of commercial enterprise that overrun the sense of clarity we believed we had gained concerning. this collective humiliation. Elizabeth Donnan's enormous, four-volume documentation becomes a case in point.

Turning directly to this source, we discover what we had not expected to find – that this aspect of the search is rendered problematic and that observations of a field of manners and its related sociometries are an outgrowth of the industry of the "exterior other" (Todorov 3), called "anthropology" later on. The European males who laded and captained these galleys and who policed and corralled these human beings, in hundreds of vessels from Liverpool to Elmina, to Jamaica; from the Cayenne Islands, to the ports at Charleston and Salem, and for three centuries of human life, were not curious about this "cargo" that bled, packed like so many live sardines among the immovable objects. Such inveterate obscene blindness might be denied, point blank, as a possibility for anyone, except that we know it happened.

Donnan's first volume covers three centuries of European "discovery" and "conquest," beginning 50 years before pious Cristobal, Christum Ferens, the bearer of Christ, laid claim to what he thought was the "Indies." From Gomes Eannes de Azurara's "Chronicle of the Discovery and Conquest of Guinea, 1441–1448" (Donnan 1:18–41), we learn that the Portuguese probably gain the dubious distinction of having introduced black Africans to the European market of servitude. We are also reminded that "Geography" is not a divine gift. Quite to the contrary, its boundaries were shifted during the European "Age of Conquest" in giddy desperation, according to the dictates of conquering armies, the edicts of prelates, the peculiar myopia of the medieval Christian mind. Looking for the "Nile River," for example, according to the fifteenth-century Portuguese notion, is someone's joke. For all that the pre-Columbian "explorers" knew about the sciences of navigation and geography, we are surprised that more parties of them did not end up "discovering" Europe. Perhaps, from a certain angle, that is precisely all that they found – an alternative reading of ego. The Portuguese, having little idea where the Nile ran, at least understood right away that there were men and women darker-skinned than themselves, but they were not specifically knowledgeable, or ingenious, about the various families and groupings represented by them. De Azurara records encounters with "Moors," "Mooresses," "Mulattoes," and people "black as Ethiops" (1: 28), but it seems that the "Land of Guinea," or of "Black Men," or of "The Negroes" (1: 35) was located anywhere southeast of Cape Verde, the Canaries, and the River Senegal, looking at an eighteenth-century European version of the subsaharan Continent along the West African coast (1: frontispiece).

Three genetic distinctions are available to the Portuguese eye, all along the riffs of melanin in the skin: in a field of captives, some of the observed are "white enough, fair to look upon, and well-proportioned." Others are less "white like mulattoes," and still others "black as Ethiops, and so ugly, both in features and in body, as almost to appear (to those who saw them) the images of a lower hemisphere" (1: 28). By implica-tion, this "third man," standing for the most aberrant phenotype to the observing eye, embodies the linguistic community most unknown to the European. Arabic translators among the Europeans could at least "talk" to the "Moors" and instruct them to ransom themselves, or else . . .

Typically, there is in this grammar of description the perspective of "declension," not of simultaneity, and its point of initiation is solipsistic – it begins with a narrative self, in an apparent unity of feeling, and unlike Equiano, who also saw "ugly" when he looked out, this collective self uncovers the means by which to subjugate the "foreign code of conscience," whose most easily remarkable and irremediable difference is perceived in skin color. By the time of De Azurara's mid-fifteenth century narrative and a century and a half before Shakespeare's "old black ram" of an Othello "tups" that "white ewe" of a Desdemona, the magic of skin color is already installed as a decisive factor in human dealings.

In De Azurara's narrative, we observe males looking at other males,

as "female" is subsumed here under the general category of estrangement. Few places in these excerpts carve out a distinct female space,
though there are moments of portrayal that perceive female captives in
the implications of socio-cultural function. When the field of captives
(referred to above) is divided among the spoilers, no heed is paid to
relations, as fathers are separated from sons, husbands from wives,
brothers from sisters and brothers, mothers from children – male and
female. It seems clear that the political program of European Christianity
promotes this hierarchical view among males, although it remains
puzzling to us exactly how this version of Christianity transforms the
"pagan" also into the "ugly." It appears that human beings came up
with degrees of "fair" and then the "hideous," in its overtones of
bestiality, as the opposite of "fair," all by themselves, without stage
direction, even though there is the curious and blazing exception of
Nietzsche's Socrates, who was Athens's ugliest and wisest and best
citizen. The intimate choreography that the Portuguese narrator sets
going between the "faithless" and the "ugly" transforms a partnership
of dancers into a single figure. Once the "faithless," indiscriminate of
the three stops of Portuguese skin color, are transported to Europe, they
become an altered human factor:

> And so their lot was now quite contrary to what it had been, since before
> they had lived in perdition of soul and body, of their souls, in that they
> were yet pagans, without the clearness and the light of the Holy Faith;
> and of their bodies, in that they lived like beasts, without any custom of
> reasonable beings – for they had no knowledge of bread and wine, and
> they were without covering of clothes, or the lodgment of houses, and
> worse than all, through the great ignorance that was in them, in that they
> had no understanding of good, but only knew how to live in bestial sloth.
> (1: 30)

The altered human factor renders an alterity of European ego, an
invention, or "discovery" as decisive in the full range of its social
implications as the birth of a newborn. According to the semantic
alignments of the excerpted passage, personhood, for this European
observer, locates an immediately outward and superficial determination,
gauged by quite arbitrarily opposed and *specular* categories: that these
"pagans" did not have "bread" and "wine" did not mean that they
were feastless, as Equiano observes about the Benin diet, c. 1745, in the
province of Essaka:

Our manner of living is entirely plain; for as yet the natives are unacquainted with those refinements in cookery which debauch the taste, bullocks, goats, and poultry supply the greatest part of their food. (These constitute likewise the principal wealth of the country, and the chief articles of its commerce.) The flesh is usually stewed in a pan; to make it savory we sometimes use pepper, and other spices, and we have salt made of wood ashes. Our vegetables are mostly plaintains, eadas, yams, beans and Indian corn. The head of the family usually eats alone, his wives and slaves have also their separate tables . . . (Equiano 8)

Just as fufu serves the Ghanaian diet today as a starch-and-bread-substitute, palm wine (an item by the same name in the eighteenth-century palate of the Benin community) need not be Heitz Cellars Martha's Vineyard and vice-versa in order for a guest, say, to imagine that she has enjoyed. That African housing arrangements of the fifteenth century did not resemble those familiar to De Azurara's narrator need not have meant that the African communities he encountered were without dwellings. Again, Equiano's narrative suggests that by the middle of the eighteenth century, at least, African living patterns were not only quite distinct in their sociometrical implications, but that also their architectonics accurately reflected the climate and availability of resources in the local circumstance: "These houses never exceed one story in height; they are always built of wood, or stakes driven into the ground, crossed with wattles, and neatly plastered within and without" (9). Hierarchical impulse in *both* De Azurara's and Equiano's narratives translates all *perceived* difference as a fundamental degradation or transcendence, but at least in Equiano's case, cultural practices are not observed in any intimate connection with skin color. For all intents and purposes, the politics of melanin, not isolated in its strange powers from the imperatives of a mercantile and competitive economics of European nation-states, will make of "transcendence" and "degradation" the basis of a historic violence that will rewrite the histories of modern Europe and black Africa. These mutually exclusive nominative elements come to rest on the same governing semantics – the ahistorical, or symptoms of the "sacred."

By August 1518, the Spanish king, Francisco de Los Covos, under the aegis of a powerful negation, could order "4000 negro slaves both male and female, provided they be Christians" to be taken to the Caribbean, "the islands and the mainland of the ocean sea already discovered or to be discovered" (Donnan 1: 42). Though the notorious "Middle Passage" be discovered" (Donnan 1: 42). Though the notorious "Middle Passage" appears to the investigator as a vast background without boundaries in time and space, we see it related in Donnan's accounts to the opening up of the entire Western hemisphere for the specific purposes of enslavement and colonization. De Azurara's narrative belongs, then, to a discourse of appropriation whose strategies will prove fatal to communities along the coastline of West Africa, stretching, according to Olaudah Equiano, "3400 miles, from Senegal to Angola, and (will include) a variety of kingdoms" (Equiano 5).

The conditions of "Middle Passage" are among the most incredible narratives available to the student, as it remains not easily imaginable. Late in the chronicles of the Atlantic Slave Trade, Britain's Parliament entertained discussions concerning possible "regulations" for slave vessels. A Captain Perry visited the Liverpool port, and among the ships that he inspected was "The Brookes," probably the most well-known image of the slave galley with its representative personae etched into the drawing like so many cartoon figures. Elizabeth Donnan's second volume carries the "Brookes Plan," along with an elaborate delineation of its dimensions from the investigative reporting of Perry himself: "Let it now be supposed ... further, that every man slave is to be allowed six feet by one foot four inches for room, every woman five feet ten by one foot four, every boy five feet by one foot two, and every girl four feet six by one foot..." (2: 592, n.). The owner of "The Brookes," James Jones, had recommended that "five females be reckoned as four males, and three boys or girls as equal to two grown persons" (2: 592).

These scaled inequalities complement the commanding terms of the dehumanizing, ungendering, and defacing project of African persons that De Azurara's narrator might have recognized. It has been pointed out to me that these measurements do reveal the application of the gender rule to the material conditions of passage, but I would suggest that "gendering" takes place within the confines of the domestic, an essential metaphor that then spreads its tentacles for male and female subject over a wider ground of human and social purposes. Domesticity appears to gain its power by way of a common origin of cultural fictions that are grounded in the specificity of proper names, more exactly, a patronymic, which, in turn, situates those persons it "covers" in a particular place. Contrarily, the cargo of a ship might not be regarded as elements of the domestic, even though the vessel that carries it is sometimes romantically (ironically?) personified as "she." The human cargo of a slave vessel – in the fundamental effacement and remission of African family and proper names – offers a counter-narrative to notions of the domestic.

Those African persons in "Middle Passage" were literally suspended in the "oceanic," if we think of the latter in its Freudian orientation as an analogy for undifferentiated identity: removed from the indigenous land and culture, and not-yet "American" either, these captive persons, without names that their captors would recognize, were in movement across the Atlantic, but they were also *nowhere* at all. Inasmuch as, on any given day, we might imagine, the captive personality did not know where s/he was, we could say that they were the culturally "unmade," thrown in the midst of a figurative darkness that "exposed" their destinies to an unknown course. Often enough for the captains of these galleys, navigational science of the day was not sufficient to guarantee the intended destination. We might say that the slave ship, its crew, and its human-as-cargo stand for a wild and unclaimed richness *of possibility* that is not interrupted, not "counted"/"accounted," or differentiated, until its movement gains the land thousands of miles, away from the point of departure. Under these conditions, one is neither female, nor male, as both subjects are taken into "account" as *quantities*. The female in "Middle Passage," as the apparently smaller physical mass, occupies "less room" in a directly translatable money economy. But she is, nevertheless, quantifiable by the same rules of accounting as her male counterpart.

It is not only difficult for the student to find "female" in "Middle Passage," but also, as Herbert S. Klein observes, "African women did not enter the Atlantic slave trade in anything like the numbers of African men. At all ages, men outnumbered women on the slave ships bound for America from Africa" (Klein 291). Though this observation does not change the reality of African women's captivity and servitude in New World communities, it does provide a perspective from which to contemplate the *internal* African slave trade, which, according to Africanists, remained a predominantly *female* market. Klein nevertheless affirms that those females forced into the trade were segregated "from men for policing purposes" ("African Women" 35). He claims that both "were allotted the same space between decks . . . and both were fed the same food" (35). It is not altogether clear from Klein's observations *for whom* the "police" kept vigil. It is certainly known from evidence presented in

Donnan's third volume ("New England and the Middle Colonies") that insurrection was both frequent and feared in passage, and we have not yet found a great deal of evidence to support a thesis that female captives participated in insurrectionary activity (see White 63–4). Because it was the rule, however – not the exception – that the African female, in both indigenous African cultures and in what becomes her "home," performed tasks of hard physical labor – so much so that the quintessential "slave" is *not* a male, but a female – we wonder at the seeming docility of the subject, granting her a "feminization" that enslavement kept at bay. Indeed, across the spate of discourse that I examined for this writing, the acts of enslavement and responses to it comprise a more or less agonistic engagement of confrontational hostilities among males. The visual and historical evidence betrays the dominant discourse on the matter as incomplete, but *counter*-evidence is inadequate as well: the sexual violation of captive females and their own express rage against their oppressors did not constitute events that captains and their crews rushed to record in letters to their sponsoring companies, or sons on board in letters home to their New England mamas.

One suspects that there are several ways to snare a mockingbird, so that insurrection might have involved, from time to time, rather more subtle means than mutiny on the "Felicity," for instance. At any rate, we get very little notion in the written record of the life of women, children, and infants in "Middle Passage," and no idea of the fate of the pregnant female captive and the unborn, which startling thematic bell hooks addresses in the opening chapter of her pathfinding work (see hooks 15–49). From hooks's lead, however, we might guess that the "reproduction of mothering" in this historic instance carries few of the benefits of a *patriarchilized* female gender, which, from one point of view, is the only female gender there is.

The relative silence of the record on this point constitutes a portion of the disquieting lacunae that feminist investigation seeks to fill. Such silence is the nickname of distortion, of the unknown human factor that a revised public discourse would both undo and reveal. This cultural subject is inscribed historically as anonymity/anomie in various public documents of European-American mal(e)venture, from Portuguese De Azurara in the middle of the fifteenth century, to South Carolina's Henry Laurens in the eighteenth.

What confuses and enriches the picture is precisely the sameness of anonymous portrayal that adheres tenaciously across the division of gender. In the vertical columns of accounts and ledgers that comprise Donnan's work, the terms "Negroes" and "Slaves" denote a common status. For instance, entries in one account, from September 1700 through September 1702, are specifically descriptive of the names of ships and the private traders in Barbados who will receive the stipulated goods, but "No. Negroes" and "Sum sold for per head" are so exactly arithmetical that it is as if these additions and multiplications belong to the other side of an equation (Donnan 2: 25). One is struck by the detail and precision that characterize these accounts, as a narrative, or story, is always implied by a man or woman's *name:* "Wm. Webster," "John Dunn," "Thos. Brownbill," "Robt. Knowles." But the "other" side of the page, as it were, equally precise, throws no *face* in view. It seems that nothing breaks the uniformity in this guise. If in no other way, the destruction of the African name, of kin, of linguistic, and ritual connections is so obvious in the vital stats sheet that we tend to overlook it. Quite naturally, the trader is not interested, in any *semantic* sense, in this "baggage" that he must deliver, but that he is not is all the more reason to search out the metaphorical implications of *naming* as one of the key sources of a bitter Americanizing for African persons.

The loss of the indigenous name/land provides a metaphor of displacement for other human and cultural features and relations, including the displacement of the genitalia, the female's and the male's desire that engenders future. The fact that the enslaved person's access to the issue of his/her own body is not entirely clear in this historic period throws in crisis all aspects of the blood relations, as captors apparently felt no obligation to acknowledge them. Actually trying to understand how the confusions of consanguinity worked becomes the project, because the outcome goes far to explain the rule of gender and its application to the African female in captivity.

III

Even though the essays in Claire C. Robertson and Martin A. Klein's *Women and Slavery in Africa* have specifically to do with aspects of the internal African slave trade, some of their observations shed light on the captivities of the Diaspora. At least these observations have the benefit of altering the kind of questions we might ask of these silent chapters.

For example, Robertson's essay, which opens the volume, discusses the term "slavery" in a wide variety of relationships. The enslaved person as property identifies the most familiar element of a most startling proposition. But to overlap *kinlessness* on the requirements of property might enlarge our view of the conditions of enslavement. Looking specifically at documents from the West African societies of Songhay and Dahomey, Claude Meillassoux elaborates several features of the property/kinless constellation that are highly suggestive for our own quite different purposes.

Meillassoux argues that "slavery creates an economic and social agent whose virtue lies in being outside the kinship system" ("Female Slavery," Robertson and Klein 501). Because the Atlantic trade involved heterogeneous social and ethnic formations in an explicit power relationship, we certainly cannot mean "kinship system" in precisely the same way that Meillassoux observes at work within the intricate calculus of descent among West African societies. However, the idea becomes useful as a point of contemplation when we try to sharpen our own sense of the African female's reproductive uses within the diasporic enterprise of enslavement and the genetic reproduction of the enslaved. In effect, under conditions of captivity, the offspring of the female does not "belong" to the Mother, nor is s/he "related" to the "owner," though the latter "possesses" it, and in the African-American instance, often fathered it, *and*, as often, without whatever benefit of patrimony. In the social outline that Meillassoux is pursuing, the offspring of the enslaved, "being unrelated both to their begetters and to their owners . . ., find themselves in the situation of being orphans" (50).

In the context of the United States, we could not say that the enslaved offspring was "orphaned," but the child does become, under the press of a patronymic, patrifocal, patrilineal, and patriarchal order, the man/ woman on the boundary, whose human and familial status, by the very nature of the case, had yet to be defined. I would call this enforced state of breach another instance of vestibular cultural formation where "kinship" loses meaning, *since it can be invaded at any given and arbitrary moment by the property relations*. I certainly do not mean to say that African peoples in the New World did not maintain the powerful ties of sympathy that bind blood-relations in a network of feeling, of continuity. It is precisely *that* relationship not customarily recognized by the code of slavery that historians have long identified as the inviolable

"Black Family" and further suggest that this structure remains one of the supreme social achievements of African-Americans under conditions of enslavement (see John Blassingame 79ff.).

Indeed, the *revised* "Black Family" of enslavement has engendered an older tradition of historiographical and sociological writings than we usually think. Ironically enough, E. Franklin Frazier's *Negro Family in the United States* likely provides the closest *contemporary* narrative of conceptualization for the "Moynihan Report." Originally published in 1939, Frazier's work underwent two redactions in 1948 and 1966. Even though Frazier's outlook on this familial configuration remains basically sanguine, I would support Angela Davis's skeptical reading of Frazier's "Black Matriarchate" (Davis 14). *"Except where the master's will was concerned,"* Frazier contends, this matriarchal figure "developed a spirit of independence and a keen sense of her personal rights" (1966: 47; emphasis mine). The "exception" in this instance tends to be overwhelming, as the African-American female's "dominance" and "strength" come to be interpreted by later generations – both black and white, oddly enough – as a "pathology," as an instrument of castration. Frazier's larger point, we might suppose, is that African-Americans developed such resourcefulness under conditions of captivity that "family" must be conceded as one of their redoubtable social attainments. This line of interpretation is pursued by Blassingame and Eugene Genovese (*Roll, Jordan, Roll* 70–5), among other US historians, and indeed assumes a centrality of focus in our own thinking about the impact and outcome of captivity.

It seems clear, however, that "Family," as we practice and understand it "in the West" – the vertical transfer of a bloodline, of a patronymic, of titles and entitlements, of real estate and the prerogatives of "cold cash," from *fathers* to *sons* and in the supposedly free exchange of affectional ties between a male and a female of *his* choice becomes the mythically revered privilege of a free and freed community. In that sense, African peoples in the historic Diaspora had nothing to prove, if the point had been that they were not capable of "family" (read "civilization"), since it is stunningly evident, in Equiano's narrative, for instance, that Africans were not only capable of the concept and the practice of "family," including "slaves," but in modes of elaboration and naming that were at least as complex as those of the "nuclear family" "in the West."

Whether or not we decide that the support systems that African-

Americans derived under conditions of captivity should be called "family," or something else, strikes me as supremely impertinent. The point remains that captive persons were forced into patterns of *dispersal*, beginning with the Trade itself, into the *horizontal* relatedness of language groups, discourse formations, bloodlines, names, and properties by the legal arrangements of enslavement. It is true that the most "well-meaning" of "masters" (and there must have been *some*) *could not*, *did not* alter the *ideological* and hegemonic mandates of dominance. It must be conceded that African-Americans, under the press of a hostile and compulsory patriarchal order, bound and determined to destroy them, or to preserve them only in the service and at the behest of the "master" class, exercised a degree of courage and will to survive that startles the imagination even now. Although it makes good revisionist history to read this tale *liberally*, it is probably truer than we know at this distance (and truer than contemporary social practice in the community would suggest on occasion) that the captive person developed, time and again, certain ethical and sentimental features that tied her and him, *across* the landscape to others, often sold from hand to hand, of the same and different blood in a common fabric of memory and inspiration.

We might choose to call this connectedness "family," or "support structure," but that is a rather different case from the moves of a dominant symbolic order, pledged to maintain the supremacy of race. It is that order that forces "family" to modify itself when it does not mean family of the "master," or dominant enclave. It is this rhetorical and symbolic move that declares primacy over any other human and social claim, and in that political order of things, "kin," just as gender formation, has no decisive legal or social efficacy.

We return frequently to Frederick Douglass's careful elaborations of the arrangements of captivity, and we are astonished each reading by two dispersed, yet poignantly related, familial enactments that suggest a connection between "kinship" and "property." Douglass tells us early in the opening chapter of the 1845 *Narrative* that he was separated in infancy from his mother: "For what this separation is (sic) done, I do not know, unless it be to hinder the development of the child's affection toward its mother, and to blunt and destroy the natural affection of the mother for the child. This is the inevitable result" (22).

Perhaps one of the assertions that Meillassoux advances concerning indigenous African formations of enslavement might be turned as a question, against the perspective of Douglass's witness: is the genetic reproduction of the slave and the recognition of the rights of the slave to his or her offspring a check on the *profitability* of slavery? And how so, if so? We see vaguely the route to framing a response, especially to the question's second half and perhaps to the first: the enslaved must not be permitted to perceive that he or she has any human rights that matter. Certainly if "kinship" were possible, the property relations would be undermined, since the offspring would then "belong" to a mother and a father. In the system that Douglass articulates, genetic reproduction becomes, then, not an elaboration of the life-principle in its cultural overlap, but an extension of the boundaries of proliferating properties. Meillassoux goes so far as to argue that "slavery exists where the slave class is reproduced through institutional apparatus: war and market" (50). Since, in the United States, the market of slavery identified the chief institutional means for maintaining a class of enforced servile labor, it seems that the biological reproduction of the enslaved was not alone sufficient to reenforce (sic) the estate of slavery. If, as Meillassoux contends, "femininity loses its sacredness in slavery" (641), then so does "motherhood" as female blood-rite/right. To that extent, the captive female body locates precisely a moment of converging political and social vectors that mark the flesh as a prime commodity of exchange. While this proposition is open to further exploration, suffice it to say now that this open exchange of female bodies in the raw offers a kind of Ur-text to the dynamics of signification and representation that the gendered female would unravel.

For Douglass, the loss of his mother eventuates in alienation from his brother and sisters, who live in the same house with him: "The early separation of us from our mother had well nigh blotted the fact of our relationship from our memories" (451). What could this mean? The *physical* proximity of the siblings survives the mother's death. They grasp their connection in the physical sense, but Douglass appears to mean a psychological bonding whose success mandates the *mother's* presence. Could we say, then, that the *feeling* of kinship is *not* inevitable? That it describes a relationship that appears "natural," but must be "cultivated" under actual material conditions? If the child's humanity is mirrored initially in the eyes of its mother, or the maternal function, then we might be able to guess that the social subject grasps the whole dynamic of resemblance and kinship by way of the same source.

There is an amazing thematic synonymity on this point between aspects of Douglass's *Narrative* and Malcolm El-Hajj Malik El-Shabazz's *Autobiography of Malcolm X* (21ff). Through the loss of the mother, in the latter contemporary instance, to the institution of "insanity" and the state – a full century after Douglass's writing and under social conditions that might be designated a post-emancipation neo-enslavement – Malcolm and his siblings, robbed of their activist father in a kkk-like ambush, are not only widely dispersed across a makeshift social terrain, but also show symptoms of estrangement and "disremembering" that require many years to heal, and even then, only by way of Malcolm's prison ordeal turned, eventually, into a redemptive occurrence.

The destructive loss of the natural mother, whose biological/genetic relationship to the child remains unique and unambiguous, opens the enslaved young to social ambiguity and chaos: the ambiguity of his/her fatherhood and to a structure of other relational elements, now threatened, that would declare the young's connection to a genetic and historic future by way of their own siblings. That the father in Douglass's case was most likely the "master," not by any means special to Douglass, involves a hideous paradox. Fatherhood, at best a supreme cultural courtesy, attenuates here on the one hand into a monstrous accumulation of power on the other. One has been "made" and "bought" by disparate currencies, linking back to a common origin of exchange and domination. The denied genetic link becomes the chief strategy of an undenied ownership, as if the interrogation into the father's identity – the blank space where his proper name will fit – were answered by the fact, *de jure* of a material possession. "And this is done," Douglass asserts, "too obviously to administer to the [masters'] own lusts, and make a gratification of their wicked desires profitable as well as pleasurable" (23).

Whether or not the captive female and/or her sexual oppressor derived "pleasure" from their seductions and couplings is not a question we can politely ask. Whether or not "pleasure" is possible at all under conditions that I would aver as non-freedom for both or either of the parties has not been settled. Indeed, we could go so far as to entertain the very real possibility that "sexuality," as a term of implied relationship and desire, is dubiously appropriate, manageable, or accurate to any of the familial arrangements under a system of enslavement, from the master's family to the captive enclave. Under these arrangements, the customary lexis of sexuality, including "reproduction," "motherhood," "pleasure," and "desire" are thrown into unrelieved crisis.

If the testimony of Linda Brent/Harriet Jacobs is to be believed, the official mistresses of slavery's "masters" constitute a privileged class of the tormented, if such contradiction can be entertained (Brent 29–35). Linda Brent/Harriet Jacobs recounts in the course of her narrative scenes from a "psychodrama," opposing herself and "Mrs. Flint," in what we have come to consider the classic alignment between captive woman and free. Suspecting that her husband, Dr. Flint, has sexual designs on the young Linda (and the doctor is nearly humorously incompetent at it, according to the story line), Mrs. Flint assumes the role of a perambulatory nightmare who visits the captive woman in the spirit of a veiled seduction. Mrs. Flint imitates the incubus who "rides" its victim in order to exact confession, expiation, and anything else that the immaterial power might want. (Gayle Jones's *Corregidora* (1975) weaves a contemporary fictional situation around the historic motif of entangled female sexualities.) This narrative scene from Brent's work, dictated to Lydia Maria Child, provides an instance of a repeated sequence, purportedly based on "real" life. But the scene in question appears to so commingle its signals with the fictive, with casebook narratives from psychoanalysis, that we are certain that the narrator has her hands on an explosive moment of New-World/US history that feminist investigation is beginning to unravel. The narrator recalls:

> Sometimes I woke up, and found her bending over me. At other times she whispered in my ear, as though it were her husband who was speaking to me, and listened to hear what I would answer. If she startled me, on such occasion, she would glide stealthily away; and the next morning she would tell me I had been talking in my sleep, and ask who I was talking to. At last, I began to be fearful for my life . . . (Brent 33)

The "jealous mistress" here (but "jealous" for whom?) forms an analogy with the "master" to the extent that male dominative modes give the male the material means to fully act out what the female might only *wish*. The mistress in the case of Brent's narrative becomes a metaphor for *his* madness that arises in the ecstasy of unchecked power. Mrs. Flint enacts a male alibi and prosthetic motion that is mobilized *at night*, at the material place of the dream work. In both male and female instances, the subject attempts to *inculcate* his or her will into the vulnerable, supine body. Though this is barely hinted on the surface of the text, we might say that Brent, between the lines of her narrative, demarcates a sexuality that is neuter-bound, inasmuch as it represents an open vulnerability to a gigantic sexualized repertoire that may be alternately expressed as male/female. Since the gendered female *exists for* the male, we might suggest that the ungendered female – in an amazing stroke of pansexual potential – might be invaded/raided by another woman or man.

If *Incidents in the Life of a Slave Girl* were a novel, and not the memoirs of an escaped female captive, then we might say that "Mrs. Flint" is also the narrator's projection, her creation, so that for all her pious and correct umbrage toward the outrage of her captivity, some aspect of Linda Brent is released in a manifold repetition crisis that the doctor's wife comes to stand in for. In the case of both an imagined fiction and the narrative we have from Brent/Jacobs/Child, published only four years before the official proclamations of Freedom, we could say that African-American women's community and Anglo-American women's community, under certain shared cultural conditions, were the twin actants on a common psychic landscape, were subject to the same fabric of dread and humiliation. Neither could claim her body and its various productions – for quite different reasons, albeit – as her own, and in the case of the doctor's wife, she appears not to have wanted her body at all, but to desire to enter someone else's, specifically, Linda Brent's, in an apparently classic instance of sexual "jealousy" and appropriation. In fact, from one point of view, we cannot unravel one female's narrative from the other's, cannot decipher one without tripping over the other. In that sense, these "threads cable-strong" of an incestuous, interracial genealogy uncover slavery in the United States as one of the richest displays of the psychoanalytic dimensions of culture before the science of European psychoanalysis takes hold.

IV

But just as we duly regard similarities between life conditions of American women – captive and free – we must observe those undeniable contrasts and differences so decisive that the African-American female's historic claim to the territory of womanhood and "femininity" still tends to rest too solidly on the subtle and shifting calibrations of a liberal ideology. Valerie Smith's reading of the tale of Linda Brent as a tale of "garreting" enables our notion that female gender for captive women's community is the tale writ between the lines and in the not-quite spaces of an American domesticity. It is this tale that we try to make clearer, or, keeping with the metaphor, "bring on line."

If the point is that the historic conditions of African-American women might be read as an unprecedented occasion in the national context, then gender and the arrangements of gender are both crucial and evasive. Holding, however, to a specialized reading of female gender as an *outcome* of a certain political, socio-cultural empowerment within the context of the United States, we would regard dispossession as the *loss* of gender, or one of the chief elements in an altered reading of gender: "Women are considered of no value, *unless* they continually increase their owner's stock. They were put on par with animals" (Brent 49; emphasis mine). Linda Brent's witness appears to contradict the point I would make, but I am suggesting that even though the enslaved female reproduced other enslaved persons, we do not read "birth" in this instance as a reproduction of mothering precisely because the female, like the male, has been robbed of the parental right, the parental function. One treads dangerous ground in suggesting an equation between female gender and mothering; in fact, feminist inquiry/praxis and the actual day-to-day living of numberless (sic) American women – black and white – have gone far to break the enthrallment of a female subject-position to the theoretical and actual situation of maternity. Our task here would be lightened considerably if we could simply slide over the powerful "No," the significant *exception*. In the historic formation to which I point, however, motherhood and female gendering/ungendering appear so intimately aligned that they seem to speak the same language. At least it is plausible to say that motherhood, while it does not exhaust the problematics of female gender, offers one prominent line of approach to it. I would go farther: Because African-American women experienced uncertainty regarding their infants' lives in the historic situation, gendering, in its coeval reference to African-American women, *insinuates* an implicit and unresolved puzzle both within current feminist discourse and within those discursive communities that investigate the entire problematics of culture. Are we mistaken to suspect that history – at least in this instance – repeats itself yet again?

Every feature of social and human differentiation disappears in public discourses regarding the African-American person, as we encounter, in the juridical codes of slavery, personality reified. William Goodell's study not only demonstrates the rhetorical and moral passions of the abolitionist project, but also lends insight into the corpus of law that underwrites enslavement. If "slave" is perceived as the essence of stillness (an early version of "ethnicity"), or of an undynamic human state, fixed in time and space, then the law articulates this impossibility as its inherent feature: "Slaves shall be deemed, sold, taken, reputed and adjudged in law to be *chattels personal*, in the hands of their owners and possessors, and their executors, administrators, and assigns, to all intents, constructions, and purposes whatsoever" (23; Goodell's emphasis).

Even though we tend to parody and simplify matters to behave as if the various civil codes of the slave-holding United States were monolithically informed, unified, and executed in their application, or that the "code" itself is spontaneously generated in an undivided historic moment, we read it nevertheless as exactly this – the *peak points*, the salient and characteristic features of a human and social procedure that evolves over a natural historical sequence and represents, consequently, the narrative *shorthand* of a transaction that is riddled, *in practice*, with contradictions, accident, and surprise. We could suppose that the legal encodations of enslavement stand for the statistically average case, that the legal code provides the *topics* of a project increasingly threatened and self-conscious. It is, perhaps, not by chance that the laws regarding slavery appear to crystallize in the precise moment when agitation against the arrangement becomes articulate in certain European and New-World communities. In that regard, the slave codes that Goodell describes are themselves an instance of the counter and isolated text that seeks to silence the contradictions and antitheses engendered by it. For example, aspects of Article 461 of the South Carolina Civil Code call attention to just the sort of uneasy oxymoronic character that the "peculiar institution" attempts to sustain in transforming *personality* into *property*.

1) The "slave" is movable by nature, but "immovable by the operation of law" (Goodell 24). As I read this, law itself is compelled to a point of saturation, or a reverse zero degree, beyond which it cannot move in the behalf of the enslaved or the free. We recall, too, that the "master," under these perversions of judicial power, is impelled to *treat* the enslaved as property, and not as person. These laws stand for the

kind of social formulation that armed forces will help excise from a living context in the campaigns of civil war. They also embody the untenable human relationship that Henry David Thoreau believed occasioned acts of "civil disobedience," the moral philosophy to which Martin Luther King, Jr. would subscribe in the latter half of the twentieth century.

2) Slaves shall be *reputed* and *considered* real estate, "subject to be mortgaged, according to the rules prescribed by law" (Goodell 24). I emphasize "reputed" and "considered" as predicate adjectives that invite attention because they denote a *contrivance*, not an intransitive "is," or the transfer of nominative property from one syntactic point to another by way a weakened copulative. The status of the "reputed" can change, as it will significantly before the nineteenth century closes. The mood here – the "shall be" – is pointedly subjunctive, or the situation devoutly to be wished. Th(at) the slave-holding class is forced, in time, to think and do something else is the narrative of violence that enslavement itself has been preparing for a couple of centuries.

Louisiana's and South Carolina's written codes offer a paradigm for praxis in those instances where a *written* text is missing. In that case, the "chattel principle has ... been affirmed and maintained by the courts, and involved in legislative acts" (Goodell 25). In Maryland, a legislative enactment of 1798 shows so forceful a synonymity of motives between branches of comparable governance that a line between "judicial" and "legislative" functions is useless to draw: "In case the personal property of a ward shall consist of specific articles, such as slaves, working beasts, animals of any kind, stock, furniture, plates, books, and so forth, the Court if it shall deem it advantageous to the ward, may at any time, pass an order for the sale thereof" (56). This inanimate and corporate ownership – the voting district of a ward – is here spoken for, or might be, as a single slave-holding male in determinations concerning property.

The eye pauses, however, not so much at the provisions of this enactment as at the details of its delineation. Everywhere in the descriptive document, we are stunned by the simultaneity of disparate items in a grammatical series: "Slave" appears in the same context with beasts of burden, all and any animal(s), various livestock, and a virtually endless profusion of domestic content from the culinary item to the book. Unlike the taxonomy of Borges's "Certain Chinese encyclopedia," whose contemplation opens Foucault's *Order of Things*, these items from a certain American encyclopedia do not sustain discrete and localized "powers of contagion," nor has the ground of their concatenation been desiccated beneath them. That imposed uniformity comprises the shock, that somehow this mix of named things, live and inanimate, collapsed by contiguity to the same text of "realism," carries a disturbingly prominent item of misplacement. To that extent, the project of liberation for African-Americans has found urgency in two passionate motivations that are twinned 1) to break apart, to rupture violently the laws of American behavior that make such syntax possible; 2) to introduce a new semantic field/fold more appropriate to his/her own historic movement. I regard this twin compulsion as distinct, though related, moments of the very same narrative process that might appear as a concentration or a dispersal. The narratives of Linda Brent, Frederick Douglass, and Malcolm El-Hajj Malik El-Shabazz (aspects of which are examined in this essay) each represent both narrative ambitions as they occur under the auspices of "author."

Relatedly, we might interpret the whole career of African-Americans, a decisive factor in national political life since the mid-seventeenth century, in light of the *intervening, intruding* tale, or the tale – like Brent's "garret" space – "between the lines," which are already inscribed, as a *metaphor* of social and cultural management. According to this reading, gender, or sex-role assignation, or the clear differentiation of sexual stuff, sustained elsewhere in the culture, does not emerge for the African-American female in this historic instance, except indirectly, except as a way to reenforce (sic) through the process of birthing, "the reproduction of the relations of production" that involves "the reproduction of the values and behavior patterns necessary to maintain the system of hierarchy in its various aspects of gender, class, and race or ethnicity" (Margaret Strobel, "Slavery and Reproductive Labor in Mombasa," Robertson and Klein 121). Following Strobel's lead, I would suggest that the foregoing identifies one of the three categories of reproductive labor that African-American females carry out under the regime of captivity. But this replication of ideology is never simple in the case of female subject-positions, and it appears to acquire a thickened layer of motives in the case of African-American females.

If we can account for an originary narrative and judicial principle that might have engendered a "Moynihan Report," many years into the twentieth century, we cannot do much better than look at Goodell's reading of the *partus sequitur ventrem*: the condition of the slave mother

is "forever entailed on all her remotest posterity." This maxim of civil
law, in Goodell's view, the "genuine and degrading principle of slavery,
inasmuch as it places the slave upon a level with brute animals, prevails
universally in the slave-holding states" (Goodell 27). But what is the
"condition" of the mother? Is it the "condition" of enslavement the
writer means, or does he mean the "mark" and the "knowledge" of the
mother upon the child that here translates into culturally forbidden and
impure? In an elision of terms, "mother" and "enslavement" are indis-
tinct categories of the illegitimate inasmuch as each if these synonymous
elements defines, in effect, a cultural situation that is *father-lacking*.
Goodell, who does not only report this maxim of law as an aspect of his
own factuality, but also regards it, as does Douglass, as a fundamental
degradation, supposes descent and identity through the female line as
comparable to a brute animality. Knowing already that there are human
communities that align social reproductive procedure according to the
line of the mother, and Goodell himself might have known it some years
later, we can only conclude that the provisions of patriarchy, here
exacerbated by the preponderant powers of an enslavng class, declare
Mother Right, by definition, a negating feature of human community.

Even though we are not even talking about any of the matriarchal
features of social production/reproduction – matrifocality, matrilinear-
ity, matriarchy – when we speak of the enslaved person, we perceive
that the dominant culture, in a fatal misunderstanding, assigns a
matriarchist value where it does not belong; actually *misnames* the
power of the female regarding the enslaved community. Such naming is
false because the female could not, in fact, claim her child, and false,
once again, because "motherhood" is not perceived in the prevailing
social climate as a legitimate procedure of cultural inheritance.

The African-American male has been touched, therefore, by the
mother, handed by her in ways that he cannot escape, and in ways that
the white American male is allowed to temporize by a fatherly reprieve.
This human and historic development – the text that has been inscribed
on the benighted heart of the continent – takes us to the center of an
inexorable difference in the depths of American women's community:
the African-American woman, the mother, the daughter, becomes historically the powerful and shadowy evocation of a cultural synthesis long
evaporated – the law of the Mother – only and precisely because legal
enslavement removed the African-American male not so much from

sight as from *mimetic* view as a partner in the prevailing social fiction of the Father's name, the Father's law.

Therefore, the female, in this order of things, breaks in upon the imagination with a forcefulness that marks both a denial and an "illegitimacy." Because of this peculiar American denial, the black American male embodies the *only* American community of males which has had the specific occasion to learn *who* the female is within itself, the infant child who bears the life against the could-be fateful gamble, against the odds of pulverization and murder, including her own. It is the heritage of the *mother* that the African-American male must regain as an aspect of his own personhood – the power of "yes" to the "female" within.

This different cultural text actually reconfigures, in historically ordained discourse, certain *representational* potentialities for African-Americans: 1) motherhood as female blood-rite is outraged, is denied, at the very *same time* that it becomes the founding term of a human and social enactment; 2) a dual fatherhood is set in motion, comprised of the African father's *banished* name and body and the captor father's mocking presence. In this play of paradox, only the female stands *in the flesh*, both mother and mother-dispossessed. This problematizing of gender places her, in my view, *out* of the traditional symbolics of female gender, and it is our task to make a place for this different social subject. In doing so, we are less interested in joining the ranks of gendered femaleness than gaining the *insurgent* ground as female social subject. Actually *claiming* the monstrosity (of a female with the potential to "name"), which her culture imposes in blindness, "Sapphire" might rewrite after all a radically different text for a female empowerment.

Works Cited

Barthes, Roland. *Mythologies*. Trans. Annette Lavers. New York: Hill and Wang, 1972.

Blassingame, John. *The Slave Community: Plantation Life in the Antebellum South*. New York: Oxford University Press, 1972.

Brent, Linda. *Incidents in the Life of a Slave Girl*. Ed. L. Maria Child. Introduced by Walter Teller. New York: Harvest, 1973.

Davis, Angela. *Women, Race, and Class*. New York: Random House, 1981.

De Azurara, Gomes Eannes. *The Chronicle of the Discovery and Conquest of*

Guinea. Trans. C. Raymond Beazley and Edgar Prestage. London: Hakluyt Society, 1896, 1897.

Donnan, Elizabeth. *Documents Illustrative of the History of the Slave Trade to America*. Washington, DC: The Carnegie Institution of Washington, 1932.

Douglass, Frederick. *Narrative of the Life of Frederick Douglass, An American Slave, Written by Himself*. New York: Signet Books, 1968.

El-Shabazz, Malcolm El-Hajj Malik. *Autobiography of Malcolm X*. With Alex Haley. Introduced by M. S. Handler. New York: Grove Press, 1966.

Equiano, Olaudah. "The Life of Olaudah Equiano, or Gustavus Vassa, the African, Written by Himself," in *Great Slave Narratives*. Introduced and selected by Arna Bontemps. Boston: Beacon Press, 1969.

Faulkner, William. *The Mansion*. New York: Vintage Books, 1965.

Frazier, E. Franklin. *The Negro Family in the United States*. Foreword by Nathan Glazer. Chicago: University of Chicago Press, 1966.

Genovese, Eugene. *Roll, Jordan, Roll: The World the Slaves Made*. New York: Pantheon Books, 1974.

Goodell, William. *The American Slave Code in Theory and Practice Shown by its Statutes, Judicial Decisions, and Illustrative Facts*. 3rd edn. New York: American and Foreign Anti-Slavery Society, 1853.

hooks, bell. *Ain't I a Woman? Black Women and Feminism*. Boston: South End Press, 1981.

Klein, Herbert. "African Women in the Atlantic Slave Trade," in Robertson and Klein, 29–39.

Meillassoux, Claude. "Female Slavery," in Robertson and Klein, 49–67.

Moynihan, Daniel P. "The Moynihan Report" (*The Negro Family: The Case for National Action*. Washington, DC: US Department of Labor, 1965), in *The Moynihan Report and the Politics of Controversy: A Transaction Social Science and Public Policy Report*. Ed. Lee Rainwater and William L. Yancey. Cambridge, MA: MIT Press, 1967.

Robertson, Claire and Martin A. Klein, eds. *Women and Slavery in Africa*. Madison: University of Wisconsin Press, 1983.

Scarry, Elaine. *The Body in Pain: The Making and Unmaking of the World*. New York: Oxford University Press, 1985.

Smith, Valerie. "Loopholes of Retreat. Architecture and Ideology in Harriet Jacob's *Incidents in the Life of a Slave Girl*," paper presented at the 1985 American Studies Association Meeting, San Diego. Cited in Henry Louis Gates, Jr., "What's Love Got to Do With It?" *New Literary History* 18: 2 (Winter 1987), 360.

Strobel, Margaret. "Slavery and Reproductive Labor in Mombasa," in Robertson and Klein, 111–30.

Suleiman, Susan, ed. *The Female Body in Western Culture*. Cambridge, MA: Harvard University Press, 1986.

Todorov, Tzvetan. *The Conquest of America: The Question of the Other*. Trans. Richard Howard. New York: Harper Colophon Books, 1984.

White, Deborah Grey. *Ar'n't I a Woman? Female Slaves in the Plantation South*. New York: W. W. Norton, 1985.

FOUR

A Black Man's Place in Black Feminist Criticism

Michael Awkward

The main theoretical task for male feminists, then, is to develop an analysis of their own position, and a strategy for how their awareness of their difficult and contradictory position in relation to feminism can be made explicit in discourse and practice.

Toril Moi, "Men Against Patriarchy"

She had been looking all along for a friend, and it took her a while to discover that a [male] lover was not a comrade and could never be – for a woman.

Toni Morrison, *Sula*

Critics eternally become and embody the generative myths of their culture by half-perceiving and half-inventing their culture, their myths, and themselves.

Houston Baker, *Afro-American Poetics*

Nor is theorizing of feminism adequate without some positioning of the person who is doing the theorizing.

Cary Nelson, "Men, Feminism: The Materiality of Discourse"

Many essays by male and female scholars devoted to exploring the subject of male critics' place in feminism generally agree about the uses and usefulness of the autobiographical male "I." Such essays suggest that citing the male critical self reflects a response to (apparent) self-difference, an exploration of the disparities between the masculine's antagonistic position in feminist discourse on the one hand and, on the other, the desire of the individual male critic to represent his difference with and from the traditional androcentric perspectives of his gender and culture. Put another way, in male feminist acts, to identify the writing self as biologically male is to emphasize the desire not to be ideologically male; it is to explore the process of rejecting the phallocentric perspectives by which men traditionally have justified the subjugation of women.[1]

In what strikes me as a particularly suggestive theoretical formulation, Joseph Boone articulates his sense of the goals of such male feminist autobiographical acts:

> In exposing the latent multiplicity and difference in the word "me(n)," we can perhaps open up a space within the discourse of feminism where a male feminist voice *can* have something to say beyond impossibilities and apologies and unresolved ire. Indeed, if the male feminist can discover a position *from which* to speak that neither elides the importance of feminism to his work nor ignores the specificity of his gender, his voice may also find that it no longer exists as an abstraction . . . but that it in fact inhabits a body: its own sexual/ textual body.[2]

Because of an awareness that androcentric perspectives are learned, are transmitted by means of specific sociocultural practices in such effective ways that they come to appear natural, male feminists such as Boone believe that, through an informed investigation of androcentric and feminist ideologies, individual men can work to resist the lure of the normatively masculine. That resistance for the aspiring male feminist requires, he says, exposing "the latent multiplicity and difference in the word 'men,' " in other words, disrupting both ideologies' unproblematized perceptions of monolithic and/or normative maleness (as villainous, antagonistic "other" for feminism, and, for androcentricism, powerful, domineering patriarch). At this early stage of male feminism's development, to speak self-consciously – autobiographically – is to explore, implicitly or explicitly, why and how the individual male experience (the "me" in men) has diverged from, has created possibilities for a rejection of, the androcentric norm.

And while there is not yet agreement as to what constitutes an identifiably male feminist act of criticism or about the usefulness of such acts for the general advancement of the feminist project, at least one possible explanation for a male critic's self-referential discourse is that it is a response to palpable mistrust – emanating from some female participants in feminism and perhaps from the writing male subject himself – about his motives. A skeptical strand of opinion with regard to male feminism is represented by Alice Jardine's "Men in Feminism: Odor di Uomo Or Campagnons de Route?" Having determined that the most useful measure of an adequately feminist text is its "*inscription of struggle – even of pain*" – an inscription of a struggle against patriarchy which Jardine finds absent from most male feminist acts, perhaps because "the historical fact that is the oppression of women [is] . . . one of their favorite blind spots" – she admits to some confusion as to the motivations for males' willing participation: "Why . . . would men want to be in feminism if it's about struggle? What do men want to be in – in pain?"[3]

In addition to seeking to cure its blindness where the history of female oppression is concerned, a male feminism must explore the motivations for its participation in what we might call, in keeping with Jardine's formulations, a discourse of (en)gendered pain. If one of the goals of male feminist self-referentiality is to demonstrate to females that individual males can indeed serve as allies in efforts to undermine androcentric power – and it seems that this is invariably the case – the necessary trust cannot be gained by insisting that motivation as such does not represent a crucial area that must be carefully negotiated. For example, I accept as accurate and, indeed, reflective of my own situation Andrew Ross's assertion that "there are those [men] for whom the *facticity* of feminism, for the most part, goes without saying . . ., who are young enough for feminism to have been a primary component of their intellectual formation."[4] However, in discussions whose apparent function is a foregrounding of both obstacles to and possibilities of a male feminism, men's relation(s) to the discourse can never go "without saying"; for the foreseeable future at least, this relation needs necessarily to be rigorously and judiciously theorized, and grounded explicitly in the experiential realm of the writing male subject.

But no matter how illuminating and exemplary one finds self-referential inscriptions of a male feminist critical self, if current views of the impossibility of a consistently truthful autobiographical act are correct, there are difficulties implicit in any such attempt to situate or inscribe that male self. Because, as recent theorizing on the subject has demonstrated, acts of discursive self-rendering unavoidably involve the creation of an idealized version of a unified or unifiable self, we can be certain only of the fact that the autobiographical impulse yields but some of the truths of the male feminist critic's experiences.[5] As is also the case for female participants, a male can never possess or be able to tell the whole truth and nothing but the truth about his relationship to feminist discourse and praxis.

But while autobiographical criticism, like the genre of autobiography itself, is poised tenuously between the poles of closure and disclosure, between representation and re-presentation, between a lived life and an invented one, I believe that even in the recoverable half-truths of my life are some of the materials that have shaped my perceptions, my beliefs, the self or selves that I bring to the interpretive act. In these half-truths is the source of my desire both to inscribe a black male feminism and to inscribe myself as a self-consciously racialized version of what Jardine considers a potentially oxymoronic entity – "male feminist" – whose literal, if not ideological or performative "blackness" is indisputable, and whose adequacy vis-à-vis feminism others must determine. By examining discussions of the phenomenon of the male feminist – that is to say, by reading male and female explorations of men's places in feminist criticism – and exploring responses of others to my own professional and personal relationships to feminism, I will identify autobiographically and textually grounded sources for my belief that while gendered difference might be said to complicate the prospect of a non-phallocentric black male feminism, it does not render such a project impossible.

At the outset, I acknowledge that mine is a necessary participation with regard to black feminist criticism in the half-invention, half-perception which, in Houston Baker's compelling formulation, represents every scholar's relationship to cultural criticism.[6] Such an acknowledgment is not intended to indicate that my male relationship to feminism is that of an illegitimate child, as it were. Rather, it is meant to suggest, like Elizabeth Weed's insistence on "the impossibility" of both men's and women's "relationship to feminism," my belief that while feminism represents a complex, sometimes self-contradictory "utopian vision" which no one can fully possess, a biological male can "develop political, theoretical [and, more generally, interpretive] strategies" which, though at most perhaps half-true to all that feminist ideologies are, nevertheless can assist in a movement toward actualizing the goals of feminism.[7]

I have been forced to think in especially serious ways about my own relationship to feminist criticism since I completed the first drafts of

Inspiriting Influence, my study of Afro-American women novelists.[8] I have questioned neither the explanatory power of feminism nor the essential importance of developing models adequate to the analysis of black female-authored texts, as my book – in harmony, I believe, with the black feminist project concerned with recovering and uncovering an Afro-American female literary tradition – attempts to provide on a limited scale. Instead, I have been confronted with suspicion about my gendered suitability for the task of explicating Afro-American women's texts, suspicion which has been manifested in the form of both specific responses to my project and general inquiries within literary studies into the phenomenon of the male feminist.

For example, a white female reader of the manuscript asserted – with undisguised surprise – that my work was "so feminist" and asked how I'd managed to offer such ideologically informed readings. Another scholar, a black feminist literary critic, recorded with no discernible hesitation her unease with my "male readings" of the texts of Zora Neale Hurston, Toni Morrison, Gloria Naylor, and Alice Walker. I wondered about the possibility of my being simultaneously "so feminist" and not so feminist (i.e., so "male"), about the meanings of these terms both for these scholars and for the larger interpretive communities in which they participate. Consequently, in what was perhaps initially an act of psychic self-protection, I began to formulate questions for which I still have found no consistently satisfactory answers. Were the differences in the readers' perceptions of the ideological adequacy of my study a function of their own views of feminist criticism, a product, in other words, of the differences not simply *within me* but *within feminism itself*? And if the differences within feminism are so significant, could I possibly satisfy everybody with "legitimate" interests in the texts of Hurston et al. by means of my own appropriated versions of black feminist discourse, my unavoidably half-true myth of what that discourse is, means, and does? Should my myth of feminism and its mobilization in critical texts be considered naturally less analytically compelling than that of a female scholar simply as a function of my biological maleness? And how could what I took to be a useful self-reflexivity avoid becoming a debilitating inquiry into a process that has come to seem for me, if not "natural," as Cary Nelson views his relationship to feminism, at least *necessary*?[9]

Compelled, and, to be frank, disturbed by such questions, I searched for answers in others' words, others' work. I purchased a copy of *Men in Feminism*, a collection which examines the possibility of men's participation as "comrades" (to use Toni Morrison's term) in feminist criticism and theory. Gratified by the appearance of such a volume, I became dismayed upon reading the editors' introductory remarks, which noted their difficulty in "locating intellectuals, who, having shown interest in the question, would offer, for instance, a gay or a black perspective on the problem."[10] While a self-consciously "gay . . . perspective" does find its way into the collection, the insights of nonwhite males and females are conspicuously absent.[11]

Even more troubling for me than the absence of black voices or, for that matter, of general inquiries into the effects of racial, cultural, and class differences on males' relationship to feminism, was the sense shared by many contributors of insurmountable obstacles to male feminism. In fact, the first essay, Stephen Heath's "Male Feminism," begins by insisting that "men's relation to feminism is an impossible one."[12] For me, Heath's formulations are insightful and provocative, if not always persuasive, as when he claims: "This is, I believe, the most any man can do today: to learn and so to try to write and talk or act in response to feminism, and so to try not in any way to be anti-feminist, supportive of the old oppressive structures. Any more, any notion of writing a feminist book or being a feminist, is a myth, a male imaginary with the reality of appropriation and domination right behind."[13] Is male participation in feminism restricted to being either appropriative and domineering or not antifeminist? Must we necessarily agree with Heath and others who claim that men cannot be feminists? To put the matter differently, is gender really an adequate determinant of "class" position?

Despite the poststructuralist tenor of Heath's work generally and of many of his perspectives here, his is an easily problematized essentialist claim – that, in effect, biology determines destiny and, therefore, one's relationship to feminist ideology, that womanhood allows one to become feminist at the same time that manhood necessarily denies that status to men. And while Heath embraces its notions of history as a narrative of male "appropriation and domination" of gendered others, he appears resistant at this point in his discourse to evidence of a powerful feminist institutional *present and presence*. I believe that we must acknowledge that feminism represents, at least in areas of the American academy, an incomparably productive, influential, and resilient ideology and institution that men, no matter how cunning, duplicitous, or culturally powerful, will neither control nor overthrow in the foreseeable future, one whose perspectives have proved and might continue to prove convincing even to biological males. In surveying the potential implications of the participation of biological men in feminism, we must therefore be honest about feminism's current persuasiveness and indomitability, about its clarifying, transformative potential, and about the fact that the corruptive possibility of both the purposefully treacherous and the only half-convinced male is, for today at least, slight indeed. Surely it is neither naive, presumptuous, nor premature to suggest that feminism as ideology and reading strategy has assumed a position of exegetical and institutional strength capable of withstanding even the most energetically masculinist acts of subversion.

Below I want to focus specifically on the question of a black male feminism. Rather than seeing it as an impossibility or as a subtle new manifestation of and attempt at androcentric domination, I want to show that certain instances of afrocentric feminism provide Afro-American men with an invaluable means of rewriting – of *re-vis(ion)*ing – our selves, our history and literary tradition, and our future.

Few would deny that black feminist literary criticism is an oppositional discourse constituted in large part as a response against black male participation in the subjugation of Afro-American women. From Barbara Smith's castigation of black male critics for their "virulently sexist . . . treatment" of black women writers and her insistence that they are "hampered by an inability to comprehend Black women's experience in sexual as well as racial terms" to Michele Wallace's characterization of the "black male Afro-Americanists who make pivotal use of Hurston's work" as "a gang," Afro-American men are generally perceived as non-allied others of black feminist discourse.[14] And, as is evident in Wallace's figuration of male Hurston scholars as intraracial street warriors, they are viewed at times as always already damned and unredeemable, even when they appear to take black women's writing seriously. We – I – must accept the fact that black male investigations informed by feminist principles, including this one, may never be good enough or ideologically correct enough for some black women who are feminists.

This sense of an unredeemable black male critic/ reader is in stark contrast to perspectives offered in such texts as Sherley Anne Williams's "Some Implications of Womanist Theory." In her essay, she embraces Alice Walker's term "womanist" – which, according to Williams, connotes a commitment "to the survival and wholeness of an entire people,

female and male, as well as a valorization of women's works in all their
varieties and multitudes" – because she considers the black feminist
project to be separatist in "its tendency to see not only a distinct black
female culture but to see that culture as a separate cultural form" from
"the facticity of Afro-American life."[15]

I believe that a black male feminism, whatever its connections to
critical theory or its specific areas of concern, can profit immensely from
what female feminists have to say about male participation. For
example, Valerie Smith's suggestion in "Gender and Afro-Americanist
Literary Theory and Criticism" that "Black male critics and theorists
might explore the nature of the contradictions that arise when they
undertake black feminist projects"[16] seems to me quite useful, as does
Alice Jardine's advice to male feminists. Speaking for white female
feminists, Jardine addresses white males who consider themselves to be
feminists: "We do not want you to *mimic* us, to become the same as us;
we don't want your pathos or your guilt; and we don't even want your
admiration (even if it's nice to get it once in a while). What we want, I
would even say what we need, is your *work*. We need you to get down
to serious work. And like all serious work, that involves struggle and
pain."[17] The womanist theoretical project that has been adopted by
Williams, Smith, and others provides aspiring Afro-American male
feminists with a useful model for the type of self-exploration that Smith
and Jardine advocate. What Williams terms "womanist theory" is
especially suggestive for Afro-American men because, while it calls for
feminist discussions of black women's texts and for critiques of black
androcentricism, womanism foregrounds a general black psychic health
as a primary objective. Williams argues that "what is needed is a
thoroughgoing examination of male images in the works of black male
writers"; her womanism, then, aims at "ending the separatist tendency
in Afro-American criticism," at leading black feminism away from "the
same hole The Brother has dug for himself – narcissism, isolation,
inarticulation, obscurity," at the creation and/ or continuation of black
"community and dialogue."[18]

If a black man is to become a useful contributor to black feminism,
he must, as Boone argues, "discover a position *from which* to speak that
neither elides the importance of feminism to his work nor ignores the
specificity of his gender." However multiply split we perceive the subject
to be, however deeply felt our sense of "maleness" and "femaleness" as
social constructions, however heightened our sense of the historical

consequences and current dangers of black androcentricism, a black male feminism cannot contribute to the continuation and expansion of the black feminist project by being so identified against or out of touch with itself as to fail to be both self-reflective and at least minimally self-interested. A black male feminist self-reflectivity of the type I have in mind necessarily would include examination of both the benefits and the dangers of a situatedness in feminist discourse. The self-interestedness of a black male feminist would be manifested in part by his concern with exploring a man's place. Clearly if convincing mimicry of female-authored concerns and interpretive strategies – speaking *like* a female feminist – is not in and of itself an appropriate goal for aspiring male participants, then a male feminism necessarily must explore males' various situations in the contexts and texts of history and the present.

Perhaps the most difficult task for a black male feminist is striking a workable balance between male self-inquiry/interest and an adequately feminist critique of patriarchy. To this point, especially in response to the commercial and critical success of contemporary Afro-American women's literature, scores of black men have proved unsuccessful in this regard. As black feminist critics such as Valerie Smith and Deborah McDowell have argued, the contemporary moment of black feminist literature has been greeted by many Afro-American males with hostility, self-interested misrepresentation, and a lack of honest intellectual intro-spection. In "Reading Family Matters," a useful discussion for black male feminism primarily as an exploration of what such a discourse ought not do and be, McDowell speaks of widely circulated androcentric male analyses of Afro-American feminist texts by writers such as Toni Morrison and Alice Walker:

> Critics leading the debate [about the representation of black men in black women's texts] have lumped all black women writers together and have focused on one tiny aspect of their immensely complex and diverse project – the image of black men – despite the fact that, if we can claim a center for these texts, it is located in the complexities of black female subjectivity and experience. In other words, though black women writers have made black women the subjects of their own family stories, these male readers/critics are attempting to usurp that place for themselves and place it at the center of critical inquiry.[19]

Although I do not believe that "the image of black men" is as microscopic an element in Afro-American women's texts as McDowell claims, I agree with her about the reprehensible nature of unabashed androcentrism found in formulations she cites by such writers as Robert Staples, Mel Watkins, and Darryl Pinckney. Nevertheless, in relation to the potential development of a black male feminism, I am troubled by what appears to be a surprisingly explicit determination to protect turf. In their unwillingness to grant that exploration of how Afro-American males are delineated by contemporary black female novelists is a legitimate concern that might produce illuminating analyses, McDowell's formulations echo in unfortunate ways those of anti-feminist male critics, white and black, who consider feminism to be an unredeemably myopic and unyielding interpretive strategy incapable of offering subtle readings of canonical, largely male-authored texts. Despite the circulation of reprehensibly masculinist responses to Afro-American women's literature, black feminist literary critics do not best serve the discourses that concern them by setting into motion homeostatic maneuvers intended to devalue all forms of inquiry except for those they hold to be most valuable (in this particular case, a female-authored scholarship that emphasizes Afro-American women's writings of black female subjectivity). If the Afro-American women's literary project is indeed "immensely complex and diverse," as McDowell claims, bringing to bear other angles of vision, including anti-patriarchal male ones, can assist in analyzing aspects of that complexity.

While the views of Staples and others are clearly problematic, those problems do not arise specifically from their efforts to place males "at the center of critical inquiry" any more than feminism is implicitly flawed because it insists, in some of its manifestations, on a gynocritical foregrounding of representations of women. Rather, these problems appear to result from the fact that the particular readers who produce these perspectives do not seem sufficiently to be, in Toril Moi's titular phrase, "men against patriarchy."[20] Certainly, in an age when both gender studies and Afro-American women's literature have achieved a degree of legitimacy within the academy and outside of it, it is unreasonable for black women either to demand that black men not be concerned with the ways in which they are depicted by Afro-American women writers, or to see that concern as intrinsically troubling in feminist terms. If female feminist calls for a non-mimicking male feminism are indeed persuasive, then black men will have very little of substance to say about contemporary Afro-American women's literature, especially if we are also to consider as transgressive any attention to figurations of black manhood. It seems to me that the most black females in feminism can insist upon in this regard is that examinations which focus on male characters treat the complexity of contemporary Afro-American women novelists' delineations of black manhood with an anti-patriarchal seriousness which the essays McDowell cites clearly lack.

From my perspective, what is potentially most valuable about the development of a black male feminism is not its capacity to reproduce black feminism as practiced by black females who focus primarily on "the complexities of black female subjectivity and experience."[21] Rather, its potential value lies in the possibility that, in being anti-patriarchal and as self-inquiring about their relationships to feminism as Afro-American women have been, black men can expand the range and utilization of feminist inquiry and explore other fruitful applications for feminist perspectives, including such topics as obstacles to a black male feminist project itself and new figurations of "family matters" and black male sexuality.

For the purpose of theorizing about a black male feminism, perhaps the most provocative, enlightening, and inviting moment in feminist or in "womanist" scholarship occurs in Hortense Spillers's "Mama's Baby, Papa's Maybe: An American Grammar Book." Indeed, Spillers's essay represents a fruitful starting point for new, potentially non-patriarchal figurations of family and of black males' relationship to the female. Toward the end of this illuminating theoretical text, which concerns itself with slavery's debilitating effects on the Afro-American family's constitution, Spillers envisions black male identity formation as a process whose movement toward successful resolution seems to require a serious engagement of black feminist principles and perspectives. Spillers asserts that as a result of those specific familial patterns which functioned during American slavery and beyond and "removed the African-American male not so much from sight as from *mimetic* view as a partner in the prevailing social fiction of the Father's name, the Father's law," the African-American male "has been touched . . . by the *mother, handed* by her in ways that he cannot escape." Because of separation from traditional American paternal name and law, "the black American male embodies the *only* American community of males which has had the specific occasion to learn *who* the female is within itself. . . . It is the heritage of the *mother* that the African-American male must regain as an aspect of his own personhood – the power of 'yes' to the 'female' within."[22]

Rather than seeing the "female" strictly as other for the Afro-American male, Spillers's afrocentric revisioning of psychoanalytic theory insists that we consider it an important aspect of the repressed in the black male self.[23] Employing Spillers's analyses as a starting point, we might regard American males' potential "in-ness" vis-à-vis feminism not, as Paul Smith insists in *Men in Feminism*, as a representation of male heterosexual desires to penetrate and violate female spaces[24] but rather as an acknowledgment of what Spillers considers the distinctive nature of the Afro-American male's connection to the "female." If Afro-American males are ever to have anything to say about or to black feminism beyond the types of reflex-action devaluations and diatribes about divisiveness that critics such as McDowell and Valerie Smith rightly decry, the investigative process of which womanist acts by Spillers and Williams speak is indispensable. Such a process, if pursued in an intellectually rigorous manner, offers a means by which black men can participate usefully in and contribute productively to the black feminist project.

Black womanism demands neither the erasure of the black gendered other's subjectivity, as have male movements to regain a putatively lost Afro-American manhood, nor the relegation of males to prone, domestic, or other limiting positions. What it does require, if it is indeed to become an ideology with widespread cultural impact, is a recognition on the part of both black females and males of the nature of the gendered inequities that have marked our past and present, and a resolute commitment to work for change. In that sense, black feminist criticism has not only created a space for an informed Afro-American male participation, but it heartily welcomes – in fact, insists upon – the joint participation of black males and females as *comrades*, to invoke, with a difference, this paper's epigraphic reference to *Sula*.

Reading "Mama's Baby, Papa's Maybe" was of special importance to me in part because it helped me to clarify and articulate my belief that my relationship to feminism need not mark me necessarily as a debilitatingly split subject. The source of that relationship can only be traced autobiographically, if at all. Having been raised by a mother who, like too many women of too many generations, was the victim of male physical and psychological brutality – a brutality which, according to my mother, resulted in large part from my father's frustrations about his inability to partake in what Spillers calls masculinity's "prevailing social fiction" – my earliest stories, my familial narratives, as it were, figured "maleness" in quite troubling terms. My mother told me horrific stories, one of which I was, in a sense, immediately involved in: my father – who left us before I was one year old and whom I never knew – kicked her in the stomach when my fetal presence swelled her body, because he believed she'd been unfaithful to him and that I was only "maybe" his baby.

As a youth, I pondered this and other such stories often and deeply, in part because of the pain I knew these incidents caused my mother, in part because, as someone without a consistent male familial role model, I actively sought a way to achieve a gendered self-definition. As one for whom maleness as manifested in the surrounding inner city culture seemed to be represented only by violence, familial abandonment, and the certainty of imprisonment, I found that I was able to define myself with regard to my gender primarily in oppositional ways. I had internalized the cautionary intent of my mother's narratives, which also served as her dearest wish for me: that I not grow up to be like my father, that I not adopt the definitions of "maleness" represented by his example and in the culture generally. Because the scars of male brutality were visibly etched – literally marked, as it were – on my mother's flesh and on her psyche, "maleness," as figured both in her stories and in my environment, seemed to me not to be a viable mimetic option. I grew up, then, not always sure of what or who I was with respect to prevailing social definitions of gender but generally quite painfully aware of what I could not become.

In order to begin to understand who my mother was, perhaps also who my father was, what "maleness" was and what extra-biological relationship I could hope to have to it, I needed answers that my mother was unable to provide. I found little of value in the black masculinist discourse of the time, which spoke endlessly of the dehumanization and castration of the Afro-American male by white men and black women – our central social narrative for too long – for this rhetoric seemed simplistic and unself-consciously concerned with justifying domestic violence and other forms of black male brutality. Afro-American women's literature, to which I was introduced along with black feminism in 1977 as a sophomore at Brandeis University, helped me move toward a comprehension of the world, of aspects of my mother's life, and of what a man against patriarchy could be and do. These discourses provided me with answers, nowhere else available, to what had been largely unresolvable mysteries. I work within the paradigm of black feminist literary criticism because it explains elements of the world about which I care most deeply. I write and read what and as I do because I am incapable of escaping the meanings of my mother's narratives for my own life, because the pain and, in the fact of their enunciation to the next generation, the sense of hope for better days that characterizes these familial texts are illuminatingly explored in many narratives by black women. Afro-American women's literature has given me parts of myself that – incapable of a (biological) "fatherly reprieve" – I would not otherwise have had.

I have decided that it is ultimately irrelevant whether these autobiographical facts, which, of course, are not, and can never be, the whole story, are deemed by others sufficient to permit me to call myself "feminist." Like Toril Moi, I come to believe that "the important thing for men is not to spend their time worrying about definitions and essences ('am I *really* a feminist?'), but to take up a recognizable anti-patriarchal position."[25] What is most important to me is that my work contribute, in however small a way, to the project whose goal is the dismantling of the phallocentric rule by which black females and, I am sure, countless other Afro-American sons have been injuriously "touched."

My indebtedness to Spillers's and other womanist perspectives is, then, great indeed, as is my sense of their potential as illuminating moments for a newborn – or not-yet-born – black male feminist discourse. But to utilize these perspectives requires that we be more inquiring than Spillers is in her formulations, not in envisioning liberating possibilities of an acknowledgment of the "female" within the black community and the male subject, but in noting potential dangers inherent in such an attempted adoption by historically brutalized Afro-American men whose relationship to a repressed "female" is not painstakingly (re)defined.

Clearly, more thinking is necessary not only about what the female within is but about what it can be said to represent for black males, as well as serious analysis of useful means and methods of interacting with a repressed female interiority and subject. Spillers's theorizing does not perform this task, in part because it has other, more compelling interests and emphases – among which is the righting/(re)writing of definitions of "woman" so that they will reflect Afro-American women's particular, historically conditioned "female social subject" status – but a black male feminism must be especially focused on exploring such issues if it is to mobilize Spillers's suggestive remarks as a means of developing a fuller understanding of the complex formulations of black manhood found in many texts and contexts, including Afro-American women's narratives.

I want to build briefly on Spillers's provocative theorizing about the Afro-American male's maturational process and situation on American shores. To this end, I will look at an illuminating moment in Toni Morrison's *Sula*, a text that is, to my mind, not only an unparalleled Afro-American woman's writing of the complexities of black female subjectivity and experience but also of black males' relationship to the female within as a consequence of their limited access to "the prevailing social fiction" of masculinity. In this novel, the difficulty of negotiating the spaces between black male lack and black female presence is plainly manifested in such figures as the undifferentiatable deweys; BoyBoy, whose name, in contrast to most of the authorial designations in *Sula*, speaks unambiguously for him; and Jude, whose difficulty in assuming the mantle of male provider leads him to view his union with Nel as that which "would make one Jude."[26]

The response of Plum, the most tragic of *Sula*'s unsuccessful nego-tiators of the so-called white man's world, vividly represents for me some of the contemporary dangers of black male "in-ness" vis-à-vis the "female." Despite a childhood which included "float[ing] in a constant swaddle of love and affection" and his mother's intention to follow the Father's law by bequeathing "everything" to him (38), Plum appears incapable of embracing hegemonic notions of masculinity. Instead, he returns from World War I spiritually fractured but, unlike a similarly devastated Shadrack, lacking the imaginative wherewithal to begin to theorize or ritualize a new relationship to his world. He turns to drugs as a method of anesthetizing himself from the horrors of his devastation and, in his mother's view, seeks to compel her resumption of familiar/familial patterns of caretaking. In the following passage, Eva explains to Hannah her perception of Plum's desires, as well as the motivation for her participation in what amounts to an act of infanticide:

> When he came back from that war he wanted to git back in. After all that carryin' on, just gettin' him out and keepin' him alive, he wanted to crawl back in my womb and well . . . I ain't got the room no more even if he could do it. There wasn't space for him in my womb. And he was crawlin' back. Being helpless and thinking baby thoughts and dreaming baby dreams and messing up his pants again and smiling all the time. I had room enough in my heart, but not in my womb, got no more. I birthed

him once. I couldn't do it again. He was growed, a big old thing.
Godhavemercy, I couldn't birth him twice . . . A big man can't be a baby
all wrapped up inside his mamma no more; he suffocate. I done everything
I could to make him leave me and go on and live and be a man but he
wouldn't and I had to keep him out so I just thought of a way he could
die like a man not all scrunched up inside my womb, but like a man.(62)[27]

What is significant about this passage for an analysis of the possibilities of a non-oppressive black male relationship to feminism – to
female experience characterized by a refusal to be subjugated to androcentric desires – is its suggestiveness for our understanding of the
obstacles to a revised male view of the repressed "female," obstacles
which result in large part from black males' relative social powerlessness.
If black feminism is persuasive in its analysis of the limitations of Afro-
American masculinist ideology, emphasizing as it does achievement of
black manhood at the expense of black female subjectivity, and if we
can best describe an overwhelming number of Africa's American male
descendants as males-in-crisis, the question a black male feminism must
ask itself is, on what basis, according to what ideological perspective,
can an Afro-American heterosexual male ground his notions of the
female? Beyond its heterosexual dimension, can the "female" truly come
to represent for a traditional black male-in-crisis more than a protective
maternal womb from which he seeks to be "birthed" again? Can it serve
as more than a site on which to find relief from or locate frustrations
caused by an inability to achieve putatively normative American male
socioeconomic status? If embracing normative masculinity requires an
escape from the protection and life-sustaining aspects symbolized by
maternal umbilical cords and apron strings and an achievement of an
economic situation wherein the male provides domestic space and
material sustenance for his dependents (including "his woman"), black
manhood generally is, like Plum, in desperate trouble. And if, as has
often been the case, a black female can be seen by an Afro-American
male-in-crisis only if she has been emptied of subjectivity and selfhood,
if she becomes visible for the male only when she is subsumed by male
desire(s), then the types of refiguration and redefinition of black male
subjectivity and engagement with the "female" central to Spillers's
formulations are highly unlikely.

This question of seeing and not seeing, of the male gaze's erasure and
recreation of the female, is crucial to *Sula*'s general thematics. It seems

to me that in all of her novels Morrison's figuration of black female subjectivity is largely incomprehensible without some serious attention both to her representation of black manhood and to her exploration of the relationships between socially constructed gendered (and racial) positions. To return explicitly to the case of Eva: What Eva fears, what appears to be a self-interested motivation for her killing of her intended male heir, is that Plum's pitiful, infantile state has the potential to reduce her to a static female function of self-sacrificing mother, which, according to Bottom legend, had already provoked her decision to lose a leg in order to collect insurance money with which to provide for her children. Having personally lost so much already, Eva chooses, instead of sacrificing other essential parts of her self, to take the life of her self-described male heir. And if Plum dies "like a man" in Eva's estimation, his achievement of manhood has nothing to do with an assumption of traditional masculine traits, nothing to do with strength, courage, and a refusal to cry in the face of death. Instead, that achievement results from Eva's creation of conditions that have become essential components of her definition of manhood: death forces him to "leave" her and to "keep . . . out" of her womb. It would appear that manhood is defined here not as presence as typically represented in Western thought, but – by and for Eva at least – as liberating (domestic and uterine) absence.

One of the intentions of this chapter is to suggest that feminism represents a fruitful and potentially not oppressive means of reconceptualizing, of figuratively birthing twice, the black male subject. But, as a close reading of the aforementioned passage from *Sula* suggests, interactions between men and women motivated by male self-interest such as necessarily characterizes an aspect of male participation in feminism are fraught with possible dangers for the biological /ideological female body of an enactment of or a capitulation to hegemonic male power. Indeed, if it is the case that, as Spillers has argued in another context, "the woman who stays in man's company keeps alive the possibility of having, one day, an unwanted guest, or the guest, deciding 'to hump the hostess,' whose intentions turn homicidal," then male proximity to feminism generally creates the threat of a specifically masculinist violation.[28] If, as I noted earlier, the dangers of a hegemonic, heterosexual Euro-American male's "in-ness" vis-à-vis feminism include (sexualized) penetration and domination, then those associated with a heterosexual black male's interactions with the ideological female body are at least doubled, and potentially involve an envisioning of the black female body as self-sacrificingly maternal or self-sacrificingly sexual. Because of a general lack of access to the full force of hegemonic male power, Afro-American men could see in increasingly influential black female texts not only serious challenges to black male fictions of the self but also an appropriate location for masculine desires for control of the types of valuable resources that the discourses of black womanhood currently represent.

But a rigorous, conscientious black male feminism need not give in to traditional patriarchal desires for control and erasure of the female. To be of any sustained value to the feminist project, a discourse must provide illuminating and persuasive readings of gender as it is consti-tuted for blacks in America and sophisticated, informed, contentious critiques of phallocentric practices in an effort to redefine our notions of black male and female textuality and subjectivity. And in its differences from black feminist texts that are produced by individual Afro-American women, a black male feminism must be both rigorous in engaging these texts and self-reflective enough to avoid, at all costs, the types of patronizing, marginalizing gestures that have traditionally characterized Afro-American male intellectuals' response to black womanhood. What a black male feminism must strive for, above all else, is to envision and enact the possibilities signaled by the differences feminism has exposed and created. In black feminist criticism, being an Afro-American male does not mean attempting to invade an/other political body like a lascivious soul snatcher or striving to erase its essence in order to replace it with one's own myth of what the discourse should be. Such a position for black men means, above all else, an acknowledgment and celebration of the incontrovertible fact that "the Father's law" is no longer the only law of the land.

Notes

1   Joseph Boone's ("Of Me[n] and Feminism: Who[se] is the Sex That Writes?") and Gerald M. MacLean's ("Citing the Subject") essays in Linda Kauffman, ed., *Gender and Theory: Dialogues on Feminist Criticism* (New York: Blackwell, 1989) assume that the foregrounding of gendered subjec-tivity is essential to the production of a male feminist critical practice. Consequently, in an effort to articulate his perspectives on the possibilities of a male feminist discourse, Boone shares with us professional secrets – he

writes of his disagreement with male-authored essays in Alice Jardine and
Paul Smith's *Men in Feminism* (New York: Methuen, 1987), and of being
excluded, because of his gender, from a Harvard feminist group discussion
of Elaine Showalter's "Critical Cross-Dressing." And MacLean's essay
discloses painfully personal information about his difficult relationship with
his mother, his unsatisfying experience with psychoanalysis, and an incident
of marital violence.

2   Boone, "Of Me(n) and Feminism," 158–80. Here and below, I quote from
p. 159. For my purposes, Boone's remarks are suggestive despite their use
of language that might seem to mark them as a hetereosexualization of
men's participation in feminism ("open up a space," "discover a position").
I believe that Boone's passage implies less about any desire for domination
on his part than it does about the pervasiveness in our language of terms
which have acquired sexual connotations and, consequently, demonstrates
the virtual unavoidability of using a discourse of penetration to describe
interactions between males and females. But it also appears to reflect a
sense of frustration motivated by Boone's knowledge that while feminism
has had a tremendous impact on his thinking about the world he inhabits,
many feminists do not see a place for himself; violation and transgression
seem to Boone to be unavoidable.

3   Alice Jardine, "Men in Feminism: Odor di Uomo or Compagnons de
Route?" in *Men in Feminism*, 58.

4   Andrew Ross, "No Question of Silence," in *Men in Feminism*, 86.

5   See Georges Poulet, "Criticism and the Experience of Interiority," in
Reader-Response Criticism: From Formalism to Post-Structuralism, ed. Jane
P. Tompkins (Baltimore: Johns Hopkins University Press, 1980), 41–9.

6   Houston A. Baker, Jr., *Afro-American Poetics: Revisions of Harlem and the
Black Aesthetic* (Madison: University of Wisconsin Press, 1988), 8.

7   Elizabeth Weed, "A Man's Place," in *Men in Feminism*, 75.

8   Michael Awkward, *Inspiriting Influences: Tradition, Revision, and Afro-
American Women's Novels* (New York: Columbia University Press, 1989).

9   About his relationship to feminism, Nelson writes: "Feminism is part of my
social and intellectual life, has been so for many years, and so, to the extent
that writing is ever 'natural,' it is natural that I write about feminism"
(153). Nelson's "Men, Feminism: The Materiality of Discourse" (*Men in
Feminism*, 153–72) is, in my estimation, a model for self-referential male
feminist inquiries that assume – or, at the very least, seek to demonstrate –
a useful place for males in the discourse of feminism.

10   Jardine and Smith, *Men in Feminism*, vii–viii.

11   See Craig Owens, "Outlaws: Gay Men in Feminism," *Men in Feminism*,
219–32. It is hard to believe that Jardine and Smith's difficulty reflected a
lack of interest among Afro-Americans in exploring the relationship of men

to black feminism. A number of texts give evidence of interest in "the problem": the 1979 *Black Scholar* special issue devoted to investigating black feminism as manifested primarily in Ntozake Shange's *for colored girls* and Michele Wallace's *Black Macho and the Myth of the Superwoman*; Mel Watkins, "Sexism, Racism, and Black Women Writers," *New York Times Book Review*, June 15, 1986, 1; Darryl Pinckney, "Black Victims, Black Villains," *New York Review of Books* 34 (January 2, 1987), 17–20; and essays by Valerie Smith and Deborah McDowell from which I draw below.

Jardine and Smith's difficulties might have stemmed from the facts that most of the men who had spoken publicly on the subject were open about their hostility to black feminism, and most of them did not speak the language of contemporary theory, a high academic idiom which demonstrates that the contributors to *Men in Feminism* are, despite significant differences among them, members of the same speech community.

12 Stephen Heath, "Male Feminism," *Men in Feminism*, 1.

13 Ibid., 9.

14 Barbara Smith, "Toward a Black Feminist Criticism," in Elaine Showalter, ed., *The New Feminist Criticism* (New York: Pantheon, 1985), 173, 172; Michele Wallace, "Who Dat Say Dat When I Say Dat? Zora Neale Hurston Then and Now," *Village Voice Literary Supplement*, April 1988, 18.

15 Sherley Anne Williams, "Some Implications of Womanist Theory," *Callaloo* 9 (1986), 304.

16 Valerie Smith, "Gender and Afro-Americanist Literary Theory and Criticism," in *Speaking of Gender*, 68.

17 Jardine, "Men in Feminism," *Men in Feminism*, 60.

18 Williams, "Some Implications," 307.

19 Deborah McDowell, "Reading Family Matters," in *Changing Our Own Words: Essays on Criticism, Theory, and Writing by Black Women*, ed. Cheryl Wall (New Brunswick: Rutgers University Press, 1989), 84.

20 Toril Moi, "Men against Patriarchy," in *Gender and Theory*, 181–8.

21 McDowell's views notwithstanding, constructions of black male and female subjectivity are too obviously interrelated in black women's narratives for feminist criticism to profit in the long run from ignoring – or urging that others ignore – the important function that delineations of black male subjectivity play in these narratives' thematics. Certainly the threat of antifeminist male critical bias is not cause to erase or minimize the significance of black male characters in these writers' works.

22 Hortense J. Spillers, "Mama's Baby, Papa's Maybe: An American Grammar Book," *Diacritics: A Review of Contemporary Criticism* 17: 2 (Summer 1987), 80.

23 In this sense, Spiller's perspectives complement those of Sherley Ann Williams, for the latter demands, in effect, that we consider the extent to

which black male repression of the "female" results from an attempt to follow the letter of the white Father's law.

24 Paul Smith, "Men in Feminism: Men and Feminist Theory," *Men in Feminism*, 33.

25 Moi, "Men against Patriarchy," 184.

26 Toni Morrison, *Sula* (New York: Plume, 1979), 71. Subsequent references to this novel appear in the text in parentheses.

27 At least one other reading of Eva's murder of her son is possible: as protection against the threat of incest. In a section of her explanation to Hannah – very little of which is contained in my textual citation of *Sula* – Eva discusses a dream she has had concerning Plum:

> I'd be laying here at night and he be downstairs in that room, but when I closed my eyes I'd see him . . . six feet tall smilin' and crawlin' up the stairs quietlike so I wouldn't hear and opening the door soft so I wouldn't hear and he'd be creepin' to the bed trying to spread my legs trying to get back up in my womb. He was a man, girl, a big old growed-up man. I didn't have that much room. I kept on dreaming it. Dreaming it and I knowed it was true. One night it wouldn't be no dream. It'd be true and I would have done it, would have let him if I'dve had the room but a big man can't be a baby all wrapped up inside his mamma no more; he suffocate.

Morrison reverses to some extent the traditional dynamics of the most prevalent form of intergenerational incest. Instead of the male parent creeping to the bed and spreading legs of his defenseless female child, in Eva's dream her man-child Plum is the active agent of violation. Eva's emphasis on Plum's immensity and her own uterus's size makes connections to incestuous creeping and crawling possible. It is not difficult to imagine, given Plum's drugged state, that frustrations caused by an inability to re-insert his whole body into his mother's womb during what Eva views as an inevitable encounter might lead to a forced insertion of a part that "naturally" fits, his penis. At any rate, a reading of this scene that notes its use of language consistent with parent-child incest serves to ground what appear to be otherwise senseless fears on Eva's part concerning both the possible effects of Plum's desire for reentry into her uterine space and her own inability to deny her son access to that space ("I would have done it, would have let him").

28 Hortense J. Spillers, "Black, White, and in Color, or Learning How to Paint: Toward an Intramural Protocol of Reading," in Jeffrey N. Cox and Larry J. Reynolds, eds., *New Historical Literacy Study: Essays on Reproducing Texts, Representing History* (Princeton: Princeton University Press, 1993), 276.

FIVE

Beyond Miranda's Meanings: Un/silencing the "Demonic Ground" of Caliban's "Woman"

Sylvia Wynter

The point of departure of this *After/Word* is to explore a central distinction that emerges as the dynamic linking sub-text of this [*Out of the Kumbla*], the first collection of critical essays written by Caribbean women. This distinction is that between Luce Irigaray's purely Western assumption of a universal category, "woman," whose "silenced" ground is the condition of what she defines as an equally universally applicable, "patriarchal discourse," and the dually Western and post-Western editorial position of a projected "womanist/feminist" critical approach as the unifying definition of the essays that constitute the anthology. The term *"womanist/feminist,"* with the qualifying attribute "womanist" borrowed from the Afro-American feminist Alice Walker, reveals the presence of a contradiction, which, whilst central to the situational frame of reference of both Afro-American and Caribbean women writers/critics, is necessarily absent from the situational frame of reference of both Western-European and Euroamerican women writers. Thus whilst at the level of the major text these essays are projected within the system of inference-making of the discourse of feminism, at the level of the sub-text which both haunts and calls in question the presuppositions of the major text, the very attempt to redefine the term *feminist* with the qualifier "womanist" expresses the paradoxical relation of Sameness and Difference which the writers of these essays, as members of the Caribbean women intelligentsia, bear to their Western European and Euroamerican peers. This dual relation is expressed by both editors if not precisely in these terms. Thus if for [Carol] Boyce Davies, the term *womanist* necessarily qualifies *feminism*, for Elaine Savory Fido, the unique positional situation of Caribbean women writers/critics, as expressed in their writings, is that of a *cross-roads*, that is, one in which they experience themselves as placed at a crossroad of three variables. These are, on the one hand, the variable of sex-gender, as well as of class, both of which they share with their European/Euroamerican counterparts – class in that many members of both intelligentsia groups are still one generation away from our non-middle-class origins, even where this is numerically truer of the intelligentsia of the still, until very recently, colonized Caribbean – and, on the other, the variable of "race" which of course strongly demarcates the situation of the Caribbean women intelligentsia, whether Black or White from that of their Western/Euroamerican counterparts.

I want to argue in this After/Word, from its projected "demonic ground" outside of our present governing system of meaning, or theory/ontology in de Nicolas' sense of the word[1] that it is precisely the variable "race" which imposes upon these essays the contradictory dualism by which the writers both work within the "regime of truth" of the discourse of feminism, at the same time as they make use of this still essentially Western discourse to point towards the epochal threshold of a new post-modern and post-Western mode of cognitive inquiry, one which goes beyond the limits of our present "human sciences," to constitute itself as a new science of human "forms of life."[2]

The German scholar Hans Blumenberg, in exploring the parallel epochal threshold which led from the European Middle Ages to the emergence of the modern world *pari passu* with the advent of Renaissance humanism and the Copernican Revolution, widens the concept of Thomas Kuhn's theory of "scientific revolutions." This theory, he argues, which describes "the breakdown of dominant systems as a result of their immanent rigorism," and the "downfall" of "the pedantic disposition of every school-like mode of thought" (with both breakdown and downfall leading "with fateful inevitability" to the "self-uncovering of the *marginal* inconsistencies from which doubt and opposition break into the consolidated field") can be capable "of generalization to a high level in relation to historical phenomena;"[3] and therefore to the shift/mutation of one age or epoch and its related, in Foucault's terms, episteme[4] to the other. And the central point I want to make in this After/Word is that the contradiction inserted into the consolidated field of meanings of the ostensibly "universal" theory of feminism by the variable "*race*," and explicitly expressed by the qualifiers of "womanist" and "cross-roads situation," of these essays points toward the emergent "downfall" of our present "school-like mode of thought" and its system of "positive knowledge" inherited from the nineteenth century and from the Industrial epoch of which it was the enabling mode of rationality and participatory epistemology[5]; and that it does this in the same way as feminist theory itself had earlier, inserted the contradiction of the variable *gender* into the ostensibly "universal" theories of Liberal Humanism and Marxism-Leninism.[6]

Because these theories and their related "universalisms" had been erected on the apriori self-description of the human on the model of a "natural organism" (as the inversion of the Euro-Christian "image of God"), the variable "race" was/is constituted as an "object of knowledge" able to function in the system of symbolic representations (Levi-Strauss's "totemic schema," Marlene Philip's system of images as the human analogue of "the DNA molecules at the heart of all life") as a central topos of our present system of meaning and its regulatory behavioral mechanism. For as such a *topos*, "race," functions to signify a system-specific mode of causality, that is, the causality of a "materialistic substrate" which not only acts so as to place genetically determined constraints on human behaviors, but also, above all, to *prescribe* a teleology – that is, to imply that "ends," now no longer, after the full-fledged secularization of the European Enlightenment, set by the most remote watchmaker of Gods, are still extra-humanly set for the human by *nature*, in our case, by the constraints of nature and/or of history.[7] Thus, if, for Freud, as Irigaray dissects with respect to the variable of "sexual difference," biology was destiny, with the functioning of the "anatomical model" being described by Freud in a manner which prescribes behaviors – "It seems" Irigaray writes, speaking ironically in Freud's voice, ". . . you take the term *masculine* to connote *active*, the term *feminine* to connote 'passive' and it is true that a relation of the kind exists for the male sex cell is actively mobile and searches out the female one, and the latter, the ovum, is immobile and waits 'passively' . . . And I, Freud, have to tell you that the behavior of the *elementary* sexual organisms is indeed a model for the conduct of sexual individuals during intercourse. My way of envisaging . . . these . . . 'things' would therefore imply that the psychic is *prescribed by the anatomical* according to a *mimetic order*, with anatomical science imposing *the truth of its*

model upon psychological *behavior*"[8] – the variable of *race/racial* difference is, since the sixteenth century, even more primarily destiny. For
with Western Europe's post-medieval expansion into the New World
(and earlier into Africa), and with its epochal shift out of primarily
religious systems of legitimation, and behaviour-regulation, her peoples'
expropriation of the land/living space of the New World peoples was to
be based on the secular concept of the "non-rational," inferior, "*nature*"
of the peoples to be expropriated and governed[9]; that is, of an ostensible
difference in "natural" substance which, for the first time in history was
no longer *primarily* encoded in the male/female gender division as it had
been hitherto in the symbolic template of all traditional and religiously
based human orders, but now in the cultural-physiognomic variations
between the dominant expanding European civilization and the non-
Western peoples that, encountering it, would now be stigmatized as
"natives." In other words, with the shift to the secular, the primary code
of difference now became that between "men" and "natives," with the
traditional "male" and "female" distinctions now coming to play a
secondary – if none the less powerful – reinforcing role within the system
of symbolic representations, Lévi-Strauss's totemic schemas,[10] by means
of which, as governing charters of meaning, all human orders are
"altruistically" integrated.[11]

Nowhere in this mutational shift from the primacy of the *anatomical*
model of sexual difference as the referential model of *mimetic* ordering,
to that of the *physiognomic* model of racial/cultural difference, more
powerfully enacted than in Shakespeare's play *The Tempest*, one of the
foundational endowing[12] texts both of Western Europe's dazzling rise to
global hegemony, and, at the level of human "life", in general, of the
mutation from primarily religiously defined modes of human being to
the first, partly secularizing ones. Whilst on the other hand, both
mutations, each as the condition of the other, are nowhere more clearly
put into play than in the relations between Miranda the daughter of
Prospero, and Caliban, the once original owner of the island now
enslaved by Prospero as a function of the latter's expropriation of the
island. That is, in the relations of enforced dominance and subordination
between Miranda, though "female," and Caliban, though "male"; relations in which *sex-gender attributes* are no longer the primary index of
"deferent" difference,[13] and in which the discourse that erects itself is no
longer primarily "patriarchal," but rather "monarchical" in its Western-
European, essentially post-Christian, post-religious definition. Therefore,

in whose context of behaviour-regulatory inferential system of meanings, as the essential condition of the mutation to the secular, Caliban, as an incarnation of a new category of the human, that of the subordinated "irrational" and "savage"[14] *native* is now constituted as the lack of the "rational" Prospero, and the now capable-of-rationality-Miranda, by the Otherness of his/its *physiognomic* "monster" difference, a difference which now takes the *coding* role of sexual-anatomical difference, with the latter now made into a mimetic parallel effect of the former, and as such a member of the *set* of differences of which the former has now become the primary "totemic operator."[15]

Correspondingly, as the play reveals, with this ontological and epistemological mutation effected in the sixteenth century, the new physiognomic model of "race" (or, in the terms of Elsa Goveiá, the Caribbean historian, used in a critical 1970 essay on the integrative principles of Caribbean societies, the "ascription of race"),[16] was to begin that ongoing transformative meaning process by which it would come to function, within our contemporary behaviour-regulatory theoretical models and systems of meaning, to provide, parallely to the earlier traditional sex-gender models of *anatomical* difference of truly "patriarchal" orders, the grounding "mimetic model" or totemic operator which now *primarily* describes/prescribes at the multiple levels of the global order, analogical behavioural relations of dominance/subordination, activity/passivity, theory-givers/theory-takers[17] between human populations/geographical races, cultures, and societal groups, i.e., ethnic, class, gender, sexual-preference, etc. The "mimetic model" or totemic operator therefore, which legitimates these relations in now *purely secular* terms, as relations ostensibly pre-ordained by the extra-human ends set by, firstly, in the narrative schema/story of the monarchical discourse of civic humanism (as enacted in *The Tempest)* by an allegedly universally applicable "natural law,"[18] and later in the Malthusian-Darwinian-Haeckelian narrative schema of a monist discourse of "social naturalism" or "biological idealism,"[19] by, allegedly, evolutionary biology. Thus, if in the first schema of "civic humanism," the model of *physiognomic* difference was still attached to the model of religio-cultural difference – with the New World peoples and African slaves defined as "pagan sacrificers of other humans and as idolatrous "cannibals,"[20] in the second, the now purely *physiognomic* difference came to provide a *somatic* mode of difference which would function from the early nineteenth century onwards as the *primary* "totemic operator" of the principle of Sameness and Difference about which our present global, and now purely secular order, auto-regulates its socio-systemic hierarchies, including those of gender, class, sexual preference, culture – including, therefore, the processes central to literary scholarship itself and to its normative system of interpretative readings, which have been defined by Cary Nelson as that of "literary idealization" by means of which, in Euro-American "humanism" processes of literary transcendence (i.e. literature as "one of the finer things on earth" one which "exhibits at once a powerful realism about the human condition and a visionary synthesis of its highest ambitions") are attached "to the experience of only one race, one sex, a restricted set of class fractions within a few national cultures." With the experiences of most of the world's peoples "having to be, rule-governedly, within the parameters of the 'play'[21] of its interpretative readings," and regulatory system of meanings, "obliterated"[22]; as the experiences of the physiognomic Other, the "natives," and in their most "primal" form *niggers*. The systemic "obliteration" is central, therefore, to the imperative which impels the counter-readings of these essays.

It is in this context that we can begin to approach the significance both of this collection of essays themselves as essays projected both from the hitherto "silenced" vantage point of the obliterated "experiences of most of the world's peoples" and from the vantage point of gender, that is of a Miranda now speaking in her own intelligentsia name – instead of in the name of her monarchical father, and of *The Tempest*'s Miranda's speech to Caliban; that we can grasp the significance of her legitimated expropriation of the right to endow his purposes – when he did not "savage" know "his own meanings" – with "words that made them known," her expropriation then of what Marlene Phillips defines as "image-making power." And here, we begin to pose in this context a new question, the question not of the absence of Caliban's legitimate father as posed by Aimé Césaire and commented on by Clarisse Zimra in her essay ["Righting the Calabash"] on Francophone Caribbean women writers, nor even the question posed by Zimra herself, that of the "silent presence of a mother not yet fully understood" which carries with it the implicit project of "discarding the logos of the Father," and of replacing it instead with "the Silent Song of the Mother," but a new question related to a new project. This question is that of the most significant absence of all, that of Caliban's Woman, of Caliban's physiognomically complementary mate. For nowhere in Shakespeare's play, and in its system of image-making, one which would be foundational to the emergence of the first form of a secular world system, our present Western world system, does Caliban's mate appear as an alternative sexual-erotic model of desire; as an alternative source of an alternative system of meanings. Rather there, on the New World island, as the only woman, Miranda and her mode of physiognomic being, defined by the philogenically "idealized" features of straight hair and thin lips is canonized as the "rational" object of desire; as the potential genitrix of a superior mode of human "life," that of "good natures" as contrasted with the ontologically absent potential genitrix – Caliban's mate – of another population of human, i.e., of a "vile race" "capable of all ill," which "any print of goodness will not take," a "race" then extra-humanly condemned by a particular mode of Original Sin which deserv-edly "confines" them to a "rock," thereby empowering the "race" of Miranda to expropriate the island, and to reduce Caliban to a labor-machine as the new "massa damnata"[23] of purely sensory nature – "He does make our fire,/fetch in our wood, and serve in offices/that profit us."[24] And since the empirical relation of rational humans to purely sensory nature humans, and its related physiognomic-cultural model of difference/deference will now serve retrospectively, as the *mimetic model* of an order whose intra-group societal hierarchical structures have been pre-ordained by an allegedly universally functioning code of natural law,[25] the "desire" of the "lower class" sailors Stephano and Trinculo can also only be *for* Miranda, with their *optimal* "desire" also trans-ferred from their own "lower class" mates to her. Hence the non-desire of Caliban for his own mate, for Caliban's "woman," is, as Maryse Condé brilliantly suggests, in another context, a founding function of the "social pyramid"[26] of the global order that will be put in place following upon the 1492 arrival of Columbus in the Caribbean; a function then of its integrating behaviour-regulatory system of meanings and "semantic closure principle."

In this first phase of Western Europe's expansion into the Americas, Caliban, as both the Arawak and African "forced" labor needed by the mutation in the land/labor ratio which followed,[27] and given the exist-ence of rapidly available fresh supplies provided by the expanding slave trade in "negroes" out of the Europe–Africa–New World triangular traffic, had no need/desire for the procreation of his own "kind," since such a mode of "desire" would only be functional in the very much later stages for the master-population group's purpose, as the only secularly-theoretically "idealized" purpose which now mattered.

Hence the empirical logic of the absence from the play's character system of Caliban's woman, for its erecting of its plot upon the "ground" not only of her absence, but also of the absence of Caliban's endogenous desire for her, of any longing. All his desire instead is "soldered"[28] on to Miranda as the only symbolically canonized potential genitrix. Hence his first act of overt rebellion is his attempt to "people this isle with Calibans": his attempt to copulate with her. However, this rebellious possibility is not to be – for if the absence of Caliban's woman is a central function of the play's foundational ontology in which Caliban "images" the human as pure sensory nature and as appetite uncurbed by reason, whilst Prospero and the prince, Fernando, "image" the human possessed of a rational nature and therefore able to curb their lustful appetites (with the ship's Boatswain and the sailors Stephano and Trinculo, lower down the scale between the two), then the metaphysically imperative elimination of *the potential* progeny of Caliban, must rule-governedly bar him from any access to Miranda as the potential genitrix of a "race" which, as the beneficiaries of both rational and sensory natures bequeathed them by Nature, must necessarily behave so as to effect the "ends," ostensibly implicit in this differential legacy; that is, must ensure the stable dominance of the "race" of good natures over the "vile race" of Caliban's purely sensory nature, if the now secularizing behaviour-regulatory system of meaning, and its related "semantic closure principle" is to be stably replicated.

The absence of Caliban's woman is therefore an ontological absence, that is, one central to the new secularizing behaviour-regulatory narrative schema, or in Clarisse Zimra's term, mode of "story-telling,"[29] by means of which the secular Laity of feudal-Christian Europe displaced the theological spirit/flesh motivational oppositions[30] and replaced it with its own first secularly constituted "humanist" motivational opposition in history. That is, the rational/sensory opposition between a projected redeemed "race" of "gentes humaniores" as the bearers of a rational nature able to master their own sensory nature at the same time as they mastered – and mistressed – the "vile race" dys-elected by Nature to be bearers of a purely sensory nature, and the new secular *massa damnata* of the "vile race" themselves.[31]

To put it in more directly political terms, the absence of Caliban's woman, is an absence which is functional to the new secularizing schema by which the peoples of Western Europe legitimated their global expansion as well as their expropriation and their marginalization of all the Other population-groups of the globe, including, partially, some of their own national groupings such as, for example, the Irish.[32] Yet it was with this same secularizing narrative schema that they were also to effect that far-reaching mutation, in which they were to displace, not only their own *religious* version of the narrative schemas of good and evil and their modes of "story-telling" – that is, their own religious version of the behaviour-motivational schemas/stories, by means of whose opiate-inducing signifying meaning systems which function to trigger the neuro-chemical processes of what Danielli defines as the internal reward system of the brain[33] and to induce and regulate the collective set of "altruistic" behaviours by means of which each human model of being and related human orders are stably brought into, and maintained in, being – but all other religious versions to the marginally private, rather than centrally public, spheres of human existence.[34] And, if the latter schemas, religious and/or mythological, together with their projection of a transcendentally ordered behaviour-regulatory definition of good and evil, had hitherto functioned to stabilize and guarantee all human "forms of life", the new narrative schema, powerfully re-enacted in the plot-line of *The Tempest*, was to initiate the first form of a secularly projected definition of Good and Evil, and therefore of a secularly guaranteed and stabilized "form of life" or human order, now dynamically brought into being by the collective behaviours motivated and induced by its (the schema's) oppositional categories of secular "good" (as rational nature incarnated in Prospero and Miranda) and of secular "evil" (as pure sensory nature outside of the control of rational nature incarnated in Caliban when his own "master, his own man").[35] In other words, in this epochal threshold shift to the secular, the physiognomic (and cultural) difference between the population groups of Prospero/Miranda and that of Caliban is now made to function, totemically, as a new, so to speak infrascendental[36] oppositional principle of good and evil which is ostensibly as extra-humanly ordained (by Natural Law), as, before, the Spirit/Flesh opposition had been ostensibly pre-ordained by supernatural decree – rather than as, in both cases ordained by the imperative of the respective narrative schemas, and the "semantic closure of principle" of their respective behaviour-regulatory systems of meanings.[37]

It is within this latter "real" imperative that the absence of Caliban's

woman as Caliban's sexual reproductive mate functions to ontologically
negate their progeny/population group, forcing this group to serve as
the allegorical incarnation of "pure" sensory nature; that is, the group
for whom the image of Caliban stands, i.e., the original owners/occupiers
of the New World lands, the American-Indians, now displaced empiri-
cally and metaphysically reduced, by the new regulatory system of
meanings, to a "native" savage Human Other status now central to the
functioning of the first secularizing behaviour-regulatory schema or
motivational apparatus in human history. Whilst with the rapid deci-
mation of the indigenous Arawaks of the Caribbean Islands, Africans
bought and sold as "trade goods" were now made to fill the same slot
in the behaviour-regulatory schema, as they were made to fill a parallel
slot in the system of forced labor. As such they too, as Caliban's women,
are reduced to having no will or desire that has not been prescribed by
Prospero/Miranda in the name of the existential interest of the popula-
tion-group for whom the "images" of Prospero/Miranda, stand. Given
that the idealization/negation of both groups is effected precisely by the
dominant group's imposition of its own mode of volition and desire
(one *necessarily* generated from the *raison d'être* of its group-existential
interests) upon the dominated; as well as by its stable enculturating of
the latter by means of its theoretical models (epistemes) and aesthetic
fields, generated from its increasingly hegemonic and secularizing systems of meanings. In consequence if, before the sixteenth century, what
Irigaray terms as *"patriarchal discourse"* had erected itself on the
"silenced ground" of women, from then on, the new primarily silenced
ground (which at the same time now enables the partial liberation of
Miranda's hitherto stifled speech), would be that of the majority population groups of the globe – all signified now as the "natives" (Calibans)
to the "men" of Prospero and Fernando, with Miranda becoming both
a co-participant, if to a lesser *derived* extent, in the power and privileges
generated by the empirical supremacy of her own population; and as
well, the beneficiary of a mode of privilege unique to her, that of being
the metaphysically invested and "idealized" object of desire for all
classes (Stephano and Trinculo) and all population groups (Caliban).[38]

This therefore is the dimension of the contradictory relation of
Sameness and Difference, of orthodoxy and heresy which these Caribbean critical essays must necessarily, if still only partially, inscribe, and
do inscribe with respect to the theory/discourse of feminism (as the latest
and last variant of the Prospero/Miranda ostensibly "universally" appli-

cable meaning and discourse-complex); the relation of *sameness and difference* which is expressed in the diacritical term *"womanist."* And if we are to understand the necessity for such an *other* term (projected both from the perspective of Black American women (US) and from that of the "native" women intelligentsia of the newly independent Caribbean ex-slave polities) as a term which, whilst developing a fully articulated theoretical/interpretative reading model of its own, nevertheless serves diacritically to draw attention to the insufficiency of all existing theoretical interpretative models, both to "voice" the hitherto silenced ground of the experience of "native" Caribbean women and Black American women as the ground of Caliban's woman, and to decode the system of meanings of that other discourse, beyond Irigaray's patriarchal one, which has imposed this mode of silence for some five centuries, as well as to make thinkable the possibility of a new "model" projected from a new "native" standpoint, we shall need to translate the variable "race", which now functions as the intra-feminist marker of difference, impelling the dually "gender/beyond gender" readings of these essays, out of the epistemic "vrai"[39] of our present order of "positive knowledge,"[40] its consolidated field of meanings and order-replicating hermeneutics. Correspondingly, since this order/field is transformative, generated from our present purely secular definition of the human on the model of a natural organism, with, in consequence, this organism's "ends" therefore being ostensibly set extra-humanly, by "nature", i.e., Haeckel's monism, neoclassical economics' Natural Scarcity, Marx's "materialist" imperative of the "mode of production," Feminism's bio-anatomical "universal" identity,[41] we shall need to move beyond this founding definition, not merely to *another* alternative one, non-consciously put in place as our present definition, but rather to a frame of reference which parallels the "demonic models" posited by physicists who seek to conceive of a vantage point outside the space-time orientation of the humuncular observer. This would be, in our case, in the context of our specific socio-human realities, a "demonic model" outside the "consolidated field" of our present mode of being/feeling/knowing, as well as of the multiple discourses, their regulatory systems of meaning and interpretative "readings", through which alone these modes, as varying expressions of human "life," including ours, can effect their respective autopeosis *as such* specific modes of being. The possibility of such a vantage point, we argue, towards which the diacritical term "womanist" (i.e., these readings as both gender, and not-gender readings, as both Caribbean/Black nationalist and not-Caribbean/Black nationalist, Marxian and not-Marxian readings)[42] point, can only be projected from a "demonic model" generated, parallely to the vantage point/demonic model with which the laity intelligentsia of Western Europe effected the first rupture of humans with their/our supernaturally guaranteed narrative schemas of origin,[43] from the situational "ground" or slot of Caliban's woman, and therefore of her systemic behaviour-regulatory role or function as the ontological "native/nigger," within the motivational apparatus by means of which our present model of being/ definition-of-the-human is given dynamic "material" existence, rather than from merely the vantage point of her/our gender, racial, class or cultural being.[44] In other words, if the laity intelligentsia of Western Europe effected a mutation by calling in question its own role as the ontological Other of "natural fallen flesh" to the theologically idealized, post-baptismal Spirit (and as such incapable of attaining to any knowl-edge of, and mastery over, either the physical processes of nature or its own social reality, except such knowledge was mediated by the then hegemonic Scholastic *theological* interpretative model), and by calling this role in question so as to clear the ground for its own self-assertion which would express itself both in the political reasons-of-state human-ism (enacted in *The Tempest*), as well as in the putting in place of the *Studia Humanitatis* (i.e., as the self-study of "natural man"), and in the laying of the basis for the rise of the natural sciences,[45] it is by a parallel calling in question of our '*native*' and, more ultimately, nigger women's role as the embodiment to varying degrees of an ostensible "primal" human nature. As well, challenging our role as a new "lay" intelligentsia ostensibly unable to know and therefore to master our present socio-systemic reality (including the reality of our "existential weightlessness" as an always "intellectually indentured"[46] intelligentsia), except as medi-ated by the theoretical models generated from the vantage point of the "normal" intelligentsia, clears the ground for a new self-assertion. This time, as one which brings together the human and natural sciences in a new projected science of the human able to constitute *demonic models* of cognition *outside* what Lemuel Johnson calls, in one of the essays in this collection, the always non-arbitrary pre-prescribed, "designs of the measuring rod" in whose parameters both our present hegemonic inter-pretative and anti-interpretative models are transformatively generated; one able in fact to take these designs of the measuring rod and their "privileged texts" as the object of our now conscious rather than reactive processes of cognition.[47] In effect, rather than only voicing the "native" woman's hitherto silenced voice[48] we shall ask: What is the systemic function of her own silencing, both as women and, more totally, as "native" women? Of what mode of speech is that absence of speech both as women (masculinist discourse) and as "native" women (feminist discourse) an imperative function?

The larger issue then is of the ontological difference and of our *human* and *"native" human* subordination, hitherto non-conscious, to the governing behaviour-regulatory codes of symbolic "life" and "death." It is an issue which calls for a second self-assertion able to respond to the new metaphysical imperative, not now of altering nature, but of altering our systems of meanings, and their privileged texts, and, therefore, of abolishing Elsa Goveiá's ascriptions of "race" and "wealth" (whose *particularisms* work to contradict the *universalism* of one-(wo)man,-one-vote), as well as those other ascriptions of the same totemic set which function to the same effect, i.e., culture, through the mechanism of literary scholarship's "idealized" (Cary Nelson) canon-ism,[49] religion, an allegedly "natural" erotic preference[50] as well as that of gender. The issue then of a second epistemological mutation – based on the new metaphysical imperative of the now conscious alterability of our governing codes, their modes of ontological difference and their rule-governedly generated behaviour-regulatory meanings, together with their always non-arbitrary "designs"[51] of interpretative readings – one able to complete the *partial* epistemological mutation of the first which ushered in our modem age as well as that first process of the non-conscious secularization of human modes/models of being, of whose order-maintaining discourses, the doubly silenced "ground" of Caliban's "native" woman, was a central meaning-coherence function; and of whose *incomplete epistemological mutation*, both the gender hierarchy of the ostensible equality of our symbolic contract, as well as of the "hard and uncomfortable life" of the, since the 1960s, now politically empowered Caribbean black and poor majority as noted by, and finely imaged in, Christine Craig's complex figure *Crow*, as both young woman metaphysically invested as the negative of normative object-desire, and old woman/Carrion bird with the garbage dump as food for both, as well as then, of the "hard and uncomfortable" life of all those who inhabit the global archipelagoes of hunger in the midst of a new technologically produced surfeit of global abundance[52] are an imperative effect and consequence.[53] That is, the paradoxical effect of that first, incomplete, and now objectified, secularizing epistemological mutation: "There are phases of objectivation" Blumenberg wrote, that loose themselves from their original motivation (*the science and technology of the later phases of the modern age provide* a stupendous example of this); and to bring them back to their human function, to subject them again to man's (the human's) purposes in relation to the world, *requires* an unavoidable counter-exertion. The medieval system ended in such a phase of objectification that has become autonomous, of hardening that is insulated from what is human. What is here called "self-assertion" is the counter-move of retrieving the lost motives, of a new concentration on man's (human) self-interest.[54]

The appeal of the Abeng is therefore to the larger issue of retrieving the lost motives of our "native" human self-interest, and, increasingly degraded in our planetary environment, of our human self-interest. This issue, which clearly calls for a second counter-exertion, has been initiated, in its first transitional phase by these diacritically "womanist" essays as the counter exertion of a "native women" intelligentsia, who, by refusing the "water with berries" strategy sets, of all our present hegemonic, theoretical models in their "pure" forms, based on their isolated "isms,"[55] has enabled the move, however preliminary, on to the "demonic" and now unsilencing trans-"isms" ground of Caliban's woman. This terrain, when fully occupied, will be that of a new science of human discourse, of human "life" beyond the "master discourse" of our governing "privileged text," and its sub/versions. Beyond Miranda's meanings.

Notes

1   See A. T. de Nicolas, "Notes on the Biology of Religion" in *Journal of Social and Biological Structures* 3, no. 2 (April 1980), 225.

2   I have put forward this proposal in two earlier essays, but most fully in the second. See Wynter, "On Disenchanting Discourse: Minority Literature and Beyond" in *Cultural Critique: The Nature and Context of Minority Discourse* 11, no. 7 (Fall 1987).

3   See Hans Blumenberg, *The Legitimacy of the Modern Age* (Cambridge, Mass.: MIT Press, 1983).

4   See Michel Foucault, *The Order of Things: An Archaeology of the Human Sciences* (New York: Vintage Books, 1973).

5 For the concept of "participatory epistemology" see Francisco Varela, *Principles of Biological Autonomy* (New York: North Holland Series in General Systems Research, 1979).

6 At the theoretical level "feminist" theory developed on the basis of its rupture with the purely economic and class-based theory of Marxism, thereby calling into question both the "universalisms" of Marxian proletarian identity and of the liberal humanist "figure of man."

7 See Blumenberg, *Legitimacy of the Modern Age*, where he discusses the function of Darwinian thought in this articulation of the concept of ends set by nature and by evolution.

8 See her *Speculum of the Other Woman* (Ithaca: Cornell University Press, 1985), 15.

9 See Anthony Pagden, *The Fall of Natural Man: The American Indian and the Origins of Comparative Ethnology* (Cambridge, UK: Cambridge University Press, 1982).

10 See C. Lévi-Strauss, *Totemism* (Harmondsworth: Penguin, 1969).

11 See J. F. Danielli, "Altruism: The Opium of the People," *Journal of Social and Biological Structures* 3, no. 2 (April 1980), 87–94.

12 See D. Halliburton, "Endowment, Enablement, Entitlement: Toward a Theory of Constitution" in *Literature and the Question of Philosophy*, ed. A. J. Cascari (Baltimore: Johns Hopkins University Press, 1986), where he develops this concept of "endowment."

13 A play on the Derridean concept of "difference" where the temporal dimension is replaced by the stratifying/status dimension, making use of the concept of "deferent" behaviour which functions to inscribe difference, and to constitute "higher" and "lower" ranking.

14 See in this respect the book by Jacob Pandian, *Anthropology and the Western Tradition: Towards an Authentic Anthropology* (Prospect Heights, Illinois: Waveland Press, 1985).

15 See for an excellent analysis of this concept, the book by Claude Jenkins, *The Social Theory of Claude Lévi-Strauss* (London: Macmillan, 1979).

16 See her essay "The Social Framework" in *Savacou*, Kingston, Jamaica, 1970.

17 The analogy here is to the always *divergent* relation of the wife-taker category to that of the wife-giver category.

18 See Anthony Pagden, *The Fall of Natural Man*, for an analysis of this intellectual process which was to lay the basis of today's concept of "international" law.

19 See my discussion of this concept/discourse which is founding to our present order of knowledge in "On Disenchanting Discourse."

20 See Pagden, *The Fall of Natural Man*.

21 The reference here is to the "freeplay" concept of the deconstructionists. As

is clear, our counter concept is that the parameters of interpretation are always set, in the last analysis, by what we develop later as the mode of ontological difference and its related code of symbolic "life" and" death."

22 See Cary Nelson, "Against English: Theory and the Limits of the Discipline in Profession," *Proceedings of the Modern Language Association* (1987).

23 The analogy here is to the Christian theological concept of the non-elect by predestination.

24 See William Shakespeare, *The Tempest*, ed. R. Langbaum (New York: Signet Classic, 1964).

25 This code, developed from Aquinas' formulation of an ontological natural law able to be detached from its Christological base, will be central to the later mutation to the secular orders of things.

26 See her book, *La parole des femmes: Essai sur les romancières des Antilles des langues françaises* (Paris: L'Harmattan, 1979).

27 Europe's expropriation of the lands of the Americas initiated a land/labor ratio of a new and unprecedented extent. Both the encomienda and hacienda and the plantation institution were the answer to this vast "enclosure system" by which the category of "native labor" and "native being" came into existence.

28 See the essay by Arnold Davidson where he quotes Freud's point about the plasticity of the "sexual instinct" and how it can be easily "soldered" on to specific objects of desire: "How to do the History of Psychoanalysis: A Reading of Freud's *Three Essays on the Theory of Sexuality*," *Critical Inquiry* 13, no. 2 (Winter 1987).

29 See the illuminating point made by Clarisse Zimra in her essay, "Righting the Calabash: Writing History in the Female Francophone Narrative," in *Out of the Kumbla: Caribbean and Literature*, ed. Carole Boyce Davies and Elaine Savory Fido (Trenton, NJ: Africa World Press, 1990).

30 The proposal here is that the Spirit/Flesh opposition of medieval Europe functioned as the motivational mechanism of desire/aversion by means of which the secular laity were made desirous of attaining to being only through the baptismal model of medieval Christianity. See Walter Ullman's book, *Medieval Foundations of Renaissance Humanism* (Ithaca, NY: Cornell University Press, 1977).

31 The roots of contemporary racism are sited in this system of speculative thought that would be "materialized" in the encomienda and the plantation systems, since these institutions were to be based on this new secular post-Christian mode of legitimation.

32 Recent work by political scientists has begun to focus on the parallels between the discourses by means of which the New World Indians were expropriated and those by which the Cromwellian conquest and partial

occupation of Ireland were also legitimated, i.e. by the projection of a "by nature difference" between the dominant and the subordinated population groups.

33 In this respect see the original and illuminating essay by James F. Danielli, "Altruism and the Internal Reward System or The Opium of the People" in *Journal of Social and Biological Structures*, 1980: 3.

34 Even where, in the case of the Ayatollah Khomeini and Islamic fundamentalism, this might seem not to be so, the religious tenets of Islam are now a *function* of a religious-nationalist ideology adapted from the West's process of secularization.

35 This then legitimates his subordination to "rational nature" incarnated in Prospero.

36 Coined on the model of transcendental, but this time, although also extra-humanly, but from below.

37 The concept of a "semantic closure principle" is borrowed from the biologist Howard Pattee's description of the integrative functioning of the cell. The proposal is that human orders *should* function according to analogous principles. See Howard H. Pattee, "Clues from Molecular Symbol Systems" in *Signed and Spoken Language: Biological Constraints on Linguistic Forms*, ed. U. Bellugi and M. Studdert-Kennedy (Berlin: Verlag Chemie, 1980), 261–74 and "Laws and Constraints, Symbols and Languages," in *Towards a Theoretical Biology*, ed. C. H. Waddington (Edinburgh: University of Edinburgh Press, 1972), 248–58.

38 The sailors' dream, too, is to be king on the island and to marry Miranda.

39 The term is used by Foucault in his talk, "The Order of Discourse," given in December 1970 and published as an appendix of the *Archaeology of Knowledge* (New York: Harper and Row, trans. A. M. Sheridan-Smith, 1972). Here Foucault notes that Mendel's findings about genetic heredity were not hearable at first because they were not within the *"vrai"* of the discipline at the time.

40 In *The Order of Things*, Foucault points out that because "Man" is an object of "positive knowledge" in Western culture, he cannot be an "object of science."

41 "Women" can only be co-identified as a universal political category on the paradoxical basis of their/our shared bio-anatomical identity.

42 The force of the term *womanist* lies in its revelation of a perspective which can only be *partially* defined by any of the definitions of our present hegemonic theoretical models.

43 With respect to the functioning of the narrative of origins in human orders, including the "evolutionary" narrative of origin of our own which also functions as "replacement material for genesis," see Glyn Isaacs, "Aspects

of Human Evolution" in D. S. Bendall, ed., *Evolution from Molecules to Men* (Cambridge and New York: Cambridge University Press, 1983), 509–43.

44 The contradiction here is between "cultural nationalism" i.e. the imperative to revalue one's gender, class, culture and to constitute one's literary counter-canon, and the scientific question. What is the function of the "obliteration" of these multiple perspectives? What role does this play in the stable bringing into being of our present human order?

45 See Ullman, *Medieval Foundations of Renaissance Humanism*, and Blumenberg, *Legitimacy of the Modern Age*, as well as Kurt Hubner, *The Critique of Scientific Reason* (Chicago: University of Chicago Press, 1983) for the linkage of the rise of the natural sciences to the overall secularizing movement of humanism.

46 The term is Henry Louis Gates's, and is central to the range of his work. See for example his variant use of a variant of this term ("interpretative indenture") in his essay "Authority (White) Power and the (Black) Critic," in *Cultural Critique* no. 7 (Fall 1987), 19–46.

47 That is, cognition outside of the parameters prescribed by our participatory epistemology (see Francisco Vorela, op. cit.) or the World View, integrative of all orders, including our own.

48 In a paper given at the 1988 March West Coast Political Science Conference, Kathy Ferguson of the University of Hawaii pointed to the contradiction, for feminist deconstructionists, between the imperative of a fixed gender identity able to facilitate a unifying identity from which to "voice" their presence, and the deconstructionist program to deconstruct gender's oppositional categories.

49 The attack on the master canon, and the thrust to devise new canons by hitherto marginalized intelligentsia groups, allow us to speak of canonism, as one of the ordering "*isms*."

50 The stigmatization of homoerotic preference plays a key role in the projection of the idea of "natural" preference, which is founding to the inferential logic of the discourse of economics.

51 Again the point here is that interpretative readings occur within parameters set by the governing code, and are never arbitrary, even if the governing codes are.

52 The problem that faces the world is one of distribution. But if, as we argue, economic distribution is a function, in the last instance of the *integration* of our present order, then the contradiction between the global surpluses of food enabled by the Green Revolution and the spread of massive world hunger reported by world agencies is an effect, not of an economic imperative, but of an order-maintaining one, i.e. of the imperative of its "altruistic" integration.

53 In *The Tempest*, Caliban accuses Prospero of having given him "water with berries" and stroked him when the latter arrived, thereby getting Caliban to show where the streams and food sources on the island were. The proposal is that all theoretical models function both as "knowledge" and as the water-with-berries strategy sets of specific groups. I have developed this more fully in a paper – "Why We Cannot Save Ourselves in a Woman's Manner Towards a Caribbean World View," presented at the First Conference of Caribbean Women Writers and Scholars, and hosted by the Black Studies Department at Wellesley College.

54 The proposal here is since all the *isms* constitute a totemic system or set, the attempt to abolish any of these as an isolated ism is everywhere a "strategy set" of the specific group for whom, as in the case of Duvalierisme for the new Haitian black middle class, the abolition of a specific *ism* will be empowering. See with respect to feminism, [Cherrie] Moraga and [Gloria] Anzaldúa, *This Bridge Called My Back: Writings by Radical Women of Color* (Watertown, MA: Persephone Press, 1981).

PART TWO

Social and Political Theory

SIX

....

Black Women:
Shaping Feminist Theory

bell hooks

Feminism in the United States has never emerged from the women who are most victimized by sexist oppression; women who are daily beaten down, mentally, physically, and spiritually – women who are powerless to change their condition in life. They are a silent majority. A mark of their victimization is that they accept their lot in life without visible question, without organized protest, without collective anger or rage. Betty Friedan's *The Feminine Mystique* is still heralded as having paved the way for contemporary feminist movement – it was written as if these women did not exist. Friedan's famous phrase, "the problem that has no name," often quoted to describe the condition of women in this society, actually referred to the plight of a select group of college-educated, middle- and upper-class, married white women – housewives bored with leisure, with the home, with children, with buying products, who wanted more out of life. Friedan concludes her first chapter by stating: "We can no longer ignore that voice within women that says: 'I want something more than my husband and my children and my house.'" That "more" she defined as careers. She did not discuss who would be called in to take care of the children and maintain the home if more women like herself were freed from their house labor and given equal access with white men to the professions. She did not speak of the needs of women without men, without children, without homes. She ignored the existence of all nonwhite women and poor white women. She did not tell readers whether it was more fulfilling to be a maid, a babysitter, a factory worker, a clerk, or a prostitute, than to be a leisure-class housewife.

She made her plight and the plight of white women like herself synonymous with a condition affecting all American women. In so doing, she deflected attention away from her classism, her racism, her sexist attitudes towards the masses of American women. In the context of her book, Friedan makes clear that the women she saw as victimized by sexism were college-educated, white women who were compelled by sexist conditioning to remain in the home. She contends:

> It is urgent to understand how the very condition of being a housewife can create a sense of emptiness, nonexistence, nothingness in women. There are aspects of the housewife role that make it almost impossible for a woman of adult intelligence to retain a sense of human identity, the firm core of self or "I" without which a human being, man or woman, is not truly alive. For women of ability, in America today, I am convinced that there is something about the housewife state itself that is dangerous.

Specific problems and dilemmas of leisure-class white housewives were real concerns that merited consideration and change but they were not the pressing political concerns of masses of women. Masses of women were concerned about economic survival, ethnic and racial discrimination, etc. When Friedan wrote *The Feminine Mystique*, more than one-third of all women were in the work force. Although many women longed to be housewives, only women with leisure time and money could actually shape their identities on the model of the feminine mystique. They were women who, in Friedan's words, were "told by the most advanced thinkers of our time to go back and live their lives as if they were Noras, restricted to the doll's house by Victorian prejudices."

From her early writing, it appears that Friedan never wondered whether or not the plight of college-educated, white housewives was an adequate reference point by which to gauge the impact of sexism or sexist oppression on the lives of women in American society. Nor did she move beyond her own life experience to acquire an expanded perspective on the lives of women in the United States. I say this not to discredit her work. It remains a useful discussion of the impact of sexist discrimination on a select group of women. Examined from a different perspective, it can also be seen as a case study of narcissism, insensitivity, sentimentality, and self-indulgence, which reaches its peak when Friedan, in a chapter titled "Progressive Dehumanization," makes a comparison between the psychological effects of isolation on white housewives and the impact of confinement on the self-concept of prisoners in Nazi concentration camps.

Friedan was a principal shaper of contemporary feminist thought. Significantly, the one-dimensional perspective on women's reality presented in her book became a marked feature of the contemporary feminist movement. Like Friedan before them, white women who dominate feminist discourse today rarely question whether or not their perspective on women's reality is true to the lived experiences of women as a collective group. Nor are they aware of the extent to which their perspectives reflect race and class biases, although there has been a greater awareness of biases in recent years. Racism abounds in the writings of white feminists, reinforcing white supremacy and negating the possibility that women will bond politically across ethnic and racial boundaries. Past feminist refusal to draw attention to and attack racial hierarchies suppressed the link between race and class. Yet class structure in American society has been shaped by the racial politic of white supremacy; it is only by analyzing racism and its function in capitalist society that a thorough understanding of class relationships can emerge. Class struggle is inextricably bound to struggle to end racism. Urging women to explore the full implication of class in an early essay, "The Last Straw," Rita Mae Brown explained:

> Class is much more than Marx's definition of relationship to the means of production. Class involves your behavior, your basic assumptions about life. Your experience (determined by your class) validates those assumptions, how you are taught to behave, how you understand problems and solve them, how you think, feel, act. It is these behavioral patterns that middle-class women resist recognizing although they may be perfectly willing to accept class in Marxist terms, a neat trick that helps them avoid really dealing with class behavior and changing that behavior in themselves. It is these behavioral patterns which must be recognized, understood, and changed.

White women who dominate feminist discourse, who for the most part make and articulate feminist theory, have little or no understanding of white supremacy as a racial politic, of the psychological impact of class, of their political status within a racist, sexist, capitalist state.

It is this lack of awareness that, for example, leads Leah Fritz to write in *Dreamers and Dealers*, a discussion of the current women's movement published in 1979:

> Women's suffering under sexist tyranny is a common bond among all
> women, transcending the particulars of the different forms that tyranny
> takes. *Suffering cannot be measured and compared quantitatively.* Is the
> enforced idleness and vacuity of a "rich" women, which leads her to
> madness and or suicide, greater or less than the suffering of a poor woman
> who barely survives on welfare but retains somehow her spirit? There is
> no way to measure such difference, but should these two women survey
> each other without the screen of patriarchal class status, they may find a
> commonality in the fact that they are both oppressed, both miserable.

Fritz's statement is another example of wishful thinking, as well as the
conscious mystification of social divisions between women that has
characterized much feminist expression. While it is evident that many
women suffer from sexist tyranny, there is little indication that this
forges "a common bond among all women." There is much evidence
substantiating the reality that race and class identity creates differences
in quality of life, social status, and lifestyle that take precedence over the
common experience women share – differences that are rarely tran-
scended. The motives of materially privileged, educated, white women
with a variety of career and lifestyle options available to them must be
questioned when they insist that "suffering cannot be measured." Fritz
is by no means the first white feminist to make this statement. It is a
statement that I have never heard a poor woman of any race make.
Although there is much I would take issue with in Benjamin Barber's
critique of the women's movement, *Liberating Feminism*, I agree with
this assertion:

> Suffering is not necessarily a fixed and universal experience that can be
> measured by a single rod: it is related to situations, needs, and aspirations.
> But there must be some historical and political parameters for the use of
> the term so that political priorities can be established and different forms
> and degrees of suffering can be given the most attention.

A central tenet of modern feminist thought has been the assertion
that "all women are oppressed." This assertion implies that women
share a common lot, that factors like class, race, religion, sexual preference, etc., do not create a diversity of experience that determines the
extent to which sexism will be an oppressive force in the lives of
individual women. Sexism as a system of domination is institutionalized,
but it has never determined in an absolute way the fate of all women in

this society. Being oppressed means the *absence of choices*. It is the primary point of contact between the oppressed and the oppressor. Many women in this society do have choices (as inadequate as they are), therefore exploitation and discrimination are words that more accurately describe the lot of women collectively in the United States. Many women do not join organized resistance against sexism precisely because sexism has not meant an absolute lack of choices. They may know they are discriminated against on the basis of sex, but they do not equate this with oppression. Under capitalism, patriarchy is structured so that sexism restricts women's behavior in some realms even as freedom from limitations is allowed in other spheres. The absence of extreme restrictions leads many women to ignore the areas in which they are exploited or discriminated against; it may even lead them to imagine that no women are oppressed.

There are oppressed women in the United States, and it is both appropriate and necessary that we speak against such oppression. French feminist Christine Delphy makes the point in her essay, "For a Materialist Feminism," that the use of the term oppression is important because it places feminist struggle in a radical political framework:

> The rebirth of feminism coincided with the use of the term "oppression." The ruling ideology, i.e. common sense, daily speech, does not speak about oppression but about a "feminine condition." It refers back to a naturalist explanation: to a constraint of nature, exterior reality out of reach and not modifiable by human action. The term "oppression," on the contrary, refers back to a choice, an explanation, a situation that is political. "Oppression" and "social oppression" are therefore synonyms or rather social oppression is a redundance: the notion of a political origin, i.e., social, is an integral part of the concept of oppression.

However, feminist emphasis on "common oppression" in the United States was less a strategy for politicization than an appropriation by conservative and liberal women of a radical political vocabulary that masked the extent to which they shaped the movement so that it addressed and promoted their class interests.

Although the impulse towards unity and empathy that informed the notion of common oppression was directed at building solidarity, slogans like "organize around your own oppression" provided the excuse many privileged women needed to ignore the differences between their

social status and the status of masses of women. It was a mark of race
and class privilege, as well as the expression of freedom from the many
constraints sexism places on working-class women, that middle-class
white women were able to make their interests the primary focus of
feminist movement and employ a rhetoric of commonality that made
their condition synonymous with "oppression." Who was there to
demand a change in vocabulary? What other group of women in the
United States had the same access to universities, publishing houses,
mass media, money? Had middle-class black women begun a movement
in which they had labeled themselves "oppressed," no one would have
taken them seriously. Had they established public forums and given
speeches about their "oppression," they would have been criticized and
attacked from all sides. This was not the case with white bourgeois
feminists for they could appeal to a large audience of women, like
themselves, who were eager to change their lot in life. Their isolation
from women of other class and race groups provided no immediate
comparative base by which to test their assumptions of common
oppression.

Initially, radical participants in women's movement demanded that
women penetrate that isolation and create a space for contact. Anthologies like *Liberation Now*, *Women's Liberation: Blueprint for the Future*,
Class and Feminism, *Radical Feminism*, and *Sisterhood Is Powerful*, all
published in the early 1970s, contain articles that attempted to address
a wide audience of women, an audience that was not exclusively white,
middle-class, college-educated, and adult (many have articles on teena-
gers). Sookie Stambler articulated this radical spirit in her introduction
to *Women's Liberation: Blueprint for the Future*:

> Movement women have always been turned off by the media's necessity
> to create celebrities and superstars. This goes against our basic philosophy.
> We cannot relate to women in our ranks towering over us with prestige
> and fame. We are not struggling for the benefit of the one woman or for
> one group of women. We are dealing with issues that concern all women.

These sentiments, shared by many feminists early in the movement, were
not sustained. As more and more women acquired prestige, fame, or
money from feminist writings or from gains from feminist movement for
equality in the work force, individual opportunism undermined appeals
for collective struggle. Women who were not opposed to patriarchy,

capitalism, classism, or racism labeled themselves "feminist." Their expectations were varied. Privileged women wanted social equality with men of their class; some women wanted equal pay for equal work; others wanted an alternative life-style. Many of these legitimate concerns were easily coopted by the ruling capitalist patriarchy. French feminist Antoinette Fouque states:

> The actions proposed by the feminist groups are spectacular, provoking. But provocation only brings to light a certain number of social contradictions. It does not reveal radical contradictions within society. The feminists claim that they do not seek equality with men, but their practice proves the contrary to be true. Feminists are a bourgeois avant-garde that maintains, in an inverted form, the dominant values. Inversion does not facilitate the passage to another kind of structure. Reformism suits everyone! Bourgeois order, capitalism, phallocentrism are ready to integrate as many feminists as will be necessary. Since these women are becoming men, in the end it will only mean a few more men. The difference between the sexes is not whether one does or doesn't have a penis, it is whether or not one is an integral part of a phallic masculine economy.

Feminists in the United States are aware of the contradictions. Carol Ehrlich makes the point in her essay, "The Unhappy Marriage of Marxism and Feminism: Can It Be Saved?" that "feminism seems more and more to have taken on a blind, safe, nonrevolutionary outlook" as "feminist radicalism loses ground to bourgeois feminism," stressing that "we cannot let this continue":

> Women need to know (and are increasingly prevented from finding out) that feminism is not about dressing for success, or becoming a corporate executive, or gaining elective office; it is not being able to share a two-career marriage and take skiing vacations and spend huge amounts of time with your husband and two lovely children because you have a domestic worker who makes all this possible for you, but who hasn't the time or money to do it for herself; it is *not* opening a Women's Bank, or spending a weekend in an expensive workshop that guarantees to teach you how to become assertive (but not aggressive); it is most emphatically not about becoming a police detective or CIA agent or Marine Corps general.

But if these distorted images of feminism have more reality than ours do, it is partly our own fault. We have not worked as hard as we should

have at providing clear and meaningful alternative analyses which relate
to people's lives, and at providing active, accessible groups in which to
work.

It is no accident that feminist struggle has been so easily coopted to
serve the interests of conservative and liberal feminists since feminism in
the United States has so far been a bourgeois ideology. Zillah Eisenstein
discusses the liberal roots of North American feminism in *The Radical
Future of Liberal Feminism*, explaining in the introduction:

> One of the major contributions to be found in this study is the role of the
> ideology of liberal individualism in the construction of feminist theory.
> Today's feminists either do not discuss a theory of individuality or they
> unselfconsciously adopt the competitive, atomistic ideology of liberal
> individualism. There is much confusion on this issue in the feminist theory
> we discuss here. Until a conscious differentiation is made between a theory
> of individuality that recognizes the importance of the individual within
> the social collectivity and the ideology of individualism that assumes a
> competitive view of the individual, there will not be a full accounting of
> what a feminist theory of liberation must look like in our Western society.

The ideology of "competitive, atomistic liberal individualism" has
permeated feminist thought to such an extent that it undermines the
potential radicalism of feminist struggle. The usurpation of feminism by
bourgeois women to support their class interests has been to a very
grave extent justified by feminist theory as it has so far been conceived.
(For example, the ideology of "common oppression.") Any movement
to resist the cooptation of feminist struggle must begin by introducing a
different feminist perspective – a new theory – one that is not informed
by the ideology of liberal individualism.

The exclusionary practices of women who dominate feminist discourse have made it practically impossible for new and varied theories
to emerge. Feminism has its party line, and women who feel a need for
a different strategy, a different foundation, often find themselves ostracized and silenced. Criticisms of or alternatives to established feminist
ideas are not encouraged, e.g., recent controversies about expanding
feminist discussions of sexuality. Yet groups of women who feel
excluded from feminist discourse and praxis can make a place for
themselves only if they first create, via critiques, an awareness of the
factors that alienate them. Many individual white women found in the
women's movement a liberatory solution to personal dilemmas. Having

directly benefited from the movement, they are less inclined to criticize it or to engage in rigorous examination of its structure than those who feel it has not had a revolutionary impact on their lives or the lives of masses of women in our society. Nonwhite women who feel affirmed within the current structure of feminist movement (even though they may form autonomous groups) seem to also feel that their definitions of the party line, whether on the issue of black feminism or on other issues, is the only legitimate discourse. Rather than encourage a diversity of voices, critical dialogue, and controversy, they, like some white women, seek to stifle dissent. As activists and writers whose work is widely known, they act as if they are best able to judge whether other women's voices should be heard. Susan Griffin warns against this overall tendency towards dogmatism in her essay, "The Way of All Ideology":

> . . . when a theory is transformed into an ideology, it begins to destroy the self and self-knowledge. Originally born of feeling, it pretends to float above and around feeling. Above sensation. It organizes experience according to itself, without touching experience. By virtue of being itself, it is supposed to know. To invoke the name of this ideology is to confer truthfulness. No one can tell it anything new. Experience ceases to surprise it, inform it, transform it. It is annoyed by any detail which does not fit into its world view. Begun as a cry against the denial of truth, now it denies any truth which does not fit into its scheme. Begun as a way to restore one's sense of reality, now it attempts to discipline real people, to remake natural beings after its own image. All that it fails to explain it records as its enemy. Begun as a theory of liberation, it is threatened by new theories of liberation; it builds a prison for the mind.

We resist hegemonic dominance of feminist thought by insisting that it is a theory in the making, that we must necessarily criticize, question, reexamine, and explore new possibilities. My persistent critique has been informed by my status as a member of an oppressed group, experience of sexist exploitation and discrimination, and the sense that prevailing feminist analysis has not been the force shaping my feminist conscious-ness. This is true for many women. There are white women who had never considered resisting male dominance until the feminist movement created an awareness that they could and should. My awareness of feminist struggle was stimulated by social circumstance. Growing up in a Southern, black, father-dominated, working-class household, I experi-enced (as did my mother, my sisters, and my brother) varying degrees of patriarchal tyranny and it made me angry – it made us all angry. Anger led me to question the politics of male dominance and enabled me to resist sexist socialization. Frequently, white feminists act as if black women did not know sexist oppression existed until they voiced feminist sentiment. They believe they are providing black women with "the" analysis and "the" program for liberation. They do not understand, cannot even imagine, that black women, as well as other groups of women who live daily in oppressive situations, often acquire an awareness of patriarchal politics from their lived experience just as they develop strategies of resistance (even though they may not resist on a sustained or organized basis).

These black women observed white feminist focus on male tyranny and women's oppression as if it were a "new" revelation and felt such a focus had little impact on their lives. To them it was just another indication of the privileged living conditions of middle- and upper-class white women that they would need a theory to inform them that they were "oppressed." The implication being that people who are truly oppressed know it even though they may not be engaged in organized resistance or are unable to articulate in written form the nature of their oppression. These black women saw nothing liberatory in party line analyses of women's oppression. Neither the fact that black women have not organized collectively in huge numbers around the issues of "feminism" (many of us do not know or use the term) nor the fact that we have not had access to the machinery of power that would allow us to share our analyses or theories about gender with the American public negate its presence in our lives or place us in a position of dependency in relationship to those white and nonwhite feminists who address a larger audience.

The understanding I had by age thirteen of patriarchal politics created in me expectations of the feminist movement that were quite different from those of young, middle-class, white women. When I entered my first women's studies class at Stanford University in the early 1970s, white women were revelling in the joy of being together – to them it was an important, momentous occasion. I had not known a life where women had not been together, where women had not helped, protected, and loved one another deeply. I had not known white women who were ignorant of the impact of race and class on their social status and consciousness. (Southern white women often have a more realistic perspective on racism and classism than white women in other areas of the United States.) I did not feel sympathetic to white peers who maintained that I could not expect them to have knowledge of or understand the life experiences of black women. Despite my background (living in racially segregated communities), I knew about the lives of white women, and certainly no white women lived in our neighborhood, attended our schools, or worked in our homes.

When I participated in feminist groups I found that white women adopted a condescending attitude towards me and other nonwhite participants. The condescension they directed at black women was one of the means they employed to remind us that the women's movement was "theirs" – that we were able to participate because they allowed it, even encouraged it; after all, we were needed to legitimate the process. They did not see us as equals. They did not treat us as equals. And though they expected us to provide firsthand accounts of black experience, they felt it was their role to decide if these experiences were authentic. Frequently, college-educated black women (even those from poor and working-class backgrounds) were dismissed as mere imitators. Our presence in movement activities did not count, as white women were convinced that "real" blackness meant speaking the patois of poor black people, being uneducated, streetwise, and a variety of other stereotypes. If we dared to criticize the movement to assume responsibility for reshaping feminist ideas and introducing new ideas, our voices were tuned out, dismissed, silenced. We could be heard only if our statements echoed the sentiments of the dominant discourse.

Attempts by white feminists to silence black women are rarely written about. All too often they have taken place in conference rooms, classrooms, or the privacy of cozy living room settings, where one lone black woman faces the racist hostility of a group of white women. From the time the women's liberation movement began, individual black women went to groups. Many never returned after a first meeting. Anita Cornwall is correct in "Three for the Price of One: Notes from a Gay Black Feminist," when she states, ". . . sadly enough, fear of encountering racism seems to be one of the main reasons that so many black womyn refuse to join the women's movement." Recent focus on the issue of racism has generated discourse but has had little impact on the behavior of white feminists towards black women. Often the white women who are busy publishing papers and books on "unlearning racism" remain patronizing and condescending when they relate to black women. This is not surprising given that frequently their discourse is aimed solely in the direction of a white audience and the focus solely on changing attitudes rather than addressing racism in a historical and political context. They make us the "objects" of their privileged discourse on race. As "objects," we remain unequals, inferiors. Even though they may be sincerely concerned about racism, their methodology suggests they are not yet free of the type of paternalism endemic to white supremacist ideology. Some of these women place themselves in the position of "authorities" who must mediate communication between racist white women (naturally they see themselves as having come to terms with their racism) and angry black women whom they believe are incapable of rational discourse. Of course, the system of racism, classism, and educational elitism [must] remain intact if they are to maintain their authoritative positions.

In 1981, I enrolled in a graduate class on feminist theory where we were given a course reading list that had writings by white women and men, one black man, but no material by or about black, Native American Indian, Hispanic, or Asian women. When I criticized this oversight, white women directed an anger and hostility at me that was so intense I found it difficult to attend the class. When I suggested that the purpose of this collective anger was to create an atmosphere in which it would be psychologically unbearable for me to speak in class discussions or even attend class. I was told that they were not angry. *I* was the one who was angry. Weeks after class ended, I received an open letter from one white female student acknowledging her anger and expressing regret for her attacks. She wrote:

> I didn't know you. You were black. In class after a while I noticed myself, that I would always be the one to respond to whatever you said. And usually it was to contradict. Not that the argument was always about racism by any means. But I think the hidden logic was that if I could prove you wrong about one thing, then you might not be right about anything at all.

And in another paragraph:

> I said in class one day that there were some people less entrapped than others by Plato's picture of the world. I said I thought we, after fifteen years of education, courtesy of the ruling class, might be more entrapped than others who had not received a start in life so close to the heart of the

monster. My classmate, once a close friend, sister, colleague, has not spoken to me since then. I think the possibility that we were not the best spokespeople for all women made her fear for her self-worth and for her Ph.D.

Often in situations where white feminists aggressively attacked individual black women, they saw themselves as the ones who were under attack, who were the victims. During a heated discussion with another white female student in a racially mixed women's group I had organized, I was told that she had heard how I had "wiped out" people in the feminist theory class, that she was afraid of being "wiped out" too. I reminded her that I was one person speaking to a large group of angry, aggressive people; I was hardly dominating the situation. It was I who left the class in tears, not any of the people I had supposedly "wiped out."

Racist stereotypes of the strong, superhuman black woman are operative myths in the minds of many white women, allowing them to ignore the extent to which black women are likely to be victimized in this society and the role white women may play in the maintenance and perpetuation of that victimization. In Lillian Hellman's autobiographical work *Pentimento*, she writes, "All my life, beginning at birth, I have taken orders from black women, wanting them and resenting them, being superstitious the few times I disobeyed." The black women Hellman describes worked in her household as family servants, and their status was never that of an equal. Even as a child, she was always in the dominant position as they questioned, advised, or guided her; they were free to exercise these rights because she or another white authority figure allowed it. Hellman places power in the hands of these black women rather than acknowledge her own power over them; hence she mystifies the true nature of their relationship. By projecting onto black women a mythical power and strength, white women both promote a false image of themselves as powerless, passive victims and deflect attention away from their aggressiveness, their power (however limited in a white supremacist, male-dominated state), their willingness to dominate and control others. These unacknowledged aspects of the social status of many white women prevent them from transcending racism and limit the scope of their understanding of women's overall social status in the United States.

Privileged feminists have largely been unable to speak to, with, and for diverse groups of women because they either do not understand fully the interrelatedness of sex, race, and class oppression or refuse to take this interrelatedness seriously. Feminist analyses of woman's lot tend to focus exclusively on gender and do not provide a solid foundation on which to construct feminist theory. They reflect the dominant tendency in Western patriarchal minds to mystify woman's reality by insisting that gender is the sole determinant of woman's fate. Certainly it has been easier for women who do not experience race or class oppression to focus exclusively on gender. Although socialist feminists focus on class and gender, they tend to dismiss race or they make a point of acknowledging that race is important and then proceed to offer an analysis in which race is not considered.

As a group, black women are in an unusual position in this society, for not only are we collectively at the bottom of the occupational ladder, but our overall social status is lower than that of any other group. Occupying such a position, we bear the brunt of sexist, racist, and classist oppression. At the same time, we are the group that has not been socialized to assume the role of exploiter/oppressor in that we are allowed no institutionalized "other" that we can exploit or oppress. (Children do not represent an institutionalized other even though they may be oppressed by parents.) White women and black men have it both ways. They can act as oppressor or be oppressed. Black men may be victimized by racism, but sexism allows them to act as exploiters and oppressors of women. White women may be victimized by sexism, but racism enables them to act as exploiters and oppressors of black people. Both groups have led liberation movements that favor their interests and support the continued oppression of other groups. Black male sexism has undermined struggles to eradicate racism just as white female racism undermines feminist struggle. As long as these two groups or any group defines liberation as gaining social equality with ruling-class white men, they have a vested interest in the continued exploitation and oppression of others.

Black women with no institutionalized "other" that we may discriminate against, exploit, or oppress often have a lived experience that directly challenges the prevailing classist, sexist, racist social structure and its concomitant ideology. This lived experience may shape our consciousness in such a way that our worldview differs from those who have a degree of privilege (however relative within the existing system). It is essential for continued feminist struggle that black women recognize

diversity, the predominant tendency of the more militant sector is probably represented by Robin Morgan when she invokes "the profoundly radical analysis beginning to emerge from revolutionary feminism: that capitalism, imperialism, and racism are *symptoms* of male supremacy – sexism.[1] Therefore, Morgan continues, "more and more, I begin to think of a worldwide Revolution as the only hope for life on the planet."[2] The potential impact of widespread female involvement and leadership in oppositional, even revolutionary, political practice should not be underestimated. Yet, the point of departure for this practice, typified by Morgan's words, has not promoted harmonious relations with other important struggles. It is against the backdrop of the unresolved tension between black liberation and women's liberation that the latter's failure to attract more than a negligible number of black women needs to be analyzed.[3]

The women's movement, as consensus has it, found its most enthusiastic adherents among young, "middle-class" white women. Intrusions of supremacy, as they were gradually brought to light, furnished, for the vast majority, the only conscious experience of the immediacy of social opposition. This may have exacerbated a theoretical inability to discover the threads connecting female oppression to the other visible social antagonisms. It hardly needs to be said that the view which accounts for class exploitation, colonial expansion, national and racial domination as symptoms of male authority has not tackled, but rather has dodged the problem.

Such a weakness – and from a Marxist viewpoint, it *is* considered weakness – attests to an inadequate theoretical basis. But it may well have a deeper, more fundamental origin. For the identical problem of uncovering the mutual interpenetration of ostensibly unrelated modes of oppression can be detected within almost every radical movement of the contemporary era. A prototypical instance is the difficult question, yet unresolved in practice, of the relation between racism and national oppression on the one hand and exploitation at the point of production on the other.

The acute disjunction of social struggles among themselves has tended to reduplicate a larger process. This is to say, it reflects the increasingly pointed and omnipresent fragmentation of capitalist social relations in an era of advanced technology.

The following reflections, however, will not include an extensive discussion of the composition of the present women's movement nor of the larger societal influences to which it is subject. Rather, they will concentrate on a less sweeping and more narrowly theoretical problem. I will seek to inferentially discover in the works of Karl Marx, after establishing his early sensitivity to the problem, the broad outlines of women's oppression and its socio-historical development. Within the framework of Marx's theoretical reconstruction of history, I will attempt to specify the ways in which the subjugation of women and their ideological relegation to the sphere of nature were indissolubly wedded to the consolidation of capitalism.

The historical development of women's oppression is a highly interesting problem. However, I chose this approach for other reasons as well – reasons related to current theoretical controversies within the women's liberation movement itself. The exponents of the theory that sexual conflict is the matrix of all other social antagonisms frequently rely on historical arguments. Kate Millett, among others, has generous recourse to the notion that the male's enslavement of the female produced the first critical cleavage of human society. According to her method, all subsequent modes of domination are direct outgrowths of this primordial conflict.[4]

Human history is far more complex than this. Unlike the sphere of nature, from which it definitively differentiates itself during its capitalist phase, history evinces few simple causal relationships. Marx made, in fact, his most significant contribution when he ferreted out the deeper meaning of history and laid the basis for theoretical categories whose abstraction would not violate the profound complexities of human development.

Alongside awesome but increasingly irrational technological achievements, women filter through the prevailing ideology as anachronisms. Men (i.e., males) have severed the umbilical cord between themselves and nature. They have deciphered its mysteries, subdued its forces, and have forged their self-definition in contradistinction to the nature they have conquered. But women are projected as embodiments of nature's unrelenting powers. In their alienated portrait, women are still primarily undifferentiated beings – sexual, childbearing, natural. Thus Erik Erikson evokes female self-realization as a function of the "somatic design [which] harbors an 'inner space' destined to bear the offspring of chosen men, and with it, a biological, psychological, and ethical commitment to take care of human infancy."[5]

As instinct is opposed to reflection, as receptivity and gratification are opposed to activity and domination, so the "female principle" is presumptuously (although sometimes in a utopian vein) counterposed to the "male principle." In the epoch of bourgeois rule, a recurring ideological motif proclaims women to be firmly anchored in nature's domain.

Such a characterization of women cannot escape the general ambivalence inherent in the bourgeois perception of nature. Nature is posited as hostility, mysterious inexorability, a resistance to be broken. In the Hobbesian model, human beings, left in the state of nature, are locked in a *bellum omnium contra omnes*. External nature and human nature alike must be conquered by science, industry, the state – and yet other social forces. Because the domination of nature by man has involved also, and above all, the domination of human being by human being, this vision of nature has been persistently accompanied by its own contradiction.

Nature is also portrayed as the realm of original innocence, the never-to-be-retrieved paradise of play, happiness, and peace. In its utopian dimensions, nature has come forth as an implicit – albeit too impotent – denunciation of social repression and the interminable antagonisms of capitalist society.

The ideology of femininity is likewise fraught with contradictions. It is an indictment of the capitalist performance principle[6] and simultaneously one of its targets. As nature, women must be at once dominated and exalted. So, for instance, the toiling black women who populate the novels of William Faulkner are worshipped by virtue of their innocent and unfathomable communion with nature. Here, however, the utopian projection of women as nature loses its progressive content. Under the impact of racism, it emerges as a thinly veiled endorsement of oppression. The authentic but naive utopian implications of a great many portraits of women are not to be ignored. But generally even these are objectively and ultimately based in ideology, although as art they may be a critique and indictment of society. The non-ideological, perhaps revolutionary function of the female as antithesis to the performance principle remains a problem to be explored.

The hypostasized notion that woman, as contrasted with man, is only a creature of nature, is blatantly false and a camouflage for the social subjugation women daily experience. But even in its falsity, there is also a hidden truth: the real oppression of women today is inextricably bound up with the capitalist mode of appropriating and mastering nature.

The definition of women as nature is ideology; it was engendered by and is a response to real conditions of oppression. As illusory consciousness, it is a distorted and obscuring representation of reality. It distorts the oppression of women by making it appear innocuous. It is at once a hint of what human relations might eventually become and a mockery of those relations. Finally, it obscures the whole history of a painful struggle between human beings and nature, the peculiar effect of this struggle on women – and specifically, on the women of the laboring classes.

In a critical, non-ideological sense, women are indeed natural beings; men, however, are equally natural. When Marx states that human beings are natural beings, this fact assumes a very precise dialectical meaning. For, armed with their biological powers and drives, living as they do in and through nature, human beings can only survive by *acting upon and transforming* the material of nature. Thus, "labor is a natural condition of human existence, a condition of material interchange between men and nature quite independent of the form of society."[7] In the course of collectively modifying nature – and labor is always social – human beings create and transform their own human nature.

Marx's *Economic and Philosophic Manuscripts* (1844) describes the "essence" of human beings as consisting in their active, creative relationship to nature through labor. In a correctly organized society, the young Marx contends, social labor would creatively appropriate external nature as the "inorganic body of man [and woman]." External nature would be humanized and the vast potential of human nature could simultaneously unfurl.

The relationships of human beings among themselves are caught up in the process which defines the human posture toward nature. Uniquely crystallized in the female–male bond is the distance human beings have traveled in this process and specifically how far they have gone in awakening the slumbering powers within themselves.

> The immediate, natural, necessary relationship of human being to human being is the *relationship* of *man* to *woman*. In this *natural* species-relationship man's relationship to nature is immediately his relationship to man, as his relationship to man is immediately his relationship to

nature, to his own *natural* condition. In this relationship the extent to which the human essence has become nature for man or nature has become the human essence of man is *sensuously manifested*, reduced to a perceptible fact. From this relationship one can thus judge the entire level of mankind's development. From the character of this relationship follows the extent to which man has comprehended himself as a *generic* being, as *man*; the relationship of man to woman is the *most natural* relationship of human being to human being. It thus indicates the extent to which man's *natural* behavior has become *human* or the extent to which his human *essence* has become a *natural* essence for him. In this relationship is also apparent the extent to which man's *need* has become *human*, thus the extent to which the *other* human being, as human being, has become a need for him, the extent to which he in his most individual existence is at the same time a social being.[8]

This passage may not be immediately transparent. It presupposes a knowledge of the categories Marx used in developing the anthropology of the 1844 *Manuscripts* – and this is not the place to elaborate on them in any detail.[9] The reproduction of this passage is nevertheless essential; it reveals that the young Marx construed the male–female bond to be a central ingredient of the social complex which must be overturned and remolded by the revolutionary process.

The *most natural* (in this sense, biologically necessary) relationship of human beings among themselves is that between woman and man. But human beings are not inexorably yoked to their biological constitution. Sexual activity, among other activities, can acquire a wealth of social meaning entirely lacking in its abstract, purely biological form. The woman–man union, in all its dimensions., is very much mutable and always subject to social transformation. But as long as social production takes place within the fetters of capitalist relations – as long as the appropriation of nature means the exploitation of human beings – this union between the sexes remains stunted and misshapen.

The worker's alienation has immediate consequences for the relationship between the sexes and, most significantly, for the woman herself. The products of labor are lost to the worker, who has brought them. He cannot creatively affirm himself as he works. He thus "feels he is acting freely only in his animal functions – eating, drinking and procreating . . . while in his human functions he feels only like an animal."[10] To be sure, eating, drinking and procreation are genuine human functions. In abstraction, however, and separated from the remaining sphere of human activities and turned into final and sole ends, they are animal functions.[11]

The implications for the woman who shares in these activities and ministers to her man's needs are formidable. Compelled to make only minimal contributions, or none whatsoever, to social production – not even in and through the alienated patterns of work – she is effectively reduced to the status of a mere *biological* need of man.

An unmistakable inference of Marx's early theory of alienation may be formulated: a critical and *explicit* mission of communism must be to shatter and recast sexual and marital relations, as production itself is transformed. It is essential, of course, that a new, more human, more creative posture toward external nature be adopted. But the man–woman union will always be disfigured unless the woman has liberated herself *as woman*. It will only be radically remolded when she is no longer defined as if she were a natural prolongation of man. The woman must first break out of the female–male union. Only then can she and man come together on a new basis, both experiencing an equal and authentically human need for one another.

This brief discussion of the 1844 *Manuscripts* has served to establish that Marx directly addressed himself – albeit not systematically – to certain dimensions of women's oppression. The bulk of this paper will be concerned with Marx's historical approach to nature and its implications for women's oppression and future liberation. A few preparatory remarks about the transition from the early to the later thought are in order.

The early writings develop the idea that the capitalist ordering of social production has erected an insurmountable hurdle between the worker on the one hand and the material and products of labor on the other. This is equivalent to saying that the human being has been severed from nature and thus, for the young Marx, from his own "inorganic body." The creative interaction with nature is the keystone of human nature. Capitalism disrupts this unity, giving rise to a non-identity between man and his essence. Communism would be the return of man to his essence, "the genuine [definitive] resolution of the antagonism between man and nature, and between man and man."[12]

The mature Marx is far more conscious of the complexity of the human being/nature relationship and its thorough-going historical character. The notion of nature – the material and fruits of labor – as the inorganic body of the human being is discovered to be a peculiar characteristic of pre-capitalist modes of production. This relationship is historically localized as the *naive unity* which binds the pre-capitalist producer to the earth and to other natural conditions of production.[13]

As general background for the remarks which follow, it should be borne in mind that in the later writings, communism is not projected as definitively eradicating the tension between the human being and nature. Social antagonisms rising out of class society are abolished. But labor, insofar as it is *necessary* labor, will always contain an element of restraint and unfreedom.[14] The vestiges of non-identity between humans and nature can never be dissolved unless technology creates a radical metamorphosis at the heart of production itself. In any event, unless and until all work is creative and unrestrained, human beings will have to seek their self-realization, in large part, outside the realm of social production. It is precisely the communist reorganization of production that permits them to do this. In anticipation, it may therefore be proposed that the *full* emancipation of women must ultimately also transcend the goal of her full and equal participation in a new and reorganized system of production.

II

Labor, in the Marxian conception, is a "natural condition of human existence."[15] In exploring the character of women's oppression during the phase of history preceding bourgeois ascendancy, the pre-capitalist function of labor should be revealing. The economic formation in question may be communal landed property, free petty land ownership, slavery, or serfdom; in all these cases, labor is geared by and large toward the production of *use-value*.

> The purpose of this labour is not the *creation of value* . . . Its purpose is the maintenance of the owner and his family as well as the communal body as a whole. The establishment of the individual as a worker, stripped of all qualities except this one, is itself a product of *history*.[16]

Or, in slightly different words, "the object of production itself is to reproduce the producer in and together with [the] objective conditions of his existence."[17] (The slave and serf are treated as "inorganic conditions of production," as animals or as appendages of the land; yet, even as they are dominated, they and their communities are in possession of the means of their subsistence and enter into corresponding social relations among themselves.)[18]

Labor is stimulated by need; its product travels a more or less uninterrupted path towards consumption. Labor functions, therefore, as a natural mediator between external nature and the human community.[19] Considering the character of their labor, pre-capitalist epochs, even the most advanced, retain certain structural features reminiscent of subhuman natural "societies." (It is, of course, capitalism which is always the measuring rod.) Thus when Marx characterizes the earth during those phases as a "natural laboratory," the community as a "natural community," the as "natural family," he is by no means romanticizing pre-capitalist history.

Through production, the needs of the community are projected onto nature; external nature is the "inorganic body" of the community.[20] The community, in turn, always bears the stamp of nature, for it is subject, in a fundamental way, to naturally imposed limitations. In appearance, the community and family are natural phenomena – eternal and indifferent to the designs of human beings. Women and men confront collective life, family life, not as human products, but rather as unchangeable preconditions of human existence. Such is the meaning of Marx's contention that whenever labor is bound, in the last instance, to agriculture, social production will always be locked in a natural unity with state, community, and family relations. This holds true with equal force where cities and city labor are ultimately dependent on agriculture.

Against this backdrop, the "natural" roles and the "natural" oppression of the women of these periods take on a significance which transcends the mere fact of their biological constitution. It is certainly conceivable that childbearing and other physiological factors might be the immediate basis for certain social roles carrying the mark of inferiority. But it is not entirely inconceivable that under different conditions these factors could be more or less unrelated to social inferiority. Moreover, even if women's oppression bore no clear relation to biological considerations, it would not, for this reason, be lacking in "natural" dimensions.

Evidence does indicate, however, that during pre-capitalist periods, women, as a rule, were socially tied to their reproductive role. A cluster of child-centered activities attached themselves to the biological fact of maternity. The woman's attachment to the child tended to confine her to the domestic sphere. This allowed, in turn, for the evolution of a whole host of uniquely female household tasks. But even here, her roles were not determined by biological causation. Other and different *social* modes of coping with then insurmountable biological constants were not necessarily excluded from the realm of possibility. Had they arisen, they too, would have been both bound to and independent of natural determination.

Although not rigidly and biologically predetermined, a *sexual* division of labor asserted itself throughout capitalism's pre-history. In those primitive formations where, for example, hunting was necessary, this was generally outside the woman's domain. Likewise her roles were usually limited in those communities maintaining themselves through the military defense of their land.[21] War is here, in Marx's words, "the great communal labor."[22] Perhaps because of what Juliet Mitchell has termed the woman's lesser capacity for violence,[23] military activity was largely performed by the community's male members. Even when the division of labor reached levels of a far greater complexity, women's labor still remained sharply distinguished from the men's.

There are two important points to be made about the pre-capitalist character of women's labor and their related social status. First, the sexual division of labor does not militate against a greater unity – a unity which asserts itself in and through this separation. Because labor is bound up with the community's and family's *needs*, the differences between female and male labor are not *qualitative* in character. The woman's labor in and around the domestic quarters was equally essential and equally constitutive of social production. Recognizing that she experienced intense and drastic forms of oppression, it still remains that she was not exiled from *social production in general*. Rather she was barred from certain *concrete* forms of labor.[24]

Secondly, insofar as the woman was anchored to a relation of servitude, she was unable to attain a critical posture from which to perceive the real meaning of this relation. Her status and attendant oppression was coated with a nature-like inexorability. And what is most important, such an attitude had its objective complement in the prevailing mode of existence. Part of her oppression consisted in her inability to contest her inferior role. The antagonisms inherent in the male–female union tended to remain dormant, lacking the *social* level which would permit their penetration into consciousness.

In a rigorous sense, the peculiar status and oppression of women during pre-capitalist history functioned not so much as a *result* of the prevailing modes of production, but rather as a concrete *precondition* of production. This does not vitiate the material origin of the status of women; the relation is formulated in this way in order to capture the blurred unity between production and the oppression of women. As Marx notes: "Where landed property and agriculture form the basis of the economic order . . ., the economic object is the production of use-values, i.e., the *reproduction of the individual* in certain definite relationships to this community, of which it forms the basis" (Marx's emphasis).[25]

In respect to women in particular, the economy was colored by and tended to support the existing structure of woman's oppression in an equally great or even greater degree than her oppression was determined by the particular mode of production.

In the earliest primitive communities, so Marx infers, the division of labor required for production must have been synonymous with "the division of labour in the sexual act."[26] Marx goes on to say (in *The German Ideology*) that during history's most primitive epochs, the social relations of production in general were the same as the social relations incorporated in the family. Certainly as more advanced economic formations evolve, natural relations are socially modified; yet Marx insisted that before the dawn of the explosive forces rushing in the direction of capitalism, natural limitations decisively conditioned men and women's entire social life.

There prevailed a natural interpenetration of individual, family, community, and even the state on the one hand, and social production on the other. Marx observes, for example, that in a rural patriarchal form of manufacture, "when spinner and weaver lived under the same roof – the women of the family spinning and the men weaving, say, for the requirements of the family – the product of labor bore the specific imprint of the family relation with its naturally evolved division of labour.[27]

In all pre-capitalist formations, according to George Lukács, "natural relations – both in the case of the 'metabolic changes' between man and nature and also in the relations between men – retained the upper hand and dominated man's social being."[28] Alfred Schmidt maintains:

> Pre-bourgeois development had a peculiarly unhistorical character because
> in it the material prerequisites of labour – the instrument as well as the

material – were not themselves the *product* of labour, but were found already to hand in the land, in nature, from which the active subject as well as the community to which it belonged did not essentially differentiate themselves. Under capitalism, however, these subjective and objective conditions of production became something created by the participants in history. Relationships were no longer determined by nature but *set up* by society.[29]

During the pre-capitalist phase of history, women's oppression, strictly construed, was heavily enshrouded in a natural determination not yet superseded or transformed by socio-historical forces. It experienced a corresponding transformation when capitalist society broke onto the scene of history. Then, it, like capitalist social relations in general, would also be *set up* by society.

III

While the pre-capitalist subjugation of women is related to socially insurmountable natural imitations, these limitations are articulated through socially prescribed roles. Highly interesting, in this connection, is the brutally unique situation into which black women were thrust during American slavery.[30] With the rise of capitalism and the subordination of slavery to an incipient commodity economy, black men and women were treated ruthlessly and literally as "inorganic conditions of production" (to use the term with which Marx describes the economic function of slaves). Other forms of slavery merely stamped with the mark of inferiority the social relations of slaves among themselves. But the American system demanded the almost total prohibition of an endemic social life within the community of slaves.

American slavery was not a natural economy based primarily on consumption; its goal was rather the production of commodities. The slaveholding class expressed its drive for profit by seeking the maximum extraction of surplus labor in utter disregard to the age or sex of the slave. Even very real biological limitations were frequently little more than occasions for flogging. As reported in slave narratives, special forms of punishment were meted out to pregnant women who were unable to meet the prescribed work pace. In some instances, a hole was carved in the ground permitting a pregnant woman to lie in a prone position while she was flogged by the overseer.

The family was either nonexistent or its sole and unmediated purpose was to produce future forgers of profit. It is true that the black woman was responsible for the domestic chores of the slave quarters. Yet, this role was not integrated into an overall structure articulating her dependence vis-à-vis the black man. External economic compulsions brought her into an equal partnership in oppression with the man. As a result, the black woman was not systematically molded into an inferior being insofar as the internal workings of the slave community – the relations of the slaves among themselves – were concerned.

This did not prevent the slave system from aspiring to foist upon her the putative inferiority of the woman. The use of her body as a breeding instrument and its sexual violation by the slave-holder were institutional assertions of the lower rank of the female slave. But this oppression was not part of a naturally conditioned order and was thus significantly different in structure from its pre-capitalist counterpart. As overt social coercion, the oppression of black women in slavery could not conceal its contingent social character.

IV

The American slave system was a notable exception in the world historical rise of capitalism. In its peculiar subordination to a commodity economy, it could only have arisen where incipient conditions of capitalism already prevailed. In the broadest sense, as Marx points out, it is the impact of economic exchange on a progressively large scale which overturns old structures and paves the way for the "free" wage laborer – the *sine qua non* of capitalism.

The ingression of exchange, when it occurs, begins to undermine fundamentally and drastically the entire texture of human life. As the central prerequisite for the genesis of capital, labor-power itself, like the products of labor, was eventually reduced to a universally exchangeable commodity. But first the producer had to be decisively severed from the land, from his implements of production, as well as from his control over the means of subsistence.[31] And the natural bonds tying producer to producer, family structures included, had to be deprived of their seemingly objective and necessary mode of existence. Their relationship to production had to take on a contingent appearance. This is to say, the reproduction of the community of producers, and of the family as its unit, could no longer be presumed to be the real goal of production. Use-value had to be supplanted by exchange-value and the aim of production had to become the reproduction of capital.

The family and community ceased to appear as extensions of nature (which has both positive and negative implications) in order to make way for a society composed of fragmented individuals, lacking any organic or human connection. Such a society, infinitely more advanced in its mode of production, is mediated by the abstract principle of exchange.

Marx never fails to accentuate the eminently progressive content of this development. There is progress in the very midst of its ruthlessness. Capitalism marked the release of productive forces which, for the first time in history, could systematically appropriate and transform the fruits of nature.[32] From the vantage point of the producer, it was also an important advance, even as it merely modified the structure of his oppression. The worker was freed from the overt domination by another human being, from the alien and unqualified control over his body and movement. He attained freedom over his body and the liberty to dispose of his labor. The new owners of the means of production would have to bargain with him for the purchase of his labor-power. His wages would not be determined by the capitalist's whim, but rather by socially necessary labor time. As a person, he would be superfluous to production; only his abstract ability to work would be pertinent. Yet, even in this contingency, he could also discover beneficial features, for, with the notable exception of racism, caste-like distinctions should not interfere when he sold his labor-power on the market. The capitalist commodity is totally indifferent to the origin of the labor which produces it; labor becomes "abstract labor-power," and each worker of similar skills should always be equal to the next.

The immanent logic of capitalist production demands the universal equivalence of labor-power. If, for the purposes of analysis, this factor is isolated from other forces at work, it latently contains profound consequences for the social status of women. In face of the dissolution of the natural rigidity of the family, and especially as mechanization progresses, women of the working class should have undergone the same process of equalization as men. In earlier periods, specific forms of labor belonged exclusively to women. Part of the quality of their products consisted precisely in the fact that they were products of *female* labor. But when the product of labor became an exchangeable commodity, all such distinctions began to vanish. An unprecedented potential thus works its way into history: *The capitalist mode of production unleashes the condition for the historical supersession of the sexually based division of labor.* The universal equivalence of labor-power conceptually implies the release of the woman from her naturally infused roles in labor.

This potentiality, needless to say, could not become more than an abstract promise of equal exploitation. Capitalism could not even proclaim for women this rudimentary egalitarianism. Instead it transmuted a more or less naturally conditioned oppression into an oppression whose content became thoroughly *socio-historical*. It was only then that women were effectively exiled from the sphere of social production – or permitted, at most, a tangential role. Their containment within the family became, not a natural necessity, but rather a peculiarly societal phenomenon. It is therefore only in bourgeois society that the oppression of women assumes a decisive *social* dimension and function.

The capitalist mode of production outstrips all previous modes in transcending virtually all extra-economic determinants. The unique status of women is not immediately implied in the capitalist organization of labor, as one of its preconditions. According to Marx: "For capital, the worker does not constitute a condition of production, but only labor. If this can be performed by machinery, or even by water or air, so much the better. And what capital appropriates is not the laborer, but his labor – and not directly, but by means of exchange."[33]

If it does not matter who does the work – only that it be done – then certainly women can be non-discriminately employed in production. Through the eyes of the commodity, in fact, women are indistinguishable from men. But, as it will be subsequently shown, their oppression is indeed a *result* of critical social forces in whose absence the mode of production could not effectively be sustained. A distinctive and indeed defining innovation of capitalist production lies in its *projection of female oppression onto a socio-historical continuum.* Once this occurs, women's liberation, like the emancipation of the producers themselves, becomes a *real* historical possibility. The concrete promise of female liberation is bound up inextricably with the overturning of the social forces fundamentally nourished by her oppression.

V

The unfettering of the historical ingredients which ushered in the capitalist form of labor in its abstract, universal equivalence, has been examined from a very specific perspective. A closer glimpse at this development, emphasizing its impact on the worker's family as it was dispossessed of its natural foundation, reveals the special basis for women's oppression under capitalism. Engels was essentially correct to link the inferior status of the female to the hierarchical make-up of the family. For the numerous material and cultural manifestations of female inferiority are predicated on the woman's dependent rank within the family unit. This derives in turn, and certainly in the final instance, from the exigencies of capitalism's productive apparatus.

Within Marxist theory, most of the discussion about the insular bourgeois family has concentrated on its mode of existence among the bourgeoisie alone. The private, individual proprietor, it is asserted, needs his own miniature "society" over which he wields unrestricted authority. His wife – and children of undisputed fatherhood – must be his uncontested possessions. The private character of his remaining property must transcend his own mortal existence: his wife, through her child-bearing, must therefore protect it from future alienation and dissolution.

While all this is true and critically important to the functioning of capitalism, the special meaning of the insular family for the worker should not go unacknowledged. Engels insisted that the worker who has nothing to sell but his ability to work cannot be overly concerned about bequeathing this meager property to his undisputed heirs. But this does not mean that the bourgeois family structure was thus *externally* foisted upon the producers, serving no *real* objective purpose. On the contrary, the hierarchical family structure, as it exists among workers, possesses a unique and necessary relationship to the capitalist mode of production. As it will later be maintained, this family also responds to certain irrepressible needs of working human beings themselves.

The central prerequisite for the constitution of capital – and thus for the ascendancy of the bourgeoisie and its family – is the historical appearance of the *private individual* worker. (The emergence of the worker as individual is simultaneously the emergence of the producing individual defined vis-à-vis production only in his capacity as worker.)[34] The further back we trace the course of history, the more does the individual, and accordingly also the producing individual, appear to be dependent and belong to a larger whole. At first the individual, in a still quite natural manner is part of the family and of the tribe which evolves from the family. Later he is a part of a community.[35] And, prior to capitalism, the producer's relation "to the natural prerequisite of his production as *his own* is mediated by his natural membership in a community" (or a state).[36] Even the slave and the serf, it should be recalled, are in direct possession of the means of their subsistence.

As capital makes its ingression into history, the worker is transfigured into an isolated private individual – isolated from the means of production (hence also from the means of subsistence) and equally isolated from the community of producers. To a hitherto unprecedented degree, workers are fragmented among themselves to the point of perceiving their own social relations as the nexus of exchange binding commodity to commodity. The fragmentation of the community of producers thus complements the fetishistic appearance of the commodity, the veiled crystallization of social relations under capitalism.

When the serf or free peasant is ejected from the land; when the artisan is divested of the implements of his labor; when they are cut off from their peers as individual units of labor-power; it is actually, they and their miniature societies which are severed from nature and the human community. The worker is sealed off in the false privacy of the insular family.

The utter disintegration of the community of producers relegates, therefore, not the individual, but rather the family unit to a distant realm which bears no organic connection to the activity of social production. Although Marx does not explicitly discuss the process of individuation undergone by the worker as it is related to the fate of the family, a direct connection between these two processes seems to be apparent nevertheless. Marx's observations seem to raise the question of whether the individual worker – carrier of abstract labor-power – demanded by production, would not have to express somewhere the authority of his individuality, an authority without which individuality would not be obtained. Assuming an affirmative answer, this authority could very well express itself in the family – but within a family whose dynamic relation to production has been annulled. If this were so, it would be clear why the woman is not permitted to experience the ruthless – although in some respects beneficial – equalizing tendencies of capitalist production. She remains inseparably anchored to the fabric necessary for the maintenance of the worker as individual.

The woman not only remains tied to the family, but must bear the major responsibility for the internal labor guaranteeing its preservation. These private domestic duties preclude more than marginal participation in *social* production. Moreover, she is enclosed within a family whose unity with social production has severely eroded; her labor within the household therefore takes on an entirely new character. In pre-bourgeois history, such work, essential to the maintenance of the family and of the larger community as well, was necessarily an important component of social production itself. With capitalism, household labor, generating only the value of utility, is no longer related to the productive apparatus. Production itself has undergone a profound metamorphosis; its fundamental aim is the creation of exchange-value. Thus, with respect to production, women experience a double inferiority. They are first prohibited, by virtue of their standing, from consistently and equally reaching the point of production. Secondly, the labor they continue to monopolize does not measure up to the characteristic labor of capitalist society.

Kinship, marital, and procreative relations are no longer balanced with the relations of production. The family itself ceases to incorporate the social – although for pre-capitalist history, natural – relations of production. But the *natural* functions of women are abstractly articulated in the family. These functions are rendered abstract exactly to the degree that they are stripped of their *immediate social character*. Through a dialectical inversion, it is the radical separation of the producer from nature that lays the basis for the *social* creation of women as eternally natural beings. This is to say, women are socially imprisoned within natural roles that are no longer naturally necessary.

Hence there occurs under capitalism a necessary dialectic between the potential equality of women, inherent in the apparatus of production, and the inevitable domination of women implied in (but not confined to) the family. This dialectic largely defines the structure of women's oppression (simultaneously signaling the negative conditions for its abolition) and confers upon this structure its overtly societal, therefore transmutable character. New relations of production render such factors as sex superfluous. But the intrinsic social necessity of these relations – the need to buttress the abstract, individual and fragmented nature of labor-power – re-establishes sexual differences in the social edifice resting on the base of production.

These social differences go so far as to apportion to women a *qualitatively* different form of labor – the labor of utility as opposed to that of exchange. Margaret Benston observes that: "The appearance of commodity production has indeed transformed the way that men labor. . . . Most household labor in capitalist society remains in the pre-market stage. This is the work which is reserved for women and it is in this fact that we can find the basis for a definition of women."[37]

Yet Benston's position implies that women are *objective* (and not just ideological) anachronisms. This dilemma can only be surmounted if their use-value producing labor is studied against the background of the objectively possible equalization of women by the commodity-producing apparatus.

As it will be subsequently shown, the equalization–repression dialectic has yet another moment, realized with the actual admission of women into capitalist social production. Female labor-power (not concrete labor), even as it is called upon for tasks identical to those performed by men, will be laden with cultural determination. This is not to mention the plethora of "female" occupations. Labor performed by women, even when it produces exchange-value, will not be "abstract labor-power in general" but rather a specific and socially inferior female ability to work.

VI

Reduced to its biological preconditions, the insular structure of the producer's family announces and fortifies the rupture of the human community of producers. In this sense, the family is essential for the ideological reproduction of capitalist society as a whole. Yet, in the course of reinforcing the alienated relations crystallized in the commodity, the family – and more specifically, the woman – must also respond to *real human needs*. "Bourgeois civilization has reduced social relations to the cash nexus. They have become emptied of affection."[38] With due consideration of the factor of sublimation, the human need for affective bonds cannot be eliminated beyond an absolute minimum. If these relations were divested of all immediate expression, human beings could hardly survive the desperate struggle for existence. Love and interpersonal emotions in general are needs which cease to demand at least minimal fulfillment only when human beings have long since ceased to be human. In capitalist society, the woman has the special mission of being both reservoir and receptacle for a whole range of human emotions otherwise banished from society. This mission is directly related to her confinement, in labor, to the production of use-values.

Forbidden to flourish in society at large, and especially at the point of production, personal relations unfolding within the family inevitably are affected adversely. Indeed, from the very outset, the "legitimate" woman–man union already bears the inexorable stamp of exchange. Its legitimacy is a contrivance of the marriage *contract*; like the labor contract, this is also an "unjust exchange." Here, of course, the woman is always victim. All this considered, it must be recognized nonetheless that in the absence of even this far from ideal occasion for interpersonal bonds, capitalist society probably would be much more grotesque than it has actually proved to be. A case in point is Nazi Germany. The unarticulated purpose behind its irrational cult of the family and mother-hood was to manipulate family-based emotions into an unmediated fusion with extreme national and racial chauvinism. In this respect, Nazi propaganda was designed, at bottom, to vitiate the family itself as a locus of personal emotions.[39]

In its "bourgeois-democratic" form, capitalism requires the family as a realm within which the natural and instinctive yearning for non-reified human relations may be expressed. Herbert Marcuse discusses their relations:

> Human relations are class relations, and their typical form is the free labor contract. This contractual character of human relationships has spread from the sphere of production to all of social life. Relationships function only in their reified form, mediated through the class distribution of the material output of the contractual partners. If this functional de-personal-ization were ever breached, not merely by that backslapping familiarity which only underscores the reciprocal functional distance separating men but rather by mutual concern and solidarity, it would be impossible for men to return to their normal social functions and positions. The contrac-tual structure upon which this society is based would be broken.[40]

Contrasted with prevailing social relations, the family and its web of personal relations add a qualitatively different dimension to social life. On precisely this basis, in fact, the woman is presented in the utopian fringes of bourgeois ideology as an antithesis to the capitalist performance principle. This positive (although still distorted) aspect of the ideology of femininity has been frequently suppressed by the women's liberation movement. In efforts to debunk the myth of the woman as an exclusively emotional being, an equally abstract position has been too often assumed. The abstract negation of "femininity" is embraced; attempts are made to demonstrate that women can be as non-emotional, reality-affirming and dominating as men are alleged to be. The model, however, is usually a concealed "masculine" one.

The most extreme case – extreme to the point of absurdity – of proposing as a solution to male supremacy the abstract negation of "femininity" is furnished by Valerie Solanas and her *SCUM Manifesto* (Society for Cutting Up Men). Her definition of sexuality is exceedingly revealing:

> Sex is not part of a relationship, on the contrary, it is a solitary experience, non-creative, a gross waste of time. The female can easily – far more easily than she may think – condition away her sex drive, leaving her completely cool and cerebral, and free to pursue truly worthy relationships and activities [sic!]. . . . When the female transcends her body, rises above animalism, the male . . . will disappear.[41]

One thing is clear in this drastic formulation of the attack against male supremacy: such a position, in the final analysis, must be a duplication – conscious or unconscious – of the reified relations which have demanded the oppression of women in the first place. This position reinstates the same relations that have engendered a situation where women are exhaustively defined as "affective" – "affective" in a way that men cannot be – and where women's emotionality is presumed to exclude rationality. In order to shatter the ideology of femininity insofar as it implies reified affection, women must also combat the ideology of reified insensibility. If, as Marx has said, liberation is to ultimately also mean "the complete *emancipation* of all the human qualities and senses,"[42] which include "not only the five senses, but the so-called spiritual senses, the practical senses (desiring, loving),"[43] then the positive qualities of femininity must be released from their sexual exclusiveness, from their distorted and distorting forms. They must be *aufgehoben* in a new and liberating socialist society.

Christopher Caudwell draws attention to the fact that within the interstices of capitalism, non-reified modes of behavior continue to exist. He describes these as vestiges of pre-capitalist history:

> Even today, in those few economic forms which still survive in a pre-bourgeois form, we can see tenderness as the essence of the relation. The commodity fetishism which sees in a relation between men only a relation between things has not yet dried it up. The economic relation of the mother to her foetus, of the child to the parent [primarily the mother] and vice versa retains its primitive form to show this clearly.[44]

Caudwell envisions "love" as capable of proposing a fierce indictment of bourgeois society. This is undoubtedly utopian idealism, unless, that is, a socio-political mediation can draw love and tenderness into the revolutionary continuum. Love alone is impotent, yet without it, no revolutionary process could ever be truly authentic. From this vantage point, a critical kernel of truth emerges out of Caudwell's vision:

> Today it is as if love and economic relations have gathered at two opposite poles. All the unused tenderness of man's instincts gather at one pole and at the other are economic relations, reduced to bare coercive rights to commodities. This polar segregation is a source of terrific tension and will give rise to a vast transformation of bourgeois society.[45]

It cannot be too strongly emphasized that in seeking to discover the precise role of such categories as Caudwell proposes in developing a revolutionary theory, and particularly as these pertain to women, much caution is necessary. In advancing the most radical construction of the revolutionary function of utopian categories in general (a function possible only with advanced capitalism), Marcuse is always careful to avoid Icarus's dilemma.[46] He reveals the threads which lead directly from utopia to science and back to utopia again.

Germaine Greer soars high with her utopian dreams of women's potential capabilities. But finally she can discover no real solutions and must turn to abstract ethical imperatives. In the last chapter of her book – the chapter entitled "Revolution" – she says, significantly:

> It would be genuine revolution if women would suddenly stop loving the victors in violent encounters . . . If soldiers were certainly faced with the withdrawal of all female favors, as Lysistrata observed so long ago, there would suddenly be less glamour in fighting.[47]

Presumably, this is a way of reaching the new society, a society free of "masculine" (she does not say "imperialist") war.

The personal relations which cluster around women contain in germ, albeit in a web of oppression and thus distortedly, the premise of the abolition of alienation, the dissolution of a compulsive performance principle, thus, ultimately, the destruction of the whole nexus of commodity exchange. But yet this utopian content is only a promise and nothing more. Its radical implications remain impotent unless they are integrated into a practical revolutionary process.

In *capitalist* society, although these personal relations are a contrast to the normal flow of social life, they are, in their present form, woven into the warp and woof of capitalist relations as a whole. Even as a negation of these relations, they actually presuppose them and foster their continuance. It is a non-subverting negation. Marcuse characterizes social relations under capitalism as creating a "reciprocal functional distance separating men." It has already been shown that the break-up of pre-capitalist economic and social life gave rise to a historically unprecedented separation of human beings among themselves – in order to separate them from the means of production. The family, it was maintained, is the direct target of these divisive forces which establish a foundation for the most advanced phase of human development by instituting the most systematic method of human exploitation. This "reciprocal functional distance separating men" both requires, and issues out of, the new family structure, closed in upon itself especially for the woman.

A progressively increasing fragmentation among human beings has accompanied an ever more developed capitalism. In the era of advanced capitalism, the insularity is virtually complete. A salient example can be seen in the recently escalated flight toward the suburbs. Workers, especially white workers, have also joined in this exodus. The closed-in cubicle-like housing is a material extension of the ever increasing distance which dissevers them from their fellow producers. (The situation of the woman worker will be discussed later in the paper.) The plight of the woman in the suburbs is especially painful, for solidarity with other human beings is hardly attainable in this isolated environment. When it occurs, it is the artificial, backslapping type. Her shopping center is in the suburb as is the school for her children (she is often opposed to "busing"), her beauty parlor, her "entertainment." She drives virtually everywhere; nothing is in walking distance from her home. There is no public transportation to speak of. If there is only one car in the family she is often confined to the house until her husband comes home from work. The husband returns each day, forgetting in this plastic environment exactly how toilsome his work has been. His comrade producers are but numbers and bodies to him – at most beer-drinking partners. The worker must thus surmount many insurmountable barriers before he can become aware that he and all other producers are the wellspring of the society. The achievement of solidarity, thus of a revolutionary class consciousness, has never been so difficult as during the present era. This particular phenomenon further attests to the inseparable unity of women's oppression and the exploitation of workers. The role society has given to women reinforces the mechanisms which guarantee the continued domination of the producers.

Perhaps the most concrete instance of the family providing an objective contrast to capitalist social relations as a whole can be sought in the oppressed communities of America. Among black people, for one, the potential for a different, more human quality of relations prevails – relations which often escape the false, "back-slapping" familiarity which is the distorted form of personal association. Families are frequently "extended" rather than "nuclear," embracing more than two generations, as well as cousins and other relatives. The increasing use of "sister" and "brother," which is by no means confined to the politically sophisticated, is an overt protest against the compartmentalization of existence. Though the use of those terms has a long tradition encompassing many and diverse associations, the fact that they now transcend political or religious affiliations and are widespread in the community as a whole, points to the yearning for human solidarity in the midst of a situation where solidarity has almost become obsolete.

As it normally functions, the family is a windowless monad of illusory satisfaction. It strengthens the distance between human beings in society. But like Leibniz's monad, it is also a reflection of a larger totality; its duplication of society is strikingly illustrated by its function in respect to the children it conceives. As the human, *natural* sphere par excellence, the family introjects society into the "human nature" of the child. Within the perimeters of the family, a psychological make-up harmonious, or at least compatible, with an exploitative and repressive environment must be reproduced. In this sense, the family's older place and role in the community has remained more or less intact. In pre-capitalist formations it was the family, the kinship group or earlier, the tribe, which regulated and perpetuated a specific metabolism between its members and nature. When "nature" is superseded by the commodity form, and human beings relate to their environment and to one another through the nexus of exchange, the family initially forges a pre-established harmony between individual and capitalist society.

The family has been divested of many of its functions as an instrument of socialization. The educational system and the media – television in particular – surpass the family's importance in the socialization process. Nevertheless, the very earliest formative months and years of the individual are still subject to the family's – and especially the mother's – guidance. As psychoanalysis has verified, the first months of childhood are critically important for the psychological constitution of the mature adult. It is not necessary to invoke the special categories of Freudian psychology to realize, for instance, that it is the mother who introduces the child to language and who first assists it to develop the powers of perception through which it will eventually "receive" the world.

The drudgery of full-time child rearing acquires, in this manner, a more profound and infinitely devastating meaning. Society assigns to women the mission of unknowingly creating human beings who will "feel at home" in a reified world.

VII

In *Capital*, Marx confidently asserted that: "modern industry, by assigning as it does an important part in the process of production, outside the domestic sphere, to women, to young persons, and to children of both sexes, creates a new economical foundation for a higher form of the family and of the relations between the sexes."[48] But, in actuality, female participation in production has remained a mere foundation whose edifice was not – and could not be – erected. It has not greatly upset the structure of the family, nor has it significantly ameliorated the social status of women. While work outside the home has furnished some women with important advantages, most have had to accept its reaffirming and amplifying effect on their oppression. In Clara Colon's words:

> The woman, pivot of home and family life, can only set one foot into the
> world of opportunity as industrial worker. The other foot is still stuck to

the household doorstep. If she tries to combine home and work, she is restricted to performing half-way in each. The working mother finds employment outside the home is a tough and tedious chore, hardly a step toward equality.[49]

As a dependent being, as someone else's "inorganic extension," the price of women's entry into production was surplus exploitation (grossly inferior wages) and jobs which, on the whole, were far less fulfilling than even the stultifying labor assigned to men. Marx pointed out that: "In England women are still occasionally used instead of horses for hauling canal boats, because the labor required to produce horses and machines is an accurately known quantity, while that required to maintain the women of the surplus population is below all calculation."[50]

In America, one-third of all married women currently work outside the home – slightly more than one-half of all working women. But considering that the median earnings of women are about half that of men (and for black women even less), it is clear that female oppression has only sunk deeper into the apparatus. For if and when women's participation in social production becomes viable and necessary, the capitalist contracts the purchase, not of "abstract labor-power in general" but rather of an already socially stigmatized female labor-power.

The family-based structure of oppression – engendered in the final instance by the capitalist mode of production – is reduplicated and exacerbated by her entry into the labor force. For as long as the woman's "natural" place is proclaimed to be the home – in concrete terms: as long as she remains chained to a man and to a private domestic economy – her servile status is inevitable. No matter how excruciating, her overly exploitative job always remains a subsidiary activity. Combined with her multitudinous domestic duties, it shrinks her realm of leisure (strictly speaking, her only freedom beyond the necessity of labor) to practically naught.

It is not to be inferred, however, that women should refrain from seeking further penetration into social production. On the contrary, the demand for job equality – equal jobs and equal pay for the same jobs – is one of the indispensable prerequisites for an effective women's liberation strategy. Such a demand, it need not be said, loses much of its meaning and can fall back into the orbit of oppression unless it is accompanied by the fight for childcare centers, maternity leaves, free abortions and the entire complex of solutions to uniquely female needs. Without such special and only apparently unequal treatment, "equality" tends towards its own negation.

The ultimate meaning of the fight for the equality of women at the point of production should transcend its immediate aim. These efforts must be seen as an essential ingredient of a broader thrust: the assault on the institutional structures which perpetuate the socially enforced inferiority of women. In the warped sexual equality foisted upon the black woman by slavery and subsequent national oppression, there is a revealing hint of the latent but radical potential of the attack on the productive apparatus. The singular status of black people from slavery to the present has forced the woman to work outside the home – at first as provider of profit for the slave-master, but later as provider for her own family. Certainly, as female, she has been objectively exploited to an even greater degree than the black man. It would therefore be cruel and extravagant to claim that the black woman has been released from the social stigma attached to women in general and particularly to the women of the laboring classes. The black woman's relative independence, emanating from her open participation in the struggle for existence, has always been but another dimension of her oppression. It has thus rendered her household and internal family responsibilities all the more onerous. From these, she had never been objectively freed. The important point, however, is the fact that she has not been – and could not be – exclusively defined by her special, "female" duties. As a result, far more meaningful social roles within the black community – oppressed from without – have been available to black women. Most importantly, black women have made critical contributions to the fight against racism and national oppression – from slavery to the present.

What has been prompted in the black woman by the utter necessity of trying to survive in face of ruthless and sustained national oppression, should be elevated by the women's movement to the status of a strategic goal. This is especially important as this movement gathers impetus within the existing social framework. Efforts to bring women into production – and always on an equal basis with men – need to be placed on the continuum of revolution. While immediate needs should be pacified, such efforts must assist in bringing to fruition among women a vast and hitherto untapped potential for anti-capitalist consciousness. As one mode of the women's struggle, the assault on sexism which permeates the productive apparatus – conjoined with agitation for all the special female needs – can help women to rid themselves of the "muck of ages," of their self-image as natural extensions of maleness. This is indispensable preparation for revolutionary consciousness and practice.

VIII

Broader strategic questions about the character and direction of women's liberation may now be posed. What ought not to be the strategy of female liberation can be clearly stated. It ought not to be reduced and confined to the abstract and isolated attempt to shift the balance of "sexual politics." In conferring absolute primacy on the sexual dimensions of woman's oppression, the narrow bourgeois feminist approach distorts its social character and functions within existing social conditions. This approach has correctly discerned the oppression of women to be a thread linking even the most disparate eras of history. It is true that even the socialist countries have not achieved the emancipation of women. But to conclude that therefore the structures of sexual oppression are primary is to ignore the changing character of women's oppression as history itself has advanced. The narrow feminist approach fails to acknowledge the specificity of the social subjugation of the women who live outside the privileged class under capitalism. It is qualitatively different from the comparatively *natural* oppression which was the lot of women in previous historical periods. And to the extent that some women continue to play subordinate roles in existing socialist societies, their oppression assumes yet another, but far less dangerous character.

Within the existing class relations of capitalism, women in their vast majority are kept in a state of familial servitude and social inferiority not by men in general, but rather by the ruling class. Their oppression serves to maximize the efficacy of domination. The objective oppression of black women in America has a class, and also a national origin. Because the structures of female oppression are inextricably tethered to capitalism, female emancipation must be simultaneously and explicitly the pursuit of black liberation and of the freedom of other nationally oppressed peoples.

An effective women's liberation movement must be cognizant of the primacy of the larger social revolution: the capitalist mode of production must be overturned, like the political and legal structures that sustain it. Conversely, the larger social revolution must be cognizant of the vital place and role of the thrust towards women's emancipation.

The socialist movement must never forget that while the economic struggle is indispensable, it is by no means the sole terrain of significant anti-capitalist activity. Thus, the unique features of the women's struggle cannot be restricted to economic agitation alone.

A socialist revolution will more or less reflect the struggles which led it to its triumphant phase. In this respect, the entire revolutionary continuum must be animated by the consciousness that the real goal of socialism is to shatter the automatism of the economic base. This, indeed, is the requisite condition for preparing the way for a sphere of freedom outside, and undetermined by, the process of production. Perhaps eventually, even work can become an expression of freedom, but this would be far in the distant future. However, even this total transfiguration of the nature of work would presuppose that the economy had long since ceased to be the center of society.

The edifice of the new society cannot spring *sui generis* from the economic and political reconstitution of its fabric. It is therefore misleading to represent women's liberation under socialism as equivalent to the achievement of full and equal female participation in production. Certainly women should perform a proportional part of social labor, but only as their necessary duties in a society oriented towards the satisfaction of its members' material and spiritual needs. Further, job discrimination under socialism attests to and fortifies the continued oppression of women.

Beyond this, women must be liberated from toilsome and time-consuming household duties; the private domestic economy must be dissolved. They must be permitted a maximum range of control over their bodies – exactly to the degree that this is objectively possible through science.

These are but a few of the negative preconditions for an affirmative release of women's human potentialities. That this release will demand an entirely new organization of the family is obvious. Most Marxists have been loath to speculate about new forms the family can assume under socialism. But, as Marcuse has emphasized on numerous occasions, utopian projections at the present phase of technological development must not necessarily lack a scientific and historical foundation. New theoretical approaches to the family – at once scientific and imaginative – can be of immense assistance to the women's movement in the formulation of its long-range goals.

Within the present fabric of domination, the women's movement is confronted with urgent oppositional tasks. For if the material and ideological supports of female inferiority are not to be carried over intact into the socialist order,[51] they must be relentlessly attacked throughout the course of building the revolutionary movement. Not only must there be agitation around the economic situation of women, but equally important, the entire superstructural nexus of women's oppression must be met with constant criticism and organized assaults. While moving towards the overthrow of capitalism, the ideology of female inferiority must be so thoroughly subverted that once the revolution is achieved, it will be impossible to refer with impunity to "my better half" or to be the "natural" place of the woman as in the home.

Perhaps the most significant message for the existing women's movement is this: the ultimate face of women's oppression is revealed precisely there where it is most drastic. In American society, the black woman is most severely encumbered by the male supremacist structures of the larger society. (This does not contradict the fact that a greater sexual equality might prevail inside the oppressed black community.) Its combination with the most devastating forms of class exploitation and national oppression clearly unmasks the socio-historical function of the subjugation of women.

Even as black women have acquired a greater equality as women within certain institutions of the black community, they have always suffered in a far greater proportion and intensity the effects of institutionalized male supremacy. "In partial compensation for [a] narrowed destiny the white world has lavished its politeness on its womankind. . . . From black women of America, however, this gauze has been withheld and without semblance of such apology they have been frankly trodden under the feet of [white] men."[52]

If the quest for black women's liberation is woven as a priority into the larger bid for female emancipation; if the women's movement begins to incorporate a socialist consciousness and forges its practice accordingly; then it can undoubtedly become a radical and subversive force of yet untold proportions. In this way the women's liberation movement may assume its well-earned and unique place among the current gravediggers of capitalism.

Notes

1 Robin Morgan, ed., *Sisterhood is Powerful* (New York: Vintage Books, 1970), xxxiv (her emphasis).
2 Ibid., xxxv.
3 Numerous critiques of the "white" women's liberation movement have been proposed by blacks – and specifically by black women. Linda La Rue, for example, cautions against an alliance with the women's movement, which she concludes would be inherently unwise (Linda La Rue, "The Black Movement and Women's Liberation," *The Black Scholar*, May 1970). Toni Morrison contends that there is something intrinsic in the experience and corresponding *Weltanschauung* of black women which renders women's liberation irrelevant and superfluous. (Toni Morrison, "What the Black Woman Thinks about Women's Lib," *The New York Times Magazine*, August 22, 1971). At the other end of the spectrum, there is, for instance, the Third World Women's Alliance, which stresses the critical importance of women's liberation for women of color, while maintaining that their organizational structure and theoretical basis must be separate from and autonomous *vis-à-vis* the women's movement among whites. (See their manifesto *Triple Jeopardy*, reprinted in *Triple Jeopardy*, vol. 1, no. 1, Sept.–Oct. 1971.)
4 The one classical Marxist text on the oppression of women – Friedrich Engels's *Origin of the Family, Private Property and the State* – has ironically been invoked by many who seek to demonstrate the socio-historical primacy of women's subjugation. Indeed, one of the flaws of this work is that Engels's entire analysis is predicated on a hypothetical pre-historical ascendancy of the woman. What he calls "the world-historical defeat of the female sex" is proposed as the first instance of human beings dominating their own kind. This is the crucial moment of his analysis and thus, in his opinion, the key to an understanding of women's oppression. While it is clearly necessary to recognize the infinitely long history of women's subjugation, the impact of capitalism on women is critical for an understanding of women's present status and oppression. Engels minimizes the qualitatively new form of socially enforced female inferiority which inserts itself into history with the advent of capitalism.
5 Erik Erikson, "Inner Space and Outer Space," *Daedalus*, no. 93, 1964, 580–606.
6 Marcuse says in *Eros and Civilization*, "We designate [the specific reality principle that has governed the origins and the growth of this civilization] as *performance principle* in order to emphasize that under its rule society is

stratified according to the competitive economic performance of its members ... The performance principle, which is that of an acquisitive and
antagonistic society in the process of constant expansion, presupposes a
long development during which domination has been increasingly rational-
ized." Herbert Marcuse, *Eros and Civilization* (London: Sphere Books,
1969), 50.

7   Karl Marx, *A Contribution to a Critique of Political Economy* (New York:
International Publishers, 1970), 36.

8   Karl Marx, *Economic and Philosophic Manuscripts* (1844), "Private Property and Communism," in Lloyd D. Easton and Kurt H. Guddat, trans. and
eds, *Writings of the Young Marx on Philosophy and Society* (New York:
Doubleday and Co./Anchor Books, 1967), 303. Some mention should be
made of the semantic problem posed, at least in the English language, by
the unavoidable use of the same term to designate both the male of the
species and the species itself. As has been repeatedly noted, the language
itself exposes how deeply male supremacy is embedded in the fabric of
society. It should that be clear that in this passage, Marx is certainly not
referring only to the male's relation to the natural human condition and
neither does he equate this with his relationship to the female. The same
principle is equally applicable to women, their inferior status under capitalism notwithstanding.

9   The notion of man [-woman] as a species-being is a key element of Marx's
early anthropology. Although the biological connotation of species is
contained within this term, this is not its essential meaning. The deeper
meaning Marx attributes to "species-being" emerges from a philosophical
tradition which sought to develop a philosophy of man [-woman], proposing various ideal definitions of the human species. "Species-being," as a
result, also has ethical implications. Human beings, social "by nature,"
strive toward the realization of their social potential (which is a creative
potential) by transforming nature and thereby making their surroundings
more human. For the early Marx, thus, labor itself acquires an ethical, even
eudaemonistic mission.

10 Marx, *Economic and Philosophic Manuscripts* (1844), "Alienated Labor,"
in Easton and Guddat, 292.

11 Ibid.

12 Marx, "Private Property and Communism," 304.

13 In analyzing pre-capitalist formations, Marx asserts that for the spontaneously evolved community, "the earth is the great laboratory, the arsenal
which provides both the means and materials of labor, and also the
location, the *basis* is the community. Men's relation to it is naive: they
regard themselves as its *communal proprietors*, and as those of the community which produces and reproduces itself by living labor." Karl Marx,

Pre-Capitalist Economic Formations (New York: International Publishers, 1965), 69.

14 Marx writes, "the realm of freedom actually begins only where labor which is determined by necessity and mundane considerations ceases; thus in the very nature of things it lies beyond the sphere of actual material production. Just as the savage must wrestle with nature to satisfy his wants, to maintain and reproduce life, so must civilized man, and he must do so in all social formations and under all possible modes of production. With his development this realm of physical necessity expands as a result of his wants; but, at the same time, the forces of production which satisfy these wants also increase. Freedom in this field can only consist in socialized man, the associated producers, rationally regulating their interrelations with nature, bringing it under their common control, instead of being ruled by it as by the blind forces of nature; and achieving this with the least expenditure of energy and under conditions most favorable to, and worthy of, their human nature. But it nonetheless still remains a realm of necessity. Beyond it begins that development of human energy which is an end in itself, the true realm of freedom, which, however, can blossom forth only with this realm of necessity as its basis. The shortening of the working-day is its basic prerequisite." Karl Marx, *Capital* (New York: International Publishers, 1968), vol. 3, 820.

15 Marx, *A Contribution to a Critique of Political Economy*, 36.

16 Marx, *Pre-Capitalist Economic Formations*, 68.

17 Ibid., 95.

18 "There is a third *possible form* [of property] which is to act as proprietor neither of the land nor of the instrument (i.e., nor of labor itself), but only of the means of subsistence, which are then found as the natural condition of the laboring subject. This is at bottom the formula of slavery and serfdom" (Marx, *Pre-Capitalist Economic Formations*, 101).

19 In describing the transition from various pre-bourgeois formations to capitalism, Marx contends that "closer analysis will show that what is dissolved in all these processes of dissolution are relations of productions in which use-value predominates; production for *immediate* use" (my emphasis) (ibid., 105).

20 Marx proposes this generalization about pre-capitalist epochs as a whole: "They all evince a unity of living and active human beings with the natural, inorganic conditions of their metabolism with nature, and therefore their appropriation of nature" (ibid., 86). Moreover, in describing "the *pre-bourgeois* relationship of the individual to the objective conditions of labor, and in the first instance to the natural objective conditions of labor," Marx says: "just as the working subject is a natural individual, a natural being, so the first objective condition of his labor appears as nature, earth, as an

inorganic body. He himself is not only the organic body, but also inorganic nature as a subject. The condition is not something he has produced, but something he finds to hand; something existing in nature and which he presupposes" (ibid., 85).

21 There are obviously exceptions to this rule. A salient example is provided by John Henrik Clarke when he discusses the critical role of African women in resisting the encroachments of the slave trade: "In the resistance to the slave trade and the colonial system that followed the death of the Queen [Nzingha of Angola], African women, along with their men helped to mount offensives all over Africa. Among the most outstanding were: Madame Tinubo of Nigeria; Nandi, the mother of the great Zulu warrior Chaka; Kaipldre of the Hereto people of South West Africa; and the female army that followed the great Dahomian King, Behanzin Howell." John Henrik Clarke, "The Black Woman: A Figure in World History," Part I, *Essence Magazine*, May 1971.

22 Marx, *Pre-Capitalist Economic Formations*, 71.

23 Juliet Mitchell, *Women: The Longest Revolution*, pamphlet reprinted from Nov.–Dec. 1966 issue of *New Left Review* (Boston: New England Press), 8.

24 Engels fails to emphasize this pre-capitalist structural necessity, a necessity which is invalidated only by capitalism. Consequently, women's oppression during both pre-capitalist and capitalist history appears, in his analysis, to be essentially homogeneous.

25 Marx, *Pre-Capitalist Economic Formations*, 81.

26 Karl Marx, *The German Ideology* (New York: International Publishers, 1963).

27 Marx, *A Contribution to a Critique of Political Economy*, 33.

28 George Lukács, *History and Class Consciousness* (London: Merlin Press, 1971), 233.

29 Alfred Schmidt, *The Concept of Nature in Marx* (London: New Left Books, 1971), 178.

30 What follows in highly condensed form is a section of a recent essay: Angela Y. Davis, "Reflections on the Black Woman's Role in the Community of Slaves," *The Black Scholar*, vol. 3, no. 4 (Dec. 1971).

31 See note 18. Also consider this paragraph: "Such historic processes of dissolution are the following: the dissolution of the servile relationship which binds the laborer to the soil, but in fact assumes his property in the means of subsistence (which amounts in truth to his separation from the soil); the dissolution of relations of property which constitute a laborer as yeoman, or free, working, petty landowner or tenant (colonus), or free peasant; the dissolution of guild relations which presuppose the laborer's property in the instrument of production and labor itself, as a certain form

of craft skill not merely as the source of property but as property itself; also the dissolution of the relations of clientship in its different types, in which *non-proprietors* appear as co-consumers of the surplus produce in the retinue of their lord, and in return wear his livery, take part in his feuds, perform real or imaginary acts of personal service, etc. Closer analysis will show that what is dissolved in all these processes of dissolution are relations of production in which use-value predominates; production of immediate use. Exchange-value and its production presuppose the dominance of the other form." Marx, *Pre-Capitalist Economic Formations*, 104–5.

32   Consider, for example, the following passage from *Pre-Capitalist Economic Formations*: "The ancient conception, in which man always appears (in however narrowly national, religious or political a definition) as the aim of production, seems very much more exalted than the modern world, in which production is the aim of man and wealth the aim of production. In fact, however, when the narrow bourgeois form has been peeled away, what is wealth, if not the universality of needs, capacities, enjoyments, productive powers, etc., of individuals, produced in universal exchange? What, if not the full development of human control over the forces of nature – those of his own nature as well as those of so-called 'nature'? What, if not the absolute elaboration of his creative dispositions, without any preconditions other than antecedent historical evolution which makes the totality of this evolution – i.e., the evolution of all human powers as such, unmeasured by *any previously established* yardstick – an end in itself? What is this, if not a situation where man does not reproduce himself in any determined form, but produces his totality? Where he does not seek to remain something formed by the past, but is in the absolute movement of becoming? In bourgeois political economy – and in the epoch of production to which it corresponds – this complete alienation, and the destruction of all fixed, one-sided purposes, is the sacrifice of the end in itself to a wholly external compulsion. Hence in one way the childlike world of the ancients appears to be superior; and this is so, in so far as we seek for closed shape, form and established limitation. The ancients provide a narrow satisfaction, whereas the modern world leaves us unsatisfied, or, where it appears to be satisfied with itself, is *vulgar* and *mean*" (84–5).

33   Ibid., 99.

34   "The establishment of the individual as a worker, stripped of all qualities except this one, is itself a product of history" (ibid., 68).

35   Marx, *A Contribution to a Critique of Political Economy*, 189. Engels comments, in a footnote to this passage, that actually the process is just the reverse. That is to say, the tribe is primary and the smaller family eventually evolves from it.

36   Marx, *Pre-Capitalist Economic Formations*, 88–9.

37   Margaret Benston, "The Political Economy of Women's Liberation," *Monthly Review*, vol. 21, no. 4 (Sept. 1969), 15. She goes on to say: "This assignment of household work, as the function of a special category, 'women,' means that this group *does* stand in a different relation to production than the group, 'men.' We will tentatively define women, then, as that group of people who are responsible for the production of simple use-values in those activities within the home and family" (15–16).

38   Christopher Caudwell, *Studies in a Dying Culture* (New York: Dodd Mead and Co., 1949), 148.

39   According to one student of Nazi culture, the Nazis regarded the family as the original social unit, the "germ cell of the people, an *aid to the state rather than a rival unit of social organization*. The ideal family is a firmly knit group rooted in the soil, contributing numerous racially pure offspring, each child reared to unswerving love for the nazi State" (my emphasis). Clifford Fitzpatrick, *Nazi Germany: Its Women and Family Life* (New York: Bobbs Merrill, 1938), 101.

40   Herbert Marcuse, "On Hedonism," *Negations* (Boston: Beacon Press, 1968), 164.

41   Valerie Solanas, *SCUM Manifesto*, quoted in *The Female State, A Journal of Female Liberation* (Somerville, Mass.), issue 4 (April 1970), 57.

42   Karl Marx, *Economic and Philosophic Manuscripts* ("Private Property and Communism"). The translation is Bottomore's: T. B. Bottomore, trans. and ed., Karl Marx, *Early Writings* (New York: McGraw-Hill, 1963), 160. Easton and Guddat translate *Eigenschaften* as "aptitudes" instead of "qualities" (308).

43   Ibid., Bottomore, 161. Easton and Guddat use "moral" instead of "practical" (309).

44   Caudwell, *Studies in a Dying Culture*, 148–9.

45   Ibid., 157.

46   "The dynamic of their productivity [i.e., the productivity of contemporary societies] deprives 'utopia' of its traditional unreal content: what is denounced as 'utopian' is no longer that which has 'no place' and cannot have any place in the historical universe, but rather that which is blocked from coming about by the power of the established societies. 'Utopian' possibilities are inherent in the technical and technological forces of advanced capitalism and socialism: the rational utilization of these forces on a global scale would terminate poverty and scarcity within a very foreseeable future." Herbert Marcuse, *An Essay on Liberation* (Boston: Beacon Press, 1969), 4–5). The unleashing of long repressed emotional potentials is objectively possible exactly to the degree that the abolition of scarcity is possible. For the latter is indeed predicated on a relaxing of the rigidity of the performance principle.

47 Germaine Greer, *The Female Eunuch* (London: Paladin, 1971), 317.

48 Marx, *Capital*, vol. 1, 495–6.

49 Clara Colon, *Enter Fighting: Today's Woman. A Marxist-Leninist View* (New York: Outlook Publishers, 1970), 8.

50 Marx, *Capital*, vol. 1, 391.

51 A socialist scholar has alluded to the family as an "instance of an alienated social institution that has been taken over lock, stock, and barrel by socialism from the capitalist system." He says that "the traditional form of the family has not only survived, but also it defies any reasonable forecasts about its further development." Adam Schaff, *Marxism and the Human Individual* (New York: McGraw-Hill, 1970), 136.

52 W. E. B. Du Bois, *Darkwater: Voices from Within the Veil* (New York: AMS Press, 1969 [original edition, 1920]), 182.

EIGHT

....

The Social Construction of Black Feminist Thought

Patricia Hill Collins

Sojourner Truth, Anna Julia Cooper, Ida Wells-Barnett, and Fannie Lou Hamer are but a few names from a growing list of distinguished African American women activists. Although their sustained resistance to black women's victimization within interlocking systems of race, gender, and class oppression is well known, these women did not act alone.[1] Their actions were nurtured by the support of countless, ordinary African American women who, through strategies of everyday resistance, created a powerful foundation for this more visible black feminist activist tradition.[2] Such support has been essential to the shape and goals of black feminist thought.

The long-term and widely shared resistance among African American women can only have been sustained by an enduring and shared standpoint among black women about the meaning of oppression and the actions that black women can and should take to resist it. Efforts to identify the central concepts of this black women's standpoint figure prominently in the works of contemporary black feminist intellectuals.[3] Moreover, political and epistemological issues influence the social construction of black feminist thought. Like other subordinate groups, African American women not only have developed distinctive interpretations of black women's oppression, but have done so by using alternative ways of producing and validating knowledge itself.

A Black Women's Standpoint

The Foundation of Black Feminist Thought

Black women's everyday acts of resistance challenge two prevailing approaches to studying the consciousness of oppressed groups.[4] One approach claims that subordinate groups identify with the powerful and have no valid independent interpretation of their own oppression.[5] The second approach assumes that the oppressed are less human than their rulers and, therefore, are less capable of articulating their own standpoints.[6] Both approaches see any independent consciousness expressed by an oppressed group as being not of the group's own making and/or inferior to the perspective of the dominant group.[7] More important, both interpretations suggest that oppressed groups lack the motivation for political activism because of their flawed consciousness of their own subordination.

Yet African American women have been neither passive victims of nor willing accomplices to their own domination. As a result, emerging work in black women's studies contends that black women have a self-defined standpoint on their own oppression.[8] Two interlocking components characterize this standpoint. First, black women's political and economic status provides them with a distinctive set of experiences that offers a different view of material reality than that available to other groups. The unpaid and paid work that black women perform, the types of communities in which they live, and the kinds of relationships they have with others suggest that African American women, as a group, experience a different world than those who are not black and female.[9] Second, these experiences stimulate a distinctive black feminist consciousness concerning that material reality.[10] In brief, a subordinate group not only experiences a different reality than a group that rules, but a subordinate group may interpret that reality differently than a dominant group.

Many ordinary African American women have grasped this connection between what one does and how one thinks. Hannah Nelson, an elderly black domestic worker, discusses how work shapes the standpoints of African American and white women: "Since I have to work, I don't really have to worry about most of the things that most of the white women I have worked for are worrying about. And if these women did their own work, they would think just like I do – about this, anyway."[11] Ruth Shays, a black inner city resident, points out how variations in men's and women's experiences lead to differences in perspective: "The mind of the man and the mind of the woman is the same. But this business of living makes women use their minds in ways that men don't even have to think about."[12] Finally, elderly domestic worker Rosa Wakefield assesses how the standpoints of the powerful and those who serve them diverge: "If you eats these dinners and don't cook 'em, if you wears these clothes and don't buy or iron them, then you might start thinking that the good fairy or some spirit did all that. . . . Black folks don't have no time to be thinking like that. . . . But when you don't have anything else to do, you can think like that. It's bad for your mind, though."[13]

While African American women may occupy material positions that stimulate a unique standpoint, expressing an independent black feminist consciousness is problematic precisely because more powerful groups have a vested interest in suppressing such thought. As Hannah Nelson notes, "I have grown to womanhood in a world where the saner you are, the madder you are made to appear."[14] Nelson realizes that those who control the schools, the media, and other cultural institutions are generally skilled in establishing their view of reality as superior to alternative interpretations. While an oppressed group's experiences may put them in a position to see things differently, their lack of control over the apparatuses of society that sustain ideological hegemony makes the articulation of their self-defined standpoint difficult. Groups unequal in power are correspondingly unequal in their access to the resources necessary to implement their perspectives outside their particular group.

One key reason that standpoints of oppressed groups are discredited and suppressed by the more powerful is that self-defined standpoints can stimulate oppressed groups to resist their domination. For instance, Annie Adams, a southern black woman, describes how she became involved in civil rights activities.

When I first went into the mill we had segregated water fountains. . . . Same thing about the toilets. I had to clean the toilets for the inspection room and then when I got ready to go to the bathroom, I had to go all the way to the bottom of the stairs to the cellar. So I asked my boss man, "What's the difference? If I can go in there and clean them toilets, why can't I use them?" Finally, I started to use that toilet. I decided I wasn't going to walk a mile to go to the bathroom.[15]

In this case, Adams found the standpoint of the "boss man" inadequate, developed one of her own, and acted upon it. In doing so, her actions exemplify the connections between experiencing oppression, developing a self-defined standpoint on that experience, and resistance.

The Significance of Black Feminist Thought

The existence of a distinctive black women's standpoint does not mean that it has been adequately articulated in black feminist thought. Peter Berger and Thomas Luckmann provide a useful approach to clarifying the relationship between a black women's standpoint and black feminist thought with the contention that knowledge exists on two levels.[16] The first level includes the everyday, taken-for-granted knowledge shared by members of a given group, such as the ideas expressed by Ruth Shays and Annie Adams. Black feminist thought, by extension, represents a second level of knowledge, the more specialized knowledge furnished by experts who are part of a group and who express the group's standpoint. The two levels of knowledge are interdependent; while black feminist thought articulates the taken-for-granted knowledge of African American women, it also encourages all black women to create new self-definitions that validate a black women's standpoint.

Black feminist thought's potential significance goes far beyond demonstrating that black women can produce independent, specialized knowledge. Such thought can encourage collective identity by offering black women a different view of themselves and their world than that offered by the established social order. This different view encourages African American women to value their own subjective knowledge base.[17] By taking elements and themes of black women's culture and traditions and infusing them with new meaning, black feminist thought rearticulates a consciousness that already exists.[18] More important, this rearticulated consciousness gives African American women another tool of resistance to all forms of their subordination.[19]

Black feminist thought, then, specializes in formulating and rearticulating the distinctive, self-defined standpoint of African American women. One approach to learning more about a black women's standpoint is to consult standard scholarly sources for the ideas of specialists on black women's experiences.[20] But investigating a black women's standpoint and black feminist thought requires more ingenuity than that required in examining the standpoints and thought of white males. Rearticulating the standpoint of African American women through black feminist thought is much more difficult since one cannot use the same techniques to study the knowledge of the dominated as one uses to study the knowledge of the powerful. This is precisely because subordinate groups have long had to use alternative ways to create an independent consciousness and to rearticulate it through specialists validated by the oppressed themselves.

The Eurocentric Masculinist Knowledge-Validation Process[21]

All social thought, including white masculinist and black feminist, reflects the interests and standpoint of its creators. As Karl Mannheim notes, "If one were to trace in detail . . . the origin and . . . diffusion of a certain thought-model, one would discover the affinity it has to the social position of given groups and their manner of interpreting the world."[22] Scholars, publishers, and other experts represent specific interests and credentialing processes and their knowledge claims must satisfy the epistemological and political criteria of the contexts in which they reside.[23]

Two political criteria influence the knowledge-validation process. First, knowledge claims must be evaluated by a community of experts whose members represent the standpoints of the groups from which they originate. Second, each community of experts must maintain its credibility as defined by the larger group in which it is situated and from which it draws its basic, taken-for-granted knowledge.

When white males control the knowledge-validation process, both political criteria can work to suppress black feminist thought. Since the general culture shaping the taken-for-granted knowledge of the community of experts is one permeated by widespread notions of black and female inferiority,[24] new knowledge claims that seem to violate these fundamental assumptions are likely to be viewed as anomalies.[25] Moreover, specialized thought challenging notions of black and female inferiority is unlikely to be generated from within a white-male-controlled academic community because both the kinds of questions that could be asked and the explanations that would be found satisfying would necessarily reflect a basic lack of familiarity with black women's reality.[26]

The experiences of African American women scholars illustrate how individuals who wish to rearticulate a black women's standpoint through black feminist thought can be suppressed by a white-male-controlled knowledge-validation process. Exclusion from basic literacy, quality educational experiences, and faculty and administrative positions has limited black women's access to influential academic positions.[27] Thus, while black women can produce knowledge claims that contest those advanced by the white male community, this community does not grant that black women scholars have competing knowledge claims based in another knowledge validation process. As a consequence, any credentials controlled by white male academicians can be denied to black women producing black feminist thought on the grounds that it is not credible research.

Those black women with academic credentials who seek to exert the authority that their status grants them to propose new knowledge claims about African American women face pressures to use their authority to help legitimate a system that devalues and excludes the majority of black women.[28] One way of excluding the majority of black women from the knowledge-validation process is to permit a few black women to acquire positions of authority in institutions that legitimate knowledge and to encourage them to work within the taken-for-granted assumptions of black female inferiority shared by the scholarly community and the culture at large. Those black women who accept these assumptions are likely to be rewarded by their institutions, often at significant personal cost. Those challenging the assumptions run the risk of being ostracized.

African American women academicians who persist in trying to rearticulate a black women's standpoint also face potential rejection of their knowledge claims on epistemological grounds. Just as the material realities of the powerful and the dominated produce separate stand-points, each group may also have distinctive epistemologies, or theories of knowledge. It is my contention that black female scholars may know that something is true but be unwilling or unable to legitimate their claims using Eurocentric masculinist criteria for consistency with sub-stantiated knowledge and Eurocentric masculinist criteria for methodo-logical adequacy.

For any particular interpretive context, new knowledge claims must be consistent with an existing body of knowledge that the group controlling the interpretive context accepts as true. The methods used to validate knowledge claims must also be acceptable to the group controlling the knowledge-validation process.

The criteria for the methodological adequacy of positivism illustrate the epistemological standards that black women scholars would have to satisfy in legitimating alternative knowledge claims.[29] Positivist approaches aim to create scientific descriptions of reality by producing objective generalizations. Since researchers have widely differing values, experiences, and emotions, genuine science is thought to be unattainable unless all human characteristics except rationality are eliminated from the research process. By following strict methodological rules, scientists aim to distance themselves from the values, vested interests, and emotions generated by their class, race sex, or unique situation and in so doing become detached observers and manipulators of nature.[30]

Several requirements typify positivist methodological approaches. First, research methods generally require a distancing of the researcher from her/ his "object" of study by defining the researcher as a "subject" with full human subjectivity and objectifying the "object" of study.[31] A second requirement is the absence of emotions from the research process.[32] Third, ethics and values are deemed inappropriate in the research process, either as the reason for scientific inquiry or as part of the research process itself.[33] Finally, adversarial debates, whether written or oral, become the preferred method of ascertaining truth – the arguments that can withstand the greatest assault and survive intact become the strongest truths.[34]

Such criteria ask African American women to objectify themselves, devalue their emotional life, displace their motivations for furthering knowledge about black women, and confront, in an adversarial relationship, those who have more social, economic, and professional power than they. It seems unlikely, therefore, that black women would use a positivist epistemological stance in rearticulating a black women's standpoint. Black women are more likely to choose an alternative epistemology for assessing knowledge claims, one using standards that are consistent with black women's criteria for substantiated knowledge and with black women's criteria for methodological adequacy. If such an epistemology exists, what are its contours? Moreover, what is its role in the production of black feminist thought?

The Contours of an Afrocentric Feminist Epistemology

Africanist analyses of the black experience generally agree on the fundamental elements of an Afrocentric standpoint. In spite of varying histories, black societies reflect elements of a core African value system that existed prior to and independently of racial oppression.[35] Moreover, as a result of colonialism, imperialism, slavery, apartheid, and other systems of racial domination, blacks share a common experience of oppression. These similarities in material conditions have fostered shared Afrocentric values that permeate the family structure, religious institutions, culture, and community life of blacks in varying parts of Africa, the Caribbean, South America, and North America.[36] This Afrocentric consciousness permeates the shared history of people of African descent through the framework of a distinctive Afrocentric epistemology.[37]

Feminist scholars advance a similar argument. They assert that women share a history of patriarchal oppression through the political economy of the material conditions of sexuality and reproduction.[38] These shared material conditions are thought to transcend divisions among women created by race, social class, religion, sexual orientation, and ethnicity and to form the basis of a women's standpoint with its corresponding feminist consciousness and epistemology.[39]

Since black women have access to both the Afrocentric and the feminist standpoints, an alternative epistemology used to rearticulate a black women's standpoint reflects elements of both traditions.[40] The search for the distinguishing features of an alternative epistemology used by African American women reveals that values and ideas that Africanist scholars identify as being characteristically "black" often bear remarkable resemblance to similar ideas claimed by feminist scholars as being characteristically "female."[41] This similarity suggests that the material conditions of oppression can vary dramatically and yet generate some uniformity in the epistemologies of subordinate groups. Thus, the significance of an Afrocentric feminist epistemology may lie in its enrichment of our understanding of how subordinate groups create knowledge that enables them to resist oppression.

The parallels between the two conceptual schemes raise a question: Is the worldview of women of African descent more intensely infused with the overlapping feminine/Afrocentric standpoints than is the case for either African American men or white women?[42] While an Afrocentric feminist epistemology reflects elements of epistemologies used by blacks as a group and women as a group, it also paradoxically demonstrates features that may be unique to black women. On certain dimensions, black women may more closely resemble black men, on others, white women, and on still others, black women may stand apart from both groups. Black feminist sociologist Deborah K. King describes this phenomenon as a "both/or" orientation, the act of being simultaneously a member of a group and yet standing apart from it. She suggests that multiple realities among black women yield a "multiple consciousness in black women's politics" and that this state of belonging yet not belonging forms an integral part of black women's oppositional consciousness.[43] Bonnie Thornton Dill's analysis of how black women live with contradictions, a situation she labels the "dialectics of black womanhood," parallels King's assertions that this "both/or" orientation is central to an Afrocentric feminist consciousness.[44] Rather than emphasizing how a black women's standpoint and its accompanying epistemology are different from those in Afrocentric and feminist analyses, I use black women's experiences as a point of contact between the two.

Viewing an Afrocentric feminist epistemology in this way challenges analyses claiming that black women have a more accurate view of oppression than do other groups. Such approaches suggest that oppression can be quantified and compared and that adding layers of oppression produces a potentially clearer standpoint. While it is tempting to claim that black women are more oppressed than everyone else and therefore have the best standpoint from which to understand the mechanisms, processes, and effects of oppression, this simply may not be the case.[45]

African American women do not uniformly share an Afrocentric feminist epistemology since social class introduces variations among black women in seeing, valuing, and using Afrocentric feminist perspectives. While a black women's standpoint and its accompanying epistemology stem from black women's consciousness of race and gender oppression, they are not simply the result of combining Afrocentric and female values – standpoints are rooted in real material conditions structured by social class.[46]

Concrete Experience as a Criterion of Meaning

Carolyn Chase, a thirty-one-year-old inner city black woman, notes, "My aunt used to say, 'A heap see, but a few know.'"[47] This saying depicts two types of knowing, knowledge and wisdom, and taps the first dimension of an Afrocentric feminist epistemology. Living life as black women requires wisdom since knowledge about the dynamics of race, gender, and class subordination has been essential to black women's survival. African American women give such wisdom high credence in assessing knowledge.

Allusions to these two types of knowing pervade the words of a range of African American women. In explaining the tenacity of racism, Zilpha Elaw, a preacher of the mid-1800s, noted: "The pride of a white skin is a bauble of great value with many in some parts of the United States, who readily sacrifice their intelligence to their prejudices, and possess more knowledge than wisdom."[48] In describing differences separating African American and white women, Nancy White invokes a similar rule: "When you come right down to it, white women just *think* they are free. Black women *know* they ain't free.[49] Geneva Smitherman, a college professor specializing in African American linguistics, suggests that "from a black perspective, written documents are limited in what they can teach about life and survival in the world. Blacks are quick to ridicule 'educated fools,' . . . they have 'book learning,' but no 'mother wit,' knowledge, but not wisdom."[50] Mabel Lincoln eloquently summarizes the distinction between knowledge and wisdom: "To black people like me, a fool is funny – you know, people who love to break bad, people you can't tell anything to, folks that would take a shotgun to a roach."[51]

Black women need wisdom to know how to deal with the "educated fools" who would "take a shotgun to a roach." As members of a subordinate group, black women cannot afford to be fools of any type, for their devalued status denies them the protections that white skin, maleness, and wealth confer. This distinction between knowledge and wisdom, and the use of experience as the cutting edge dividing them, has been key to black women's survival. In the context of race, gender, and class oppression, the distinction is essential since knowledge without wisdom is adequate for the powerful, but wisdom is essential to the survival of the subordinate.

For ordinary African American women, those individuals who have lived through the experiences about which they claim to be experts are more believable and credible than those who have merely read or thought about such experiences. Thus, concrete experience as a criterion for credibility frequently is invoked by black women when making knowledge claims. For instance, Hannah Nelson describes the importance that personal experience has for her: "Our speech is most directly personal, and every black person assumes that every other black person has a right to a personal opinion. In speaking of grave matters, your personal experience is considered very good evidence. With us, distant statistics are certainly not as important as the actual experience of a sober person."[52] Similarly, Ruth Shays uses her concrete experiences to challenge the idea that formal education is the only route to knowledge: "I am the kind of person who doesn't have a lot of education, but both my mother and my father had good common sense. Now, I think that's all you need. I might not know how to use thirty-four words where three would do, but that does not mean that I don't know what I'm talking about . . . I know what I'm talking about because I'm talking about myself. I'm talking about what I have lived."[53] Implicit in Shays's self-assessment is a critique of the type of knowledge that obscures the truth, the "thirty-four words" that cover up a truth that can be expressed in three.

Even after substantial mastery of white masculinist epistemologies, many black women scholars invoke their own concrete experiences and those of other black women in selecting topics for investigation and methodologies used. For example, Elsa Barkley Brown subtitles her essay on black women s history, "how my mother taught me to be a historian in spite of my academic training."[54] Similarly, Joyce Ladner maintains that growing up as a black woman in the South gave her special insights in conducting her study of black adolescent women.[55]

Henry Mitchell and Nicholas Lewter claim that experience as a criterion of meaning with practical images as its symbolic vehicles is a fundamental epistemological tenet in African American thought-systems.[56] Stories, narratives, and Bible principles are selected for their applicability to the lived experiences of African Americans and become symbolic representations of a whole wealth of experience. For example, Bible tales are told for their value to common life, so their interpretation involves no need for scientific historical verification. The narrative method requires that the story be "told, not torn apart in analysis, and trusted as core belief, not admired as science."[57] Any biblical story contains more than characters and a plot – it presents key ethical issues salient in African American life.

June Jordan's essay about her mother's suicide exemplifies the multiple levels of meaning that can occur when concrete experiences are used as a criterion of meaning. Jordan describes her mother, a woman who literally died trying to stand up, and the effect that her mother's death had on her own work:

> I think all of this is really about women and work. Certainly this is all about me as a woman and my life work. I mean I am not sure my mother's suicide was something extraordinary. Perhaps most women must deal with a similar inheritance, the legacy of a woman whose death you cannot possibly pinpoint because she died so many, many times and because, even before she became your mother, the life of that woman was taken. . . . I came too late to help my mother to her feet. By way of everlasting thanks to all of the women who have helped me to stay alive, I am working never to be late again.[58]

While Jordan has knowledge about the concrete act of her mother's death, she also strives for wisdom concerning the meaning of that death.

Some feminist scholars offer a similar claim that women, as a group, are more likely than men to use concrete knowledge in assessing knowledge claims. For example, a substantial number of the 135 women in a study of women's cognitive development were "connected knowers" and were drawn to the sort of knowledge that emerges from firsthand observation. Such women felt that since knowledge comes from experience, the best way of understanding another person's ideas was to try to share the experiences that led the person to form those ideas. At the heart of the procedures used by connected knowers is the capacity for empathy.[59]

In valuing the concrete, African American women may be invoking not only an Afrocentric tradition, but a women's tradition as well. Some feminist theorists suggest that women are socialized in complex relational nexuses where contextual rules take priority over abstract principles in governing behavior. This socialization process is thought to stimulate characteristic ways of knowing.[60] For example, Canadian sociologist Dorothy Smith maintains that two modes of knowing exist, one located in the body and the space it occupies and the other passing beyond it. She asserts that women, through their child-rearing and nurturing activities, mediate these two modes and use the concrete experiences of their daily lives to assess more abstract knowledge claims.[61]

Amanda King, a young black mother, describes how she used the concrete to assess the abstract and points out how difficult mediating these two modes of knowing can be:

> The leaders of the ROC [a labor union] lost their jobs too, but it just seemed like they were used to losing their jobs. . . . This was like a lifelong thing for them, to get out there and protest. They were like, what do you call them – intellectuals. . . . You got the ones that go to the university that are supposed to make all the speeches, they're the ones that are supposed to lead, you know, put this little revolution together, and then you got the little ones . . . that go to the factory everyday, they be the ones that have to fight. I had a child, and I thought I don't have the time to be running around with these people . . . I mean I understand some of that stuff they were talking about, like the bourgeoisie, the rich and the poor and all that, but I had surviving on my mind for me and my kid.[62]

For King, abstract ideals of class solidarity were mediated by the concrete experience of motherhood and the connectedness it involved.

In traditional African American communities, black women find considerable institutional support for valuing concrete experience. Black extended families and black churches are two key institutions where black women experts with concrete knowledge of what it takes to be self-defined black women share their knowledge with their younger, less experienced sisters. This relationship of sisterhood among black women can be seen as a model for a whole series of relationships that African American women have with each other, whether it is networks among women in extended families, among women in the black church, or among women in the African American community at large.[63]

Since the black church and the black family are both woman-centered and Afrocentric institutions, African American women traditionally have found considerable institutional support for this dimension of an Afro-centric feminist epistemology in ways that are unique to them. While white women may value the concrete, it is questionable whether white families, particularly middle-class nuclear ones, and white community institutions provide comparable types of support. Similarly, while black men are supported by Afrocentric institutions, they cannot participate in black women's sisterhood. In terms of black women's relationships with one another then, African American women may indeed find it easier than others to recognize connectedness as a primary way of knowing, simply because they are encouraged to do so by black women's tradition of sisterhood.

Epistemology and Black Feminist Thought

Living life as an African American woman is a necessary prerequisite for producing black feminist thought because within black women's communities thought is validated and produced with reference to a particular set of historical, material, and epistemological conditions.[64] African American women who adhere to the idea that claims about black women must be substantiated by black women's sense of their own experiences, and who anchor their knowledge claims in an Afrocentric feminist epistemology, have produced a rich tradition of black feminist thought.

Traditionally, such women were blues singers, poets, autobiographers, storytellers, and orators validated by the larger community of black women as experts on a black women's standpoint. Only a few unusual African American feminist scholars have been able to defy Eurocentric masculinist epistemologies and explicitly embrace an Afrocentric feminist epistemology. Consider Alice Walker's description of Zora Neale Hurston: "In my mind, Zora Neale Hurston, Billie Holiday, and Bessie Smith form a sort of unholy trinity. Zora *belongs* in the tradition of black women singers, rather than 'the literati.' . . . Like Billie and Bessie she followed her own road, believed in her own gods, pursued her own dreams, and refused to separate herself from 'common' people."[65]

Zora Neale Hurston is an exception for, prior to 1950, few black women earned advanced degrees, and most of those who did complied with Eurocentric masculinist epistemologies. While these women worked on behalf of black women, they did so within the confines of pervasive race and gender oppression. Black women scholars were in a position to see the exclusion of black women from scholarly discourse, and the thematic content of their work often reflected their interest in examining a black women's standpoint. However, their tenuous status in academic institutions led then to adhere to Eurocentric masculinist epistemologies so that their work would be accepted as scholarly. As a result, while they produced black feminist thought, those black women most likely to gain academic credentials were often least likely to produce black feminist thought that used an Afrocentric feminist epistemology.

As more black women earn advanced degrees, the range of black feminist scholarship is expanding. Increasing numbers of African American women scholars are explicitly choosing to ground their work in black women's experiences, and, by doing so, many implicitly adhere to an Afrocentric feminist epistemology. Rather than being restrained by their "both/ and" status of marginality, these women make creative use of their outsider-within status and produce innovative black feminist thought. The difficulties these women face lie less in demonstrating the technical components of white male epistemologies than in resisting the hegemonic nature of these patterns of thought in order to see, value, and use existing alternative Afrocentric feminist ways of knowing.

In establishing the legitimacy of their knowledge claims, black women scholars who want to develop black feminist thought may encounter the often conflicting standards of three key groups. First, black feminist thought must be validated by ordinary African American women who grow to womanhood "in a world where the saner you are, the madder you are made to appear."[66] To be credible in the eyes of this group, scholars must be personal advocates for their material, be accountable for the consequences of their work, have lived or experienced their material in some fashion, and be willing to engage in dialogues about their findings with ordinary, everyday people. Second, if it is to establish its legitimacy, black feminist thought also must be accepted by the community of black women scholars. These scholars place varying amounts of importance on rearticulating a black women's standpoint using an Afrocentric feminist epistemology. Third, black feminist thought within academia must be prepared to confront Eurocentric masculinist political and epistemological requirements.

The dilemma facing black women scholars engaged in creating black feminist thought is that a knowledge claim that meets the criteria of adequacy for one group and thus is judged to be an acceptable knowledge claim may not be translatable into the terms of a different group. Using the example of Black English, June Jordan illustrates the difficulty of moving among epistemologies: "You cannot 'translate' instances of Standard English preoccupied with abstraction or with nothing/nobody evidently alive into Black English. That would warp the language into uses antithetical to the guiding perspective of its community of users.

Rather you must first change those Standard English sentences themselves into ideas consistent with the person-centered assumptions of Black English."[67] While the worldviews share a common vocabulary, the ideas themselves defy direct translation.

Once black feminist scholars face the notion that, on certain dimensions of a black women's standpoint, it may be fruitless to try to translate ideas from an Afrocentric feminist epistemology into a Eurocentric masculinist epistemology, then the choices become clearer. Rather than trying to uncover universal knowledge claims that can withstand the translation from one epistemology to another, time might be better spent rearticulating a black women's standpoint in order to give African American women the tools to resist their own subordination. The goal here is not one of integrating black female "folk culture" into the substantiated body of academic knowledge, for that substantiated knowledge is, in many ways, antithetical to the best interests of black women. Rather, the process is one of rearticulating a preexisting black women's standpoint and recentering the language of existing academic discourse to accommodate these knowledge claims. For those black women scholars engaged in this rearticulation process, the social construction of black feminist thought requires the skill and sophistication to decide which knowledge claims can be validated using the epistemological assumptions of one but not both frameworks, which claims can be generated in one framework and only partially accommodated by the other, and which claims can be made in both frameworks without violating the basic political and epistemological assumptions of either.

Black feminist scholars offering knowledge claims that cannot be accommodated by both frameworks face the choice between accepting the taken-for-granted assumptions that permeate white-male-controlled academic institutions or leaving academia. Those black women who choose to remain in academia must accept the possibility that their knowledge claims will be limited to their claims about black women that are consistent with a white male worldview. And yet those African American women who leave academia may find their work is inaccessible to scholarly communities.

Black feminist scholars offering knowledge claims that can be partially accommodated by both epistemologies can create a body of thought that stands outside of either. Rather than trying to synthesize competing worldviews that, at this point in time, defy reconciliation, their task is to point out common themes and concerns. By making creative use of their status as mediators, their thought becomes an entity unto itself that is rooted in two distinct political and epistemological contexts.[68]

Those black feminists who develop knowledge claims that both epistemologies can accommodate may have found a route to the elusive goal of generating so-called objective generalizations that can stand as universal truths. Those ideas that are validated as true by African American women, African American men, white men, white women, and other groups with distinctive standpoints, with each group using the epistemological approaches growing from its unique standpoint, thus become the most objective truths.[69]

Alternative knowledge claims, in and of themselves, are rarely threatening to conventional knowledge. Such claims are routinely ignored, discredited, or simply absorbed and marginalized in existing paradigms. Much more threatening is the challenge that alternative epistemologies offer to the basic process used by the powerful to legitimate their knowledge claims. If the epistemology used to validate knowledge comes into question, then all prior knowledge claims validated under the dominant model become suspect. An alternative epistemology challenges all certified knowledge and opens up the question of whether what has been taken to be true can stand the test of alternative ways of validating truth. The existence of an independent black women's standpoint using an Afrocentric feminist epistemology calls into question the content of what currently passes as truth and simultaneously challenges the process of arriving at that truth.

Notes

1   For analyses of how interlocking systems of oppression affect black women, see Frances Beale, "Double Jeopardy: To Be Black and Female," in *The Black Woman: An Anthology*, ed. Toni Cade (New York: Signet, 1970); Angela Y. Davis, *Women, Race, and Class* (New York: Random House, 1981); Bonnie Thornton Dill, "Race, Class, and Gender: Prospects for an All-Inclusive Sisterhood," *Feminist Studies* 9, no. 1 (1983), 13–50; bell hooks, *Ain't I a Woman? Black Women and Feminism* (Boston: South End Press, 1981); Diane Lewis, "A Response to Inequality: Black Women, Racism, and Sexism," *Signs: Journal of Women in Culture and Society* 3,

no. 2 (Winter 1977), 339–61; Pauli Murray, "The Liberation of Black Women," in *Voices of the New Feminism*, ed. Mary Lou Thompson (Boston: Beacon Press, 1970), 87–102; and the introduction in Filomina Chioma Steady, *The Black Woman Cross-Culturally* (Cambridge, MA: Schenkman, 1981), 7–41.

2　See the introduction in Steady, *The Black Woman*, for an overview of black women's strengths. This strength-resiliency perspective has greatly influenced empirical work on African American women. See e.g. Joyce Ladner's study of low-income black adolescent girls, *Tomorrow's Tomorrow* (New York: Doubleday, 1971); and Lena Wright Myers's work on black women's self-concept, *Black Women: Do They Cope Better?* (Englewood Cliffs, NJ: Prentice-Hall, 1980). For discussions of black women's resistance, see Elizabeth Fox-Genovese, "Strategies and Forms of Resistance: Focus on Slave Women in the United States," in *In Resistance: Studies in African, Caribbean and Afro-American History*, ed. Gary Y. Okihiro (Amherst: University of Massachusetts Press, 1986), 143–65; and Rosalyn Terborg-Penn, "Black Women in Resistance: A Cross-Cultural Perspective," in Okihiro, *In Resistance*, 188–209. For a comprehensive discussion of everyday resistance, see James C. Scott, *Weapons of the Weak: Everyday Forms of Peasant Resistance* (New Haven, CT: Yale University Press, 1985).

3　See Patricia Hill Collins's analysis of the substantive content of black feminist thought in "Learning from the Outsider Within: The Sociological Significance of Black Feminist Thought," *Social Problems* 33, no. 6 (1986), 14–32.

4　Scott describes consciousness as the meaning that people give to their acts through the symbols, norms, and ideological forms they create.

5　This thesis is found in scholarship of varying theoretical perspectives. For example, Marxist analyses of working-class consciousness claim that "false consciousness" makes the working class unable to penetrate the hegemony of ruling-class ideologies. See Scott's critique of this literature.

6　For example, in Western societies, African Americans have been judged as being less capable of intellectual excellence, more suited to manual labor, and therefore less human than whites. Similarly, white women have been assigned roles as emotional, irrational creatures ruled by passions and biological urges. They too have been stigmatized as being less than fully human, as being objects. For a discussion of the importance that objectification and dehumanization play in maintaining systems of domination, see Arthur Brittan and Mary Maynard, *Sexism, Racism and Oppression* (New York: Basil Blackwell, 1984).

7　The tendency for Western scholarship to assess black culture as pathological and deviant illustrates this process. See Rhett S. Jones, "Proving Blacks

Inferior: The Sociology of Knowledge," in *The Death of White Sociology*, ed. Joyce Ladner (New York: Vintage, 1973), 114–35.

8 The presence of an independent standpoint does not mean that it is uniformly shared by all black women or even that black women fully recognize its contours. By using the concept of standpoint, I do not mean to minimize the rich diversity existing among African American women. I use the phrase "black women's standpoint" to emphasize the plurality of experiences within the overarching term "standpoint." For discussions of the concept of standpoint, see Nancy M. Hartsock, "The Feminist Standpoint: Developing the Ground for a Specifically Feminist Historical Materialism," in *Discovering Reality*, ed. Sandra Harding and Merrill Hintikka (Boston: D. Reidel, 1983), 283–310, and *Money, Sex, and Power* (Boston: Northeastern University Press, 1983); and Alison M. Jaggar, *Feminist Politics and Human Nature* (Totowa, NJ: Rowman & Allanheld, 1983), 377–89. My use of the standpoint epistemologies as an organizing concept in this essay does not mean that the concept is problem-free. For a helpful critique of standpoint epistemologies, see Sandra Harding, *The Science Question in Feminism* (Ithaca, NY: Cornell University Press, 1986).

9 One contribution of contemporary black women's studies is its documentation of how race, class, and gender have structured these differences. For representative works surveying African American women's experiences, see Paula Giddings, *When and Where I Enter: The Impact of Black Women on Race and Sex in America* (New York: William Morrow, 1984); and Jacqueline Jones, *Labor of Love, Labor of Sorrow: Black Women, Work, and the Family from Slavery to the Present* (New York: Basic Books, 1985).

10 For example, Judith Rollins, *Between Women: Domestics and their Employers* (Philadelphia: Temple University Press, 1985); and Bonnie Thornton Dill, " 'The Means to Put My Children Through': Child-Rearing Goals and Strategies among Black Female Domestic Servants," in *The Black Woman*, ed. LaFrances Rodgers-Rose (Beverly Hills, CA: Sage Publications, 1980), 107–23, report that black domestic workers do not see themselves as being the devalued workers that their employers perceive and construct their own interpretations of the meaning of their work. For additional discussions of how black women's consciousness is shaped by the material conditions they encounter, see Ladner, *Tomorrow's Tomorrow*; Myers, *Black Women*; and Cheryl Townsend Gilkes, " 'Together and in Harness': Women's Traditions in the Sanctified Church," *Signs*, no. 4 (Summer 1985), 678–99. See also Marcia Westkott's discussion of consciousness as a sphere of freedom for "Feminist Criticism of the Social Sciences," *Harvard Educational Review* 49, no. 4 (1979), 422–30.

11 John Langston Gwaltney, *Drylongso: A Self-Portrait of Black America* (New York: Vintage, 1980), 4–12.

12   Ibid., 33.

13   Ibid., 88.

14   Ibid., 7.

15   Victoria Byerly, *Hard Times Cotton Mill Girls: Personal Histories of Womanhood and Poverty in the South* (New York: ILR Press, 1986), 134.

16   See Peter L. Berger and Thomas Luckmann, *The Social Construction of Reality* (New York: Doubleday, 1966), for a discussion of everyday thought and the role of experts in articulating specialized thought.

17   See Michael Omi and Howard Winant, *Racial Formation in the United States* (New York: Routledge & Kegan Paul, 1986), especially 93.

18   In discussing standpoint epistemologics, Hartsock, in *Money, Sex, and Power*, notes that a standpoint is "achieved rather than obvious, a mediated rather than immediate understanding" (132).

19   See Scott, *Weapons of the Weak*; and Hartsock, *Money, Sex, and Power*.

20   Some readers may question how one determines whether the ideas of any given African American woman are "feminist" and "Afrocentric." I offer the following working definitions. I agree with the general definition of feminist consciousness provided by black feminist sociologist Deborah K. King: "Any purposes, goals, and activities that seek to enhance the potential of women, to ensure their liberty, afford them equal opportunity, and to permit and encourage their self-determination represent a feminist consciousness, even if they occur within a racial community" (in "Race, Class and Gender Salience in Black Women's Womanist Consciousness," typescript, Dartmouth College, Department of Sociology, Hanover, NH, 1987, 22). To be black or Afrocentric, such thought must not only reflect a similar concern for the self-determination of African American people, but must in some way draw upon key elements of an Afrocentric tradition as well.

21   The Eurocentric masculinist process is defined here as the institutions, paradigms, and any elements of the knowledge-validation procedure controlled by white males and whose purpose is to represent a white male standpoint. While this process represents the interests of powerful white males, various dimensions of the process are not necessarily managed by white males themselves.

22   Karl Mannheim, *Ideology and Utopia: An Introduction to the Sociology of Knowledge* (1936; reprint, New York: Harcourt, Brace & Co., 1954), 276.

23   The knowledge-validation model used in this essay is taken from Michael Mulkay, *Science and the Sociology of Knowledge* (Boston: Allen & Unwin, 1979). For a general discussion of the structure of knowledge, see Thomas Kuhn, *The Structure of Scientific Revolutions* (Chicago: University of Chicago Press, 1962).

24   For analyses of the content and functions of images of black female

inferiority, see Mae King, "The Politics of Sexual Stereotypes," *Black Scholar* 4, nos. 6–7 (1973), 12–23; Cheryl Townsend Gilkes, "From Slavery to Social Welfare: Racism and the Control of Black Women," in *Class, Race, and Sex: The Dynamics of Control*, eds. Amy Smerdlow and Helen Lessinger (Boston: G. K. Hall, 1981), 288–300; and Elizabeth Higginbotham, "Two Representative Issues in Contemporary Sociological Work on Black Women," in *All the Women Are White, All the Blacks Are Men, But Some of Us Are Brave*, eds. Gloria T. Hull, Patricia Bell Scott, and Barbara Smith (Old Westbury, NY: Feminist Press, 1982).

25 Kuhn, *The Structure*.

26 Evelyn Fox Keller, *Reflections on Gender and Science* (New Haven, CT: Yale University Press, 1985), 167.

27 Maxine Baca Zinn, Lynn Weber Cannon, Elizabeth Higginbotham, and Bonnie Thornton Dill, "The Cost of Exclusionary Practices in Women's Studies," *Signs* 1, no. 2 (Winter 1986), 290–303.

28 Berger and Luckmann (in *The Social Construction of Reality*) note that if an outsider group, in this case African American women, recognizes that the insider group, namely, white men, requires special privileges from the larger society, a special problem arises of keeping the outsiders out and at the same time having them acknowledge the legitimacy of this procedure. Accepting a few "safe" outsiders is one way of addressing this legitimation problem. Collins's discussion (in "Learning from the Outsider Within") of black women as "outsiders within" addresses this issue. Other relevant works include Frantz Fanon's analysis of the role of the national middle class in maintaining colonial systems, in *The Wretched of the Earth* (New York: Grove, 1963); and William Tabb's discussion of the use of "bright natives" in controlling African American communities, *The Political Economy of the Black Ghetto* (New York: W. W. Norton, 1970).

29 While I have been describing Eurocentric masculinist approaches as a single process, there are many schools of thought or paradigms subsumed under this one process. Positivism represents one such paradigm. See Harding, *The Science Question*, for an overview and critique of this literature. The following discussion depends heavily on Jaggar, *Feminist Politics*, 355–8.

30 Jaggar, *Feminist Politics*, 356.

31 See Keller, *Reflections on Gender*, 67–126, especially her analysis of static autonomy and its relation to objectivity.

32 Ironically, researchers must "objectify" themselves to achieve this lack of bias. See Arlie Russell Hochschild, "The Sociology of Feeling and Emotion: Selected Possibilities," in *Another Voice: Feminist Perspectives on Social Life and Social Science*, eds. Marcia Millman and Rosabeth Kanter (Garden City, NY: Anchor, 1975), 280–307. Also, see Jaggar, *Feminist Politics*.

33 See *Social Science as Moral Inquiry*, eds. Norma Haan, Robert Bellah, Paul

Rabinow, and William Sullivan (New York: Columbia University Press, 1983), especially Michelle Z. Rosaldo's "Moral/Analytic Dilemmas Posed by the Intersection of Feminism and Social Science," 76–96; and Robert Bellah's "The Ethical Aims of Social Inquiry," 360–81.

34   Janice Moulton, "A Paradigm of Philosophy: The Adversary Method," in Harding and Hintikka, *Discovering Reality*, 149–64.

35   For detailed discussions of the Afrocentric worldview, see John S. Mbiti, *African Religions and Philosophy* (London: Heinemann, 1969); Dominique Zahan, *The Religion, Spirituality, and Thought of Traditional Africa* (Chicago: University of Chicago Press, 1979); and Mechal Sobel, *Trabelin' On': The Slave Journey to an Afro-Baptist Faith* (Westport, CT: Greenwood Press, 1979), 1–76.

36   For representative works applying these concepts to African American culture, see Niara Sudarkasa, "Interpreting the African Heritage in Afro-American Family Organization," in *Black Families*, ed. Harriette Pipes McAdoo (Beverly Hills, CA: Sage Publications, 1981); Henry H. Mitchell and Nicholas Cooper Lewter, *Soul Theology: The Heart of American Black Culture* (San Francisco: Harper & Row, 1986); Robert Farris Thompson, *Flash of the Spirit: African and Afro-American Art and Philosophy* (New York: Vintage, 1983); and Ortiz M.Walton, "Comparative Analysis of the African and the Western Aesthetics," in *The Black Aesthetic*, ed. Addison Gayle (Garden City, NY: Doubleday, 1971), 154–64.

37   One of the best discussions of an Afrocentric epistemology is offered by James E. Turner, "Foreword: Africana Studies and Epistemology; a Discourse in the Sociology of Knowledge," in *The Next Decade: Theoretical and Research Issues in Africana Studies*, ed. James E. Turner (Ithaca, NY: Cornell University Africana Studies and Research Center, 1984), v–xxv. See also Vernon Dixon, "World Views and Research Methodology," summarized in Harding, *The Science Question*, 170.

38   See Hester Eisenstein, *Contemporary Feminist Thought* (Boston: G. K. Hall, 1983). Nancy Hartsock's *Money, Sex, and Power*, 145–209, offers a particularly insightful analysis of women's oppression.

39   For discussions of feminist consciousness, see Dorothy Smith, "A Sociology for Women," in *The Prism of Sex: Essays in the Sociology of Knowledge*, eds. Julia A. Sherman and Evelyn T. Beck (Madison: University of Wisconsin Press, 1979); and Michelle Z. Rosaldo, "Women, Culture, and Society: A Theoretical Overview," in *Woman, Culture, and Society*, eds. Michelle Z. Rosaldo and Louise Lamphere (Stanford, CA: Stanford University Press, 1974), 17–42. Feminist epistemologies are surveyed by Jaggar, *Feminist Politics*.

40   One significant difference between Afrocentric and feminist standpoints is that much of what is termed women's culture is, unlike African American

culture, treated in the context of and produced by oppression. Those who argue for a women's culture are electing to value, rather than denigrate, those traits associated with females in white patriarchal societies. While this choice is important, it is not the same as identifying an independent, historical culture associated with a society. I am indebted to Deborah K. King for this point.

41   Critiques of the Eurocentric masculinist knowledge-validation process by both Africanist and feminist scholars illustrate this point. What one group labels "white" and "Eurocentric," the other describes as "male-dominated" and "masculinist." Although he does not emphasize its patriarchal and racist features, Morris Berman's *The Reenchantment of the World* (New York: Bantam Books, 1981) provides a historical discussion of Western thought. Afrocentric analyses of this same process can be found in Molefi Kete Asante, "International/Intercultural Relations," in *Contemporary Black Thought*, eds. Molefi Kete Asante and Abdulai S. Vandi (Beverly Hills, CA: Sage Publications, 1980), 43–58; and Dona Richards, "European Mythology: The Ideology of 'Progress,'" in Asante and Vandi, *Contemporary Black Thought*, 59–79. For feminist analyses, see Hartsock, *Money, Sex, and Power*. Harding also discusses this similarity (see ch. 7, "Other 'Others' and Fractured Identities: Issues for Epistemologists," 63–96).

42   Harding, *The Science Question*, 166.

43   King, "Race, Class and Gender Salience."

44   Bonnie Thornton Dill, "The Dialectics of Black Womanhood," *Signs* 4, no. 3 (Spring 1979), 543–55.

45   One implication of standpoint approaches is that the more subordinate the group, the purer the vision of the oppressed group. This is an outcome of the origins of standpoint approaches in Marxist social theory, itself a dualistic analysis of social structure. Because such approaches rely on quantifying and ranking human oppressions – familiar tenets of positivist approaches – they are rejected by blacks and feminists alike. See Harding, *The Science Question*, for a discussion of this point. See also Elizabeth V. Spelman's discussion of the fallacy of additive oppression in "Theories of Race and Gender: The Erasure of Black Women," *Quest* 5, no. 4 (1982), 36–62.

46   Class differences among black women may be marked. For example, see Paula Giddings's analysis (in *When and Where I Enter*) of the role of social class in shaping black women's political activism; or Elizabeth Higginbotham's study of the effects of social class in black women's college attendance in "Race and Class Barriers to Black Women's College Attendance," *Journal of Ethnic Studies* 13, no. 1 (1985), 89–107. Those African American women who have experienced the greatest degree of convergence

of race, class, and gender oppression may be in a better position to recognize and use an alternative epistemology.

47 Gwaltney, *Drylongso*, 83.

48 William L. Andrews, *Sisters of the Spirit: Three Black Women's Autobiographies of the Nineteenth Century* (Bloomington: Indiana University Press, 1986), 85.

49 Gwaltney, *Drylongso*, 147.

50 Geneva Smitherman, *Talkin and Testifyin: The Language of Black America* (Detroit: Wayne State University Press, 1986), 76.

51 Gwaltney, *Drylongso*, 68.

52 Ibid., 7.

53 Ibid., 27, 33.

54 Elsa Barkley Brown, "Hearing Our Mothers' Lives" (paper presented at the Fifteenth Anniversary Faculty Lecture Series, African American and African Studies, Emory University, Atlanta, 1986).

55 Ladner, *Tomorrow's Tomorrow*.

56 Mitchell and Lewter, *Soul Theology*. The use of the narrative approach in African American theology exemplifies an inductive system of logic alternately called "folk wisdom" or a survival-based, need-oriented method of assessing knowledge claims.

57 Ibid., 8.

58 June Jordan, *On Call: Political Essays* (Boston: South End Press, 1985), 26.

59 Mary Belenky, Blythe Clinchy, Nancy Goldberger, and Jill Tarule, *Women's Ways of Knowing* (New York: Basic Books, 1986), 113.

60 Hartsock, *Money, Sex, and Power*, 237; and Nancy Chodorow, *The Reproduction of Mothering* (Berkeley and Los Angeles: University of California Press, 1978).

61 Dorothy Smith, *The Everyday World as Problematic* (Boston: Northeastern University Press, 1987).

62 Byerly, *Hard Times Colton Mill Girls*, 198.

63 For black women's centrality in the family, see Steady, *The Black Woman*; Ladner, *Tomorrow's Tomorrow*; Brown, "Hearing Our Mothers' Lives"; and McAdoo, *Black Families*. See Gilkes, " 'Together and in Harness,' " for black women in the church; and chapter 4 of Deborah Gray White, *Arn't I a Woman? Female Slaves in the Plantation South* (New York: W. W. Norton, 1985). See also Gloria Joseph, "Black Mothers and Daughters: Their Roles and Functions in American Society," in *Common Differences: Conflicts in Black and White Feminist Perspectives*, eds. Gloria Joseph and Jill Lewis (Garden City, NY: Anchor, 1981), 75–126. Even though black women play essential roles in black families and black churches, these institutions are not free from sexism.

64 Black men, white women, and members of other race, class, and gender

groups should be encouraged to interpret, teach, and critique the black feminist thought produced by African American women.

65 Walker, *In Search of Our Mothers' Gardens* (New York: Harcourt Brace Jovanovich, 1974), 91.
66 Gwaltney, *Drylongso*.
67 Jordan, *On Call*, 130.
68 Collins, "Learning from the Outsider Within."
69 This point addresses the question of relativity in the sociology of knowledge and offers a way of regulating competing knowledge claims.

NINE

Demarginalizing the Intersection of Race and Sex: A Black Feminist Critique of Antidiscrimination Doctrine, Feminist Theory and Antiracist Politics

Kimberlé Crenshaw

One of the very few Black women's studies books is entitled *All the Women Are White, All the Blacks Are Men, But Some of Us are Brave.*[1] I have chosen this title as a point of departure in my efforts to develop a Black feminist criticism[2] because it sets forth a problematic consequence of the tendency to treat race and gender as mutually exclusive categories of experience and analysis.[3] [. . .] I want to examine how this tendency is perpetuated by a single-axis dominant in antidiscrimination law [. . . one] also reflected in feminist theory and antiracist politics.

I will center Black women in this analysis in order to contrast the multidimensionality of Black women's experience with the single-axis analysis that distorts these experiences. Not only will this juxtaposition reveal how Black women are theoretically erased, it will also illustrate how this framework imports its own theoretical limitations that undermine efforts to broaden feminist and antiracist analyses. With Black women as the starting point, it becomes more apparent how dominant conceptions of discrimination condition us to think about subordination as disadvantage occurring along a single categorical axis. I want to suggest further that this single-axis framework erases Black women in the conceptualization, identification and remediation of race and sex

[...]n in promotions to upper-level craft positions and to supervisory [...] Moore introduced statistical evidence establishing a significant [...]ity between men and women, and somewhat less of a disparity [...]en Black and white men in supervisory jobs.[16]

[...]firming the district court's refusal to certify Moore as the class [...]entative in the sex discrimination complaint on behalf of all [...]n at Hughes, the Ninth Circuit noted approvingly: ". . . Moore [...]ever claimed before the EEOC that she was discriminated against [...]emale, *but only* as a Black female. . . . [T]his raised serious doubts [...]Moore's ability to adequately represent white female employees."[17] [...]curious logic in *Moore* reveals not only the narrow scope of [...]scrimination doctrine and its failure to embrace intersectionality, [...]lso the centrality of white female experiences in the conceptualiza- [...]f gender discrimination. One inference that could be drawn from [...]urt's statement that Moore's complaint did not entail a claim of [...]mination "against females" is that discrimination against Black [...]es is something less than discrimination against females. More than [...], however, the court meant to imply that Moore did not claim that [...]nales were discriminated against *but only* Black females. But even [...]recast, the court's rationale is problematic for Black women. The [...] rejected Moore's bid to represent all females apparently because [...]ttempt to specify her race was seen as being at odds with the [...]ard allegation that the employer simply discriminated "against [...]es."

[...]e court failed to see that the absence of a racial referent does not [...]sarily mean that the claim being made is a more inclusive one. A [...] woman claiming discrimination against females may be in no [...] position to represent all women than a Black woman who claims [...]mination as a Black female and wants to represent all females. The [...]'s preferred articulation of "against females" is not necessarily [...] inclusive – it just appears to be so because the racial contours of [...]aim are not specified. The court's preference for "against females" [...]r than "against Black females" reveals the implicit grounding of [...] female experiences in the doctrinal conceptualization of sex dis- [...]nation. For white women, claiming sex discrimination is simply a [...]nent that but for gender, they would not have been disadvantaged. [...]hem there is no need to specify discrimination as *white* females [...]se their race does not contribute to the disadvantage for which

discrimination by limiting inquiry to the experiences of otherwise-privileged members of the group. In other words, in race discrimination cases, discrimination tends to be viewed in terms of sex- or class-privileged Blacks; in sex discrimination cases, the focus is on race- and class-privileged women.

This focus on the most privileged group members marginalizes those who are multiply-burdened and obscures claims that cannot be understood as resulting from discrete sources of discrimination. I suggest further that this focus on otherwise-privileged group members creates a distorted analysis of racism and sexism because the operative conceptions of race and sex become grounded in experiences that actually represent only a subset of a much more complex phenomenon.

After examining the doctrinal manifestations of this single-axis framework, I will discuss how it contributes to the marginalization of Black women in feminist theory and in antiracist politics. I argue that Black women are sometimes excluded from feminist theory and antiracist policy discourse because both are predicated on a discrete set of experiences that often does not accurately reflect the interaction of race and gender. These problems of exclusion cannot be solved simply by including Black women within an already established analytical structure. Because the intersectional experience is greater than the sum of racism and sexism, any analysis that does not take intersectionality into account cannot sufficiently address the particular manner in which Black women are subordinated. Thus, for feminist theory and antiracist policy discourse to embrace the experiences and concerns of Black women, the entire framework that has been used as a basis for translating "women's experience" or "the Black experience" into concrete policy demands must be rethought and recast.

As examples of theoretical and political developments that miss the mark with respect to Black women because of their failure to consider intersectionality, I will briefly discuss the feminist critique of rape and separate spheres ideology, and the public policy debates concerning female-headed households within the Black community.

I The Antidiscrimination Framework

A *The Experience of Intersectionality and the Doctrinal Response*

One way to approach the problem of intersectionality is to examine how courts frame and interpret the stories of Black women plaintiffs. While I cannot claim to know the circumstances underlying the cases that I will discuss, I nevertheless believe that the way courts interpret claims made by Black women is itself part of Black women's experience and, consequently, a cursory review of cases involving Black female plaintiffs is quite revealing. To illustrate the difficulties inherent in judicial treatment of intersectionality, I will consider three Title VII[4] cases: *DeGraffenreid v General Motors*,[5] *Moore v Hughes Helicopter*,[6] and *Payne v Travenol*.[7]

1 *DeGraffenreid v General Motors* In *DeGraffenreid*, five Black women brought suit against General Motors, alleging that the employer's seniority system perpetuated the effects of past discrimination against Black women. Evidence adduced at trial revealed that General Motors simply did not hire Black women prior to 1964 and that all of the Black women hired after 1970 lost their jobs in a seniority-based layoff during a subsequent recession. The district court granted summary judgment for the defendant, rejecting the plaintiffs' attempt to bring a suit not on behalf of Blacks or women, but specifically on behalf of Black women. The court stated:

> [P]laintiffs have failed to cite any decisions which have stated that Black women are a special class to be protected from discrimination. The Court's own research has failed to disclose such a decision. The plaintiffs are clearly entitled to a remedy if they have been discriminated against. However, they should not be allowed to combine statutory remedies to create a new "super-remedy" which would give them relief beyond what the drafters of the relevant statutes intended. Thus, this lawsuit must be examined to see if it states a cause of action for race discrimination, sex discrimination, or alternatively either, but not a combination of both.[8]

Although General Motors did not hire Black women prior to 1964, the court noted that "General Motors has hired . . . female employees

for a number of years prior to the enactment of th[e] 1964."[9] Because General Motors did hire women – – during the period that no Black women were hir[ed,] court's view, no sex discrimination that the se[niority system] conceivably have perpetuated.

After refusing to consider the plaintiffs' sex disc[rimination,] court dismissed the race discrimination complaint[s] consolidation with another case alleging race disc[rimination] same employer.[10] The plaintiffs responded that suc[h a] defeat the purpose of their suit since theirs was n[ot] but an action brought specifically on behalf of [Black women for] race *and* sex discrimination. The court, however, [12]

> The legislative history surrounding Title VII does [not indicate that the] goal of the statute was to create a new classificati[on of] who would have greater standing than, for examp[le] prospect of the creation of new classes of protecte[d] only by the mathematical principles of permutat[ion] clearly raises the prospect of opening the hackneye[d]

Thus, the court apparently concluded that [Congress did not] contemplate that Black women could be discrimi[nated against as "Black] women" or did not intend to protect them wh[en such discrimination] occurred.[12] The court's refusal in *DeGraffenre[id* to acknowledge that] Black women encounter combined race and se[x discrimination implies] that the boundaries of sex and race discriminat[ion are defined] respectively by white women's and Black men's [experiences. Under this] view, Black women are protected only to the [extent that their experi]ences coincide with those of either of the tw[o groups. Where their] experiences are distinct, Black women can ex[pect little protection as] long as approaches, such as that in *DeGraffe[nreid*, which] obscure problems of intersectionality prevail.

2 *Moore v Hughes Helicopter, Inc.* *Moore [v Hughes Helicopter,] Inc.*[14] presents a different way in which cour[ts fail to] recognize Black women's claims. *Moore* is typ[ical of the way in which courts] in which courts refused to certify Black femal[es as class representatives] in race and sex discrimination actions.[15] In *M[oore*, the plaintiff alleged] that the employer, Hughes Helicopter, practic[ed]

they seek redress. The view of discrimination that is derived from this grounding takes race privilege as a given.

Discrimination against a white female is thus the standard sex discrimination claim; claims that diverge from this standard appear to present some sort of hybrid claim. More significantly, because Black females' claims are seen as hybrid, they sometimes cannot represent those who may have "pure" claims of sex discrimination. The effect of this approach is that even though a challenged policy or practice may clearly discriminate against all females, the fact that it has particularly harsh consequences for Black females places Black female plaintiffs at odds with white females.

Moore illustrates one of the limitations of antidiscrimination law's remedial scope and normative vision. The refusal to allow a multiply-disadvantaged class to represent others who may be singularly-disadvantaged defeats efforts to restructure the distribution of opportunity and limits remedial relief to minor adjustments within an established hierarchy. Consequently, "bottom-up" approaches, those which combine all discriminatees in order to challenge an entire employment system, are foreclosed by the limited view of the wrong and the narrow scope of the available remedy. If such "bottom-up" intersectional representation were routinely permitted, employees might accept the possibility that there is more to gain by collectively challenging the hierarchy rather than by each discriminate individually seeking to protect her source of privilege within the hierarchy. But as long as antidiscrimination doctrine proceeds from the premise that employment systems need only minor adjustments, opportunities for advancement by disadvantaged employees will be limited. Relatively privileged employees probably are better off guarding their advantage while jockeying against others to gain more. As a result, Black women – the class of employees which, because of its intersectionality, is best able to challenge all forms of discrimination – are essentially isolated and often required to fend for themselves.

In *Moore*, the court's denial of the plaintiff's bid to represent all Blacks and females left Moore with the task of supporting her race and sex discrimination claims with statistical evidence of discrimination against Black females alone.[18] Because she was unable to represent white women or Black men, she could not use overall statistics on sex disparity at Hughes, nor could she use statistics on race. Proving her claim using statistics on Black women alone was no small task, due to the fact that she was bringing the suit under a disparate impact theory of discrimination.[19]

The court further limited the relevant statistical pool to include only Black women who it determined were qualified to fill the openings in upper-level labor jobs and in supervisory positions.[20] According to the court, Moore had not demonstrated that there were any qualified Black women within her bargaining unit or the general labor pool for either category of jobs.[21] Finally, the court stated that even if it accepted Moore's contention that the percentage of Black females in supervisory positions should equal the percentage of Black females in the employee pool, it still would not find discriminatory impact. [22] Because the promotion of only two Black women into supervisory positions would have achieved the expected mean distribution of Black women within that job category, the court was "unwilling to agree that a prima facie case of disparate impact ha[d] been proven."[23]

The court's rulings on Moore's sex and race claim left her with such a small statistical sample that even if she had proved that there were qualified Black women, she could not have shown discrimination under a disparate impact theory. *Moore* illustrates yet another way that antidiscrimination doctrine essentially erases Black women's distinct experiences and, as a result, deems their discrimination complaints groundless.

3 *Payne v Travenol* Black female plaintiffs have also encountered difficulty in their efforts to win certification as class representatives in some race discrimination actions. This problem typically arises in cases where statistics suggest significant disparities between Black and white workers and further disparities between Black men and Black women. Courts in some cases[24] have denied certification based on logic that mirrors the rationale in *Moore*. The sex disparities between Black men and Black women created such conflicting interests that Black women could not possibly represent Black men adequately. In one such case, *Payne v Travenol*,[25] two Black female plaintiffs alleging race discrimination brought a class action suit on behalf of all Black employees at a pharmaceutical plant.[26] The court refused, however, to allow the plaintiffs to represent Black males and granted the defendant's request to narrow the class to Black women only. Ultimately, the district court found that there had been extensive racial discrimination at the plant and awarded back pay and constructive seniority to the class of Black

female employees. But, despite its finding of general race discrimination, the court refused to extend the remedy to Black men for fear that their conflicting interests would not be adequately addressed;[27] the Fifth Circuit affirmed.[28]

Notably, the plaintiffs in *Travenol* fared better than the similarly situated plaintiff in *Moore*: They were not denied use of meaningful statistics showing an overall pattern of race discrimination simply because there were no men in their class. The plaintiffs' bid to represent all Black employees, however, like Moore's attempt to represent all women employees, failed as a consequence of the court's narrow view of class interest.

Even though Travenol was a partial victory for Black women, the case specifically illustrates how antidiscrimination doctrine generally creates a dilemma for Black women. It forces them to choose between specifically articulating the intersectional aspects of their subordination, thereby risking their ability to represent Black men, or ignoring intersectionality in order to state a claim that would not lead to the exclusion of Black men. When one considers the political consequences of this dilemma, there is little wonder that many people within the Black community view the specific articulation of Black women's interests as dangerously divisive.

In sum, several courts have proved unable to deal with intersectionality, although for contrasting reasons. In *DeGraffenreid*, the court refused to recognize the possibility of compound discrimination against Black women and analyzed their claim using the employment of white women as the historical base. As a consequence, the employment experiences of white women obscured the distinct discrimination that Black women experienced.

Conversely, in *Moore*, the court held that a Black woman could not use statistics reflecting the overall sex disparity in supervisory and upper-level labor jobs because she had not claimed discrimination as a woman, but "only" as a Black woman. The court would not entertain the notion that discrimination experienced by Black women is indeed sex discrimination – provable through disparate impact statistics on women.

Finally, courts, such as the one in *Travenol*, have held that Black women cannot represent an entire class of Blacks due to presumed class conflicts in cases where sex additionally disadvantaged Black women. As a result, in the few cases where Black women are allowed to use overall statistics indicating racially disparate treatment Black men may not be able to share in the remedy.

Perhaps it appears to some that I have offered inconsistent criticisms of how Black women are treated in antidiscrimination law: I seem to be saying that in one case, Black women's claims were rejected and their experiences obscured because the court refused to acknowledge that the employment experience of Black women can be distinct from that of white women, while in other cases, the interests of Black women were harmed because Black women's claims were viewed as so distinct from the claims of either white women or Black men that the court denied to Black females representation of the larger class. It seems that I have to say that Black women are the same and harmed by being treated differently or that they are different and harmed by being treated the same. But I cannot say both.

This apparent contradiction is but another manifestation of the conceptual limitations of the single-issue analyses that intersectionality challenges. The point is that Black women can experience discrimination in any number of ways and that the contradiction arises from our assumptions that their claims of exclusion must be unidirectional. Consider an analogy to traffic in an intersection, coming and going in all four directions. Discrimination, like traffic through an intersection, may flow in one direction, and it may flow in another. If an accident happens in an intersection, it can be caused by cars traveling from any number of directions and, sometimes, from all of them. Similarly, if a Black woman is harmed because she is in the intersection, her injury could result from sex discrimination or race discrimination.

Judicial decisions which premise intersectional relief on a showing that Black women are specifically recognized as a class are analogous to a doctor's decision at the scene of an accident to treat an accident victim only if the injury is recognized by medical insurance. Similarly, providing legal relief only when Black women show that their claims are based on race or on sex is analogous to calling an ambulance for the victim only after the driver responsible for the injuries is identified. But it is not always easy to reconstruct an accident: Sometimes the skid marks and the injuries simply indicate that they occurred simultaneously, frustrating efforts to determine which driver caused the harm. In these cases the tendency seems to be that no driver is held responsible, no treatment is administered, and the involved parties simply get back in their cars and zoom away.

To bring this back to a non-metaphorical level, I am suggesting that Black women can experience discrimination in ways that are both similar to and different from those experienced by white women and Black men. Black women sometimes experience discrimination in ways similar to white women's experiences; sometimes they share very similar experiences with Black men. Yet often they experience double-discrimination – the combined effects of practices which discriminate on the basis of race and on the basis of sex. And sometimes, they experience discrimination as Black women – not the sum of race and sex discrimination, but as Black women.

Black women's experiences are much broader than the general categories that discrimination discourse provides. Yet the continued insistence that Black women's demands and needs be filtered through categorical analyses that completely obscure their experiences guarantees that their needs will seldom be addressed.

B   The Significance of Doctrinal Treatment of Intersectionality

DeGraffenreid, Moore, and Travenol are doctrinal manifestations of a common political and theoretical approach to discrimination which operates to marginalize Black women. Unable to grasp the importance of Black women's intersectional experiences, not only courts, but feminist and civil rights thinkers as well have treated Black women in ways that deny both the unique compoundedness of their situation and the centrality of their experiences to the larger classes of women and Blacks. Black women are regarded either as too much like women or Blacks and the compounded nature of their experience is absorbed into the collective experiences of either group or as too different, in which case Black women's Blackness or femaleness sometimes has placed their needs and perspectives at the margin of the feminist and Black liberationist agendas.

While it could be argued that this failure represents an absence of political will to include Black women, I believe that it reflects an uncritical and disturbing acceptance of dominant ways of thinking about discrimination. Consider first the definition of discrimination that seems to be operative in antidiscrimination law: Discrimination which is wrongful proceeds from the identification of a specific class or category; either a discriminator intentionally identifies this category, or a process is adopted which somehow disadvantages all members of this category.[29] According to the dominant view, a discriminator treats all people within a race or sex category similarly. Any significant experiential or statistical variation within this group suggests either that the group is not being discriminated against or that conflicting interests exist which defeat any attempts to bring a common claim.[30] Consequently, one generally cannot combine these categories. Race and sex, moreover, become significant only when they operate to explicitly *disadvantage* the victims; because the *privileging* of whiteness or maleness is implicit, it is generally not perceived at all.

Underlying this conception of discrimination is a view that the wrong which antidiscrimination law addresses is the use of race or gender factors to interfere with decisions that would otherwise be fair or neutral. This process-based definition is not grounded in a bottom-up commitment to improve the substantive conditions for those who are victimized by the interplay of numerous factors. Instead, the dominant message of antidiscrimination law is that it will regulate only the limited extent to which race or sex interferes with the process of determining outcomes. This narrow objective is facilitated by the top-down strategy of using a singular "but for" analysis to ascertain the effects of race or sex. Because the scope of antidiscrimination law is so limited, sex and race discrimination have come to be defined in terms of the experiences of those who are privileged *but for* their racial or sexual characteristics. Put differently, the paradigm of sex discrimination tends to be based on the experiences of white women; the model of race discrimination tends to be based on the experiences of the most privileged Blacks. Notions of what constitutes race and sex discrimination are, as a result, narrowly tailored to embrace only a small set of circumstances, none of which include discrimination against Black women.

To the extent that this general description is accurate, the following analogy can be useful in describing how Black women are marginalized in the interface between antidiscrimination law and race and gender hierarchies: Imagine a basement which contains all people who are disadvantaged on the basis of race, sex, class, sexual preference, age and/or physical ability. These people are stacked – feet standing on shoulders – with those on the bottom being disadvantaged by the full array of factors, up to the very top, where the heads of all those disadvantaged by a singular factor brush up against the ceiling. Their ceiling is actually the floor above which only those who are not disadvantaged in any way reside. In efforts to correct some aspects of domination, those above the ceiling admit from the basement only those who can say that "but for" the ceiling, they too would be in the upper room. A hatch is developed through which those placed immediately below can crawl. Yet this hatch is generally available only to those who – due to the singularity of their burden and their otherwise privileged position relative to those below – are in the position to crawl through. Those who are multiply burdened are generally left below unless they can somehow pull themselves into the groups that are permitted to squeeze through the hatch.

As this analogy translates for Black women, the problem is that they can receive protection only to the extent that their experiences are recognizably similar to those whose experiences tend to be reflected in antidiscrimination doctrine. If Black women cannot conclusively say that "but for" their race or "but for" their gender they would be treated differently, they are not invited to climb through the hatch but told to wait in the unprotected margin until they can be absorbed into the broader, protected categories of race and sex.

Despite the narrow scope of this dominant conception of discrimination and its tendency to marginalize those whose experiences cannot be described within its tightly-drawn parameters, this approach has been regarded as the appropriate framework for addressing a range of problems. In much of feminist theory and, to some extent, in antiracist politics, this framework is reflected in the belief that sexism or racism can be meaningfully discussed without paying attention to the lives of those other than the race-, gender- or class-privileged. As a result, both feminist theory and antiracist politics have been organized, in part, around the equation of racism with what happens to the Black middle-class or to Black men, and the equation of sexism with what happens to white women.

Looking at historical and contemporary issues in both the feminist and the civil rights communities, one can find ample evidence of how both communities' acceptance of the dominant framework of discrimination has hindered the development of an adequate theory and praxis to address problems of intersectionality. This adoption of a single-issue framework for discrimination not only marginalizes Black women within the very movements that claim them as part of their constituency but it also makes the elusive goal of ending racism and patriarchy even more difficult to attain.

II Feminism and Black Women: "Ain't We Women?"

Oddly, despite the relative inability of feminist politics and theory to address Black women substantively, feminist theory and tradition borrow considerably from Black women's history. For example, "Ain't I a Woman?" has come to represent a standard refrain in feminist discourse.[31] Yet the lesson of this powerful oratory is not fully appreciated because the context of the delivery is seldom examined. I would like to tell part of the story because it establishes some themes that have characterized feminist treatment of race and illustrates the importance of including Black women's experiences as a rich source for the critique of patriarchy.

In 1851, Sojourner Truth declared "Ain't I a Woman?" and challenged the sexist imagery used by male critics to justify the disenfranchisement of women.[32] The scene was a Women's Rights Conference in Akron, Ohio; white male hecklers, invoking stereotypical images of "womanhood," argued that women were too frail and delicate to take on the responsibilities of political activity. When Sojourner Truth rose to speak, many white women urged that she be silenced, fearing that she would divert attention from women's suffrage to emancipation. Truth, once permitted to speak, recounted the horrors of slavery, and its particular impact on Black women:

> Look at my arm! I have ploughed and planted and gathered into barns, and no man could head me – and ain't I a woman? I could work as much and eat as much as a man – when I could get it – and bear the lash as well! And ain't I a woman? I have born thirteen children, and seen most of 'em sold into slavery, and when I cried out with my mother's grief, none but Jesus heard me – and ain't I a woman?[33]*

By using her own life to reveal the contradiction between the ideological myths of womanhood and the reality of Black women's experience, Truth's oratory provided a powerful rebuttal to the claim that women were categorically weaker than men. Yet Truth's personal challenge to the coherence of the cult of true womanhood was useful only to the extent that white women were willing to reject the racist

---

* Editors' note: Historian Nell Painter's *Sojourner Truth: A Life, A Symbol* examines the accuracy of this speech being attributed to Truth.

attempts to rationalize the contradiction – that because Black women were something less than real women, their experiences had no bearing on true womanhood. Thus, this nineteenth-century Black feminist challenged not only patriarchy, but she also challenged white feminists wishing to embrace Black women's history to relinquish their vestedness in whiteness.

Contemporary white feminists inherit not the legacy of Truth's challenge to patriarchy but, instead, Truth's challenge to their forbearers. Even today, the difficulty that white women have traditionally experienced in sacrificing racial privilege to strengthen feminism renders them susceptible to Truth's critical question. When feminist theory and politics that claim to reflect *women's* experience and *women's* aspirations do not include or speak to Black women, Black women must ask: "Ain't We Women?" If this is so, how can the claims that "women are," "women believe" and "women need" be made when such claims are inapplicable or unresponsive to the needs, interests and experiences of Black women?

The value of feminist theory to Black women is diminished because it evolves from a white racial context that is seldom acknowledged. Not only are women of color in fact overlooked, but their exclusion is reinforced when *white* women speak for and as *women*. The authoritative universal voice – usually white male subjectivity masquerading as non-racial, non-gendered objectivity[34] – is merely transferred to those who, but for gender, share many of the same cultural, economic and social characteristics. When feminist theory attempts to describe women's experiences through analyzing patriarchy, sexuality, or separate spheres ideology, it often overlooks the role of race. Feminists thus ignore how their own race functions to mitigate some aspects of sexism and moreover, how it often privileges them over and contributes to the domination of other women.[35] Consequently, feminist theory remains *white*, and its potential to broaden and deepen its analysis by addressing non-privileged women remains unrealized.

An example of how some feminist theories are narrowly constructed around white women's experiences is found in the separate spheres literature. The critique of how separate spheres ideology shapes and limits women's roles in the home and in public life is a central theme in feminist legal thought.[36] Feminists have attempted to expose and dismantle separate spheres ideology by identifying and criticizing the stereotypes that traditionally have justified the disparate societal roles assigned to men and women.[37] Yet this attempt to debunk ideological justifications for *women's* subordination offers little insight into the domination of *Black* women. Because the experiential base upon which many feminist insights are grounded is white, theoretical statements drawn from them are over generalized at best, and often wrong.[38] Statements such as "men and women are taught to see men as independent, capable, powerful; men and women are taught to see women as dependent, limited in abilities, and passive,"[39] are common within this literature. But this "observation" overlooks the anomalies created by crosscurrents of racism and sexism. Black men and women live in a society that creates sex-based norms and expectations which racism operates simultaneously to deny; Black men are not viewed as powerful, nor are Black women seen as passive. An effort to develop an ideological explanation of gender domination in the Black community should proceed from an understanding of how crosscutting forces establish gender norms and how the conditions of Black subordination wholly frustrate access to these norms. Given this understanding, perhaps we can begin to see why Black women have been dogged by the stereotype of the pathological matriarch[40] or why there have been those in the Black liberation movement who aspire to create institutions and to build traditions that are intentionally patriarchal.[41]

Because ideological and descriptive definitions of patriarchy are usually premised upon white female experiences, feminists and others informed by feminist literature may make the mistake of assuming that since the role of Black women in the family, and in other Black institutions does not always resemble the familiar manifestations of patriarchy in the white community, Black women are somehow exempt from patriarchal norms. For example, Black women have traditionally worked outside the home in numbers far exceeding the labor participation rate of white women.[42] An analysis of patriarchy that highlights the history of white women's exclusion from the workplace might permit the inference that Black women have not been burdened by this particular gender-based expectation. Yet the very fact that Black women must work conflicts with norms that women should not, often creating personal, emotional and relationship problems in Black women's lives. Thus, Black women are burdened not only because they often have to take on responsibilities that are not traditionally feminine but, moreover, their assumption of these roles is sometimes interpreted within the Black community as either Black women's failure to live up to such norms or as another manifestation of racism's scourge upon the Black community.[43] This is one of the many aspects of intersectionality that cannot be understood through an analysis of patriarchy rooted in white experience.

Another example of how theory emanating from a white context obscures the multidimensionality of Black women's lives is found in feminist discourse on rape. A central political issue on the feminist agenda has been the pervasive problem of rape. Part of the intellectual and political effort to mobilize around this issue has involved the development of a historical critique of the role that law has played in establishing the bounds of normative sexuality and in regulating female sexual behavior.[44] Early carnal knowledge statutes and rape laws are understood within this discourse to illustrate that the objective of rape statutes traditionally has not been to protect women from coercive intimacy but to protect and maintain a property-like interest in female chastity.[45] Although feminists quite rightly criticize these objectives, to characterize rape law as reflecting male control over female sexuality is for Black women an oversimplified account and an ultimately inadequate account.

Rape statutes generally do not reflect male control over *female* sexuality, but *white* male regulation of *white* female sexuality.[46] Historically, there has been absolutely no institutional effort to regulate Black female chastity.[47] Courts in some states had gone so far as to instruct juries that, unlike white women, Black women were not presumed to be chaste.[48] Also, while it was true that the attempt to regulate the sexuality of white women placed unchaste women outside the law's protection, racism restored a fallen white woman's chastity where the alleged assailant was a Black man.[49] No such restoration was available to Black women.

The singular focus on rape as a manifestation of male power over female sexuality tends to eclipse the use of rape as a weapon of racial terror.[50] When Black women were raped by white males, they were being raped not as women generally, but as Black women specifically: their femaleness made them sexually vulnerable to racist domination, while their Blackness effectively denied them any protection.[51] This white male power was reinforced by a judicial system in which the successful conviction of a white man for raping a Black woman was virtually unthinkable.[52]

In sum, sexist expectations of chastity and racist assumptions of sexual promiscuity combined to create a distinct set of issues confronting Black women.[53] These issues have seldom been explored in feminist literature nor are they prominent in antiracist politics. The lynching of Black males, the institutional practice that was legitimized by the regulation of white women's sexuality, has historically and contemporaneously occupied the Black agenda on sexuality and violence. Consequently, Black women are caught between a Black community that, perhaps understandably, views with suspicion attempts to litigate questions of sexual violence, and a feminist community that reinforces those suspicions by focusing on white female sexuality.[54] The suspicion is compounded by the historical fact that the protection of white female sexuality was often the pretext for terrorizing the Black community. Even today some fear that anti-rape agendas may undermine antiracist objectives. This is the paradigmatic political and theoretical dilemma created by the intersection of race and gender: Black women are caught between ideological and political currents that combine first to create and then to bury Black women's experiences.

III   When and Where I Enter: Integrating an Analysis of Sexism into Black Liberation Politics

Anna Julia Cooper, a nineteenth-century Black feminist, coined a phrase that has been useful in evaluating the need to incorporate an explicit analysis of patriarchy in any effort to address racial domination.[55] Cooper often criticized Black leaders and spokespersons for claiming to speak for the race, but failing to speak for Black women. Referring to one of Martin Delaney's public claims that where he was allowed to enter, the race entered with him. Cooper countered: "Only the Black Woman can say, when and where I enter . . . then and there the whole Negro race enters with me."[56]

Cooper's words bring to mind a personal experience involving two Black men with whom I had formed a study group during our first year of law school. One of our group members, a graduate from Harvard College, often told us stories about a prestigious and exclusive men's club that boasted memberships of several past United States presidents and other influential white males. He was one of its very few Black members. To celebrate completing our first-year exams, our friend invited us to join him at the club for drinks. Anxious to see this fabled place, we approached the large door and grasped the brass door ring to announce our arrival. But our grand entrance was cut short when our friend sheepishly slipped from behind the door and whispered that he had forgotten one very important detail. My companion and I bristled, our training as Black people having taught us to expect yet another barrier; even an informal one-Black-person quota at the establishment was not unimaginable. The tension broke, however, we learned that we would not be excluded because of our race but that I would have to go around to the back door because I was a female. I entertained the idea of making a scene to dramatize the fact that my humiliation as a female was no less painful and my exclusion no more excusable than had we all been sent to the back door because we were Black. But, sensing no general assent to this proposition, and also being of the mind that due to our race a scene would in some way jeopardize all of us, I failed to stand my ground. After all, the Club was about to entertain its first Black guests – even though one would have to enter through the back door.[57]

Perhaps this story is not the best example of the Black community's failure to address problems related to Black women's intersectionality seriously. The story would be more apt if Black women, and only Black women, had to go around to the back door of the club and if the restriction came from within, and not from the outside of the Black community. Still this story does reflect a markedly decreased political and emotional vigilance toward barriers to Black women's enjoyment of privileges that have been won on the basis of race but continue to be denied on the basis of sex.[58]

The story also illustrates the ambivalence among Black women about the degree of political and social capital that ought to be expended toward challenging gender barriers, particularly when the challenges might conflict with the antiracism agenda. While there are a number of reasons – including antifeminist ones – why gender has not figured directly in analyses of the subordination of Black Americans, a central reason is that race is still seen by many as the primary oppositional force in Black lives.[59] If one accepts that the social experience of race creates both a primary group identity as well as a shared sense of being under collective assault, some of the reasons that Black feminist theory and politics have not figured prominently in the Black political agenda may be better understood.[60]

The point is not that African Americans are simply involved in a more important struggle. Although some efforts to oppose Black feminism are based on this assumption, a fuller appreciation of the problems of the Black community will reveal that gender subordination does contribute significantly to the destitute conditions of so many African Americans and that it must therefore be addressed. Moreover, the foregoing critique of the single-issue framework renders problematic the claim that the struggle against racism is distinguishable from, much less prioritized over, the struggle against sexism. Yet it is also true that the politics of racial otherness that Black women experience along with Black men prevent Black feminist consciousness from patterning the development of white feminism. For white women, the creation of a consciousness that was distinct from and in opposition to that of white men figured prominently in the development of white feminist politics. Black women, like Black men, live in a community that has been defined and subordinated by color and culture.[61] Although patriarchy clearly operates within the Black community, presenting yet another source of domination to which Black women are vulnerable, the racial context in which Black women find themselves makes the creation of a political consciousness that is oppositional to Black men difficult.

Yet while it is true that the distinct experience of racial otherness militates against the development of an oppositional feminist consciousness, the assertion of racial community sometimes supports defensive priorities that marginalize Black women. Black women's particular interests are thus relegated to the periphery in public policy discussions about the presumed needs of the Black community. The controversy over the movie *The Color Purple* is illustrative. The animating fear behind much of the publicized protest was that by portraying domestic abuse in a Black family, the movie confirmed the negative stereotypes of Black men.[62] The debate over the propriety of presenting such an image on the screen overshadowed the issue of sexism and patriarchy in the Black community. Even though it was sometimes acknowledged that the Black community was not immune from domestic violence and other manifestations of gender subordination, some nevertheless felt that in the absence of positive Black male images in the media, portraying such images merely reinforced racial stereotypes.[63] The struggle against racism seemed to compel the subordination of certain aspects of the Black female experience in order to ensure the security of the larger Black community.

The nature of this debate should sound familiar to anyone who recalls

Daniel Moynihan's diagnosis of the ills of Black America.[64] Moynihan's report depicted a deteriorating Black family, foretold the destruction of the Black male householder and lamented the creation of the Black matriarch. His conclusions prompted a massive critique from liberal sociologists[65] and from civil rights leaders.[66] Surprisingly, while many critics characterized the report as racist for its blind use of white cultural norms as the standard for evaluating Black families, few pointed out the sexism apparent in Moynihan's labeling Black women as pathological for their "failure" to live up to a white female standard of motherhood.[67]

The latest versions of a Moynihanesque analysis can be found in the Moyers televised special, *The Vanishing Black Family*,[68] and, to a lesser extent, in William Julius Wilson's *The Truly Disadvantaged*.[69] In *The Vanishing Black Family*, Moyers presented the problem of female-headed households as a problem of irresponsible sexuality, induced in part by government policies that encouraged family breakdown.[70] The theme of the report was that the welfare state reinforced the deterioration of the Black family by rendering the Black male's role obsolete. As the argument goes, because Black men know that someone will take care of their families, they are free to make babies and leave them. A corollary to the Moyers view is that welfare is also dysfunctional because it allows poor women to leave men upon whom they would otherwise be dependent.

Most commentators criticizing the program failed to pose challenges that might have revealed the patriarchal assumptions underlying much of the Moyers report. They instead focused on the dimension of the problem that was clearly recognizable as racist.[71] White feminists were equally culpable. There was little, if any published response to the Moyers report from the white feminist community. Perhaps feminists were under the mistaken assumption that since the report focused on the Black community, the problems highlighted were racial, not gender based. Whatever the reason, the result was that the ensuing debates over the future direction of welfare and family policy proceeded without significant feminist input. The absence of a strong feminist critique of the Moynihan/Moyers model not only impeded the interests of Black women, but it also compromised the interests of growing numbers of white women heads of household who find it difficult to make ends meet.[72]

William Julius Wilson's *The Truly Disadvantaged* modified much of the moralistic tone of this debate by reframing the issue in terms of a lack of marriageable Black men.[73] According to Wilson, the decline in Black marriages is not attributable to poor motivation, bad work habits or irresponsibility but instead is caused by structural economics which have forced Black unskilled labor out of the work force. Wilson's approach represents a significant move away from that of Moynihan/ Moyers in that he rejects their attempt to center the analysis on the morals of the Black community. Yet, he too considers the proliferation of female-headed households as dysfunctional *per se* and fails to explain fully why such households are so much in peril. Because he incorporates no analysis of the way the structure of the economy and the workforce subordinates the interests of women, especially childbearing Black women, Wilson's suggested reform begins with finding ways to put Black men back in the family.[74] In Wilson's view, we must change the economic structure with an eye toward providing more Black jobs for Black men. Because he offers no critique of sexism, Wilson fails to consider economic or social reorganization that directly empowers and supports these single Black mothers.[75]

Notes

1   Gloria T. Hull, et al., eds., *All the Women are White, All the Blacks are Men, But Some of Us Are Brave* (The Feminist Press, 1982).
2   For other work setting forth a Black feminist perspective on law, see Judy Scales-Trent, *Black Women and the Constitution: Finding Our Place, Asserting Our Rights (Voices of Experience: New Responses to Gender Discourse)* 24 Harv CR-CL L Rev 9 (1989); Regina Austin, *Sapphire-Bound!* in Wise Women's L.J. (1989); Angela Harris, *Race and Essentialism in Feminist Legal Theory* (unpublished manuscript on file with author [published in *Stanford Law Review* 42 (1990); and Paulette M. Caldwell, *A Hair Piece* (unpublished manuscript on file with author [published in *Duke Law Journal* 1991).
3   The most common linguistic manifestation of this analytical dilemma is represented in the conventional usage of the term "Blacks and women." Although it may be true that some people mean to include Black women in either "Blacks" or "women" the context in which the term is used actually suggests that often Black women are not considered. See, for example, Elizabeth Spelman, *The Inessential Woman: Problems of Exclusion in Feminist Thought* 114–15 (Beacon Press, 1988), discussing an article on Blacks and women in the military where the racial identity of those

identified as "women" does not become explicit until reference is made to Black women, at which point it also becomes clear that the category of women excludes Black women [except where] explicitly included; the preferred term would be either "Blacks and white women" or "Black men and all women."

4 Civil Rights Act of 1964, 42 USC §2000e, et seq as amended (1982).

5 413 F Suppl 142 (E D Mo 1976).

6 708 F2d 475 (9th Cir 1983).

7 673 F2d 798 (5th Cir 1982).

8 *DeGraffenreid*, 413 F Supp at 143.

9 Id at 144.

10 Id at 145. In *Mosley v General Motors*, 497 F Supp 583 (E D Mo 1980), plaintiffs, alleging broad-based racial discrimination at General Motors' St. Louis facility, prevailed in a portion of their Title VII claim. The senority system challenged in *DeGraffenreid*, however, was not considered in *Mosley*.

11 Id at 145.

12 Interestingly, no case has been discovered in which a court denied a white male's attempt to bring a reverse discrimination claim on similar grounds – that is, that sex and race claims cannot be combined because Congress did not intend to protect compound classes. White males in a typical reverse discrimination case are in no better position that the frustrated plaintiffs in *DeGraffenreid*: If they are required to make their claims separately, white males cannot prove race discrimination because white women are not discriminated against, and they cannot prove sex discrimination because Black males are not discriminated against. Yet it seems that courts do not acknowledge the compound nature of most reverse discrimination cases. That Black women's claims automatically raise the question of compound discrimination and white males' "reverse discrimination" cases do not suggest that the notion of compoundedness is somehow contingent upon an implicit norm, that is not neutral but is white male. Thus, Black women are perceived as a compound class because they are two steps removed from a white male norm, while white males are apparently not perceived to be a compound class because they somehow represent the norm.

13 I do not mean to imply that all courts that have grappled with this problem have adopted the *DeGraffenreid* approach. Indeed, other courts have concluded that Black women are protected by Title VII. See, for example, *Jefferies v Harris Community Action Ass'n.*, 615 F2d 1025 (5th Cir 1980). I do mean to suggest that the very fact that the Black women's claims are seen as aberrant suggests that sex discrimination doctrine is still centered in the experiences of white women. Even those courts that have held that Black women are protected seem to accept that Black women's claims [involve]

issues that the "standard" sex discrimination claims do not. See Elaine W. Schoben, *Compound Discrimination: the Interaction of Race and Sex in Employment Discrimination*, 55 NYU L Rev 793, 803–4 (1980) (criticizing the *Jefferies* use of a sex-plus analysis to create a subclass of Black women).

14   708 F2d 475.

15   See also *Moore v National Association of Securities Dealers*, 27 EPD (CCH) 32,238 (D DC 1981); but see *Edmondson v Simon*, 86 FRD 375 (N D Ill 1980) (where the court was unwilling to hold as a matter of law that no Black female could represent without conflicts of interests both Blacks and females).

16   708 F2d at 479. Between January 1976 and June 1979, the three years in which Moore claimed that she was passed over for promotion, the percentage of white males occupying first-level supervisory positions ranged from 70.3 to 76.8%; Black males from 8.9 to 10.9%; white women from 1.8 to 3.3%; and Black females from 0 to 2.2% The overall male/female ratio in the top five labor grades ranged from 100/0% in 1976 to 98/1.8% in 1979. The white/Black ratio was 85/3.3% in 1076 and 79.6/8% in 1979; the Black to white ratio during the same time period was 78.6 to 8.9% and 73.6 to 13.1%. For promotions to the top five labor grades, the percentages were worse. Between 1976 and 1979, the percentage of white males in these positions ranged from 85.3 to 77.9%; Black males 3.3 to 8%; white females from 0 to 1.4%, and Black females from 0 to 0%. Overall, in 1979, 98,25 of the highest level employees were male; 1.8% were female.

17   708 F2d at 480 (emphasis added).

18   Id at 484–6.

19   Under the disparate impact theory that prevailed at the time, the plaintiff had to introduce statistics suggesting that a policy or procedure disparately affects the members of a protected group. The employer could rebut that evidence by showing that there was a business necessity supporting the rule. The plaintiff then countered the rebuttal by showing that there was a less discriminatory alternative. See, for example, *Griggs v Duke Power*, 401 US 424 (1971); *Connecticut v Teal*, 457 US 440 (1982). A central issue in a disparate impact case is whether the impact proved is statistically significant. A related issue is how the protected group is defined. In many cases a Black female plaintiff would prefer to use statistics which include white women and/or Black men to indicate that the policy in question does in fact disparately affect the protected class. If, as in *Moore*, the plaintiff may use only statistics involving Black women, there may not be enough Black women employees to create a statistically significant sample.

20   Id at 484.

21   The court buttressed its finding with respect to the upper-level labor jobs with statistics for the Los Angeles Metropolitan Area which indicated the

there were only 0.2% Black women within comparable job categories. Id at 485 n 9.

22   Id at 486.

23   Id.

24   See *Strong v Arkansas Blue Cross & Blue Shield, Inc.*, 87 FRD 496 (E D Ark 1980); *Hammons v Folger Coffee Co.*, 87 FRD 600 (W D Mo 1980); *Edmondson v Simon*, 86 FRD 375 (N D Ill 1980); *Vuyanich v Republic National Bank of Dallas*, 82 FRD 420 (N D Tex 1979); *Colston v Maryland Cup Corp.*, 26 Fed Rules Serv 940 (D Md 1978).

25   416 F Supp 248 (N D Miss 1976).

26   The suit commenced on March 2, 1972, with the filing of a complaint by three employees seeking to represent a class of persons allegedly subjected to racial discrimination at the hands of the defendants. Subsequently, the plaintiffs amended the complaint to add an allegation of sex discrimination. Of the original named plaintiffs, one was a Black male and two were Black females. In the course of the three-year period between the filing of the complaint and the trial, the only named male plaintiff received permission of the court to withdraw for religious reasons. Id at 250.

27   As the dissent in *Travenol* pointed out, there was no reason to exclude Black males from the scope of the remedy *after* counsel had presented sufficient evidence to support a finding of discrimination against Black men. If the rationale for excluding Black males was the potential conflict between Black males and Black females, then "in this case, to paraphrase an old adage, the proof of plaintiffs' ability to represent the interests of Black males was in the presentation thereof." 673 F2d at 837–8.

28   673 F2d 798 (5th Cir 1982).

29   In much of antidiscrimination doctrine, the presence of intent to discriminate distinguishes unlawful from lawful discrimination. See *Washington v Davis*, 426 US 229, 239–45 (1976) (proof of discriminatory purpose required to substantiate Equal Protection violation). Under Title VII, however, the Court has held that statistical data showing a disproportionate impact can suffice to support a finding of discrimination. See *Griggs*, 401 US at 432. Whether the distinction between the two analyses will survive is an open question. See *Wards Cove Packing Co., Inc. v Atonio*, 109 S Ct 2115, 2122–3 (1989) (plaintiffs must show more than mere disparity to support a prima facie case of disparate impact). For a discussion of the competing normative visions that underlie the intent and effects analyses, see Alan David Freeman, *Legitimizing Racial Discrimination, Through Antidiscrimination Law: A Critical Review of Supreme Court Doctrine*, 62 Minn L Rev 1049 (1978).

30   See, for example, *Moore*, 708 F2d at 479.

31   See Phyliss Palmer, *The Racial Feminization of Poverty: Women of Color*

as Portents of the Future for All Women, Women's Studies Quarterly 11: 3–4 (Fall 1983).

32 See Paula Giddings, *When and Where I Enter: The Impact of Black Women on Race and Sex in America* 54 (William Morrow and Co, Inc, 1ˢᵗ ed 1984).

33 Eleanor Flexner, *Century of Struggle: The Women's Rights Movement in the United States* 91 (Belknap Press of Harvard University Press, 1975). See also bell hooks, *Ain't I a Woman? Black Women and Feminism* 159–60 (South End Press, 1981).

34 "'Objectivity'" is itself an example of the reification of white male thought." Hull et al., eds., *But Some of Us Are Brave* at xxv (cited in note 1).

35 For example, many white females were able to gain entry into previously all white male enclaves not through bringing about a fundamental reordering of male versus female work, but in large part by shifting their "female" responsibilities to poor and minority women.

36 Feminists often discuss how gender-based stereotypes and norms reinforce the subordination of women by justifying their exclusion from public life and glorifying their roles within the private sphere. Law has historically played a role in maintaining this subordination by enforcing the exclusion of women from public life and by limiting its reach into the private sphere. See, for example, Deborah L. Rhode, *Association and Assimilation*, 81 Nw U L Rev 106 (1986); Frances Olsen, *From False Paternalism to False Equality: Judicial Assaults on Feminist Community, Illinois 1869–95*, 84 Mich L Rev 1518 (1986); Martha Minow, *Foreword: Justice Engendered*, 101 Harv L Rev 10 (1987); Nadine Taub and Elizabeth M. Schneider, *Perspectives on Women's Subordination and the Role of Law*, in David Kairys, ed, *The Politics of Law* 117–39 (Pantheon Books, 1982).

37 See works cited in note 36.

38 This criticism is a discrete illustration of a more general claim that feminism has been premised on white middle-class women's experience. For example, early feminist texts such as Betty Friedan's *The Feminine Mystique* (W. W. Norton, 1963), placed white middle-class problems at the center of feminism and thus contributed to its rejection within the Black community. See hooks, *Ain't I a Woman?* at 185–96 (cited in note 33) (noting that feminism was eschewed by Black women because its white middle-class agenda ignored Black women's concerns).

39 Richard A. Wasserstrom, *Racism, Sexism and Preferential Treatment: An Approach to the Topics*, 24 UCLA L Rev 581, 588 (1977). I chose this phrase not because it is typical of most feminist statements of separate spheres; indeed, most discussions are not as simplistic as the bold statement

presented here. See, for example, Taub and Schneider, *Perspectives on Women's Subordination and the Role of Law* at 117–39 (cited in note 36).

40 For example, Black families have sometimes been cast as pathological largely because of Black women's divergence from the white middle-class female norm. The most infamous rendition of this view is found in the Moynihan report that blamed many of the Black community's ills on a supposed pathological family structure. For a discussion of the report and its contemporary reincarnation, see 163–5.

41 See hooks, *Ain't I a Woman?* at 94–9 (cited in note 33) (discussing the elevation of sexist imagery in the Black liberation movement during the 1960s).

42 See generally Jacqueline Jones, *Labor of Love, Labor of Sorrow; Black Women Work, and the Family from Slavery to the Present* (Basic Books, 1985); Angela Davis, *Women, Race and Class* (Random House, 1981).

43 As Elizabeth Higginbotham noted, "women, who often fail to conform to 'appropriate' sex roles, have been pictured as, and made to feel, inadequate – even though as women they possess traits recognized as positive when held by men in the wider society. Such women are stigmatized because their lack of adherence to expected gender roles is seen as a threat to the value system." Elizabeth Higginbotham, *Two Representative Issues in Contemporary Sociological Work on Black Women*, in Hull, et al., eds., *But Some of Us Are Brave* at 95 (cited in note 1).

44 See generally Susan Brownmiller, *Against Our Will* (Simon and Schuster, 1975); Susan Estrich, *Real Rape* (Harvard University Press, 1987).

45 See Brownmiller, *Against Our Will* at 17; see generally Estrich, *Real Rape*.

46 One of the central theoretical dilemmas of feminism that is largely obscured by universalizing the white female experience is that experiences that are described as a manifestation of male control over females can be instead a manifestation of dominant group control over all subordinates. The significance is that other non-dominant men may not share in, participate in or connect with the behavior, beliefs or actions at issue, and may be victimized themselves by "male" power. In other contexts, however, "male authority" might include nonwhite men, particularly in private sphere contexts. Efforts to think more clearly about when Black women are dominated as *women* and when they are dominated as *Black women* are directly related to the question of when power is *male* and when it is *white male*.

47 See Note, *Rape, Racism and the Law*, 5 Harv Women's L J 103, 117–23 (1983) (discussing the historical and contemporary evidence suggesting that Black women are generally not thought to be chaste). See also hooks, *Ain't I a Woman?* at 54 (cited in note 33) (stating that stereotypical images of Black womanhood during slavery were based on the myth that "all black

women were immoral and sexually loose"); Beverly Smith, *Black Women's Health: Notes for a Course*, in Hull et al., eds., *But Some of Us Are Brave* at 110 (cited in note 1) (noting that ". . . white men for centuries have justified their sexual abuse of Black women by claiming that we are licentious, always 'ready' for any sexual encounter").

48 The following statement is probably unusual only in its candor: "What has been said by some of our courts about an unchaste female being a comparatively rare exception is no doubt true where the population is composed largely of the Caucasian race, but we would blind ourselves to actual conditions if we adopted this rule where another race that is largely immoral constitutes an appreciable part of the population." *Dallas v State*, 7 6 Fla 358, 79 So 690 (1918), quoted in Note, 6 Harv Women's L J at 121 (cited in note 47). Espousing precisely this view, one commentator stated in 1902: "I sometimes hear of a virtuous Negro woman but the idea is so absolutely inconceivable to me . . . I cannot imagine such a creature as a virtuous Negro Woman." Id at 82. Such images persist in popular culture. See Paul Grein, *Taking Stock of the Latest Pop Record Surprises, LA Times* § 6 at 1 (July 7, 1988) (recalling the controversy in the late 70s over a Rolling Stone recording which included the line "Black girls just wanna get fucked all night"). Opposition to such negative stereotypes has sometimes taken the form of sexual conservatism. "A desperate reaction to this slanderous myth is the attempt . . . to conform to the strictest versions of patriarchal morality." Smith, *Black Women's Health*, in Hull et al., eds., *But Some of Us Are Brave* at 111 (cited in Note 1). Part of this reaction is reflected in the attitudes and policies of Black schools which have been notoriously strict in regulating the behavior of female students. See Gail Elizabeth Wyatt, *The Sexual Experience of Afro-American Women*, in Martha Kirkpatrick, ed., *Women's Sexual Experience Exploration of the Dark Continent* 24 (Plenum, 1982) (noting "the differences between the predominantly Afro-American universities, where there was far more super-vision regarding sexual behavior, and the majority of white colleges, where there were fewer curfews and restrictions placed on the resident"). Any attempt to understand and critique the emphasis on Black virtue without focusing on the racist ideology that places virtue beyond the reach of Black women would be incomplete and probably incorrect.

49 Because of the way the legal system viewed chastity, Black women could not be victims of forcible rape. One commentator has noted that "[a]ccording to governing stereotypes [sic], chastity could not be possessed by Black women. Thus, Black women's rape charges were automatically discounted, and the issue of chastity was contested only in cases where the rape complainant was a white woman." Note, 6 Harv Women's L J at 126 (cited in note 47). Black women's claims of rape were not taken seriously

regardless of the offender's race. A judge in 1912 said: "This court will never take the word of a nigger against the word of a white man [concerning rape]." Id at 120. On the other hand, lynching was considered an effective remedy for a Black man's rape of a white woman. Since rape of a white woman by a Black man was "a crime more horrible than death," the only way to assuage society's rage and to make the woman whole again was to brutally murder the black man. Id at 125.

50   See *The Rape of Black Women as a Weapon of Terror* in Gerda Lerner, ed., *Black Women in White America: A Documentary History*, 172–93 (Pantheon Books, 1972). See also Brownmiller, *Against Our Will* (cited in note 44.) Even where Brownmiller acknowledges the use of rape as racial terrorism, she resists making a "special case" for Black Women by offering evidence that white women were raped by the Klan as well. Id at 139. Whether or not one considers the racist rape of Black women a "special case," such experiences are probably different. In any case, Brownmiller's treatment of the issue raises serious questions about the ability to sustain an analysis of patriarchy without understanding its multiple intersections with racism.

51   Lerner, *Black Women in White America* at 173.

52   See generally, Note, 6 Harv Women's L J at 103 (cited in note 47).

53   Paula Giddings notes the combined effect of sexual and racial stereotypes: "Black women were seen having all of the inferior qualities of white women without any of their virtues." Giddings, *When and Where I Enter* at 82 (cited in note 32).

54   Susan Brownmiller's treatment of the Emmett Till case illustrates why antirape politicization makes some African Americans uncomfortable. Despite Brownmiller's quite laudable efforts to discuss elsewhere the rape of Black women and the racism involved in much of the hysteria over the Black male threat, her analysis of the Till case places the sexuality of white women, rather than racial terrorism, at center stage. Brownmiller states: "Rarely has one single case exposed so clearly as Till's the underlying group-male antagonisms over access to women, for what began in Bryant's store should not be misconstrued as an innocent flirtation . . . In concrete terms, the accessibility of all white women was on review." Brownmiller, *Against Our Will* at 272 (cited in note 44). Later, Brownmiller argues: "And what of the wolf whistle, Till's 'gesture of adolescent bravado'? We are rightly aghast that a whistle could be cause for murder but we must also accept that Emmett Till and J. W. Millam shared something in common. They both understood that the whistle was no small tweet of hubba-hubba or melodious approval for a well-turned ankle. Given the deteriorated situation . . . it was a deliberate insult just short of physical assault, a last reminder to Carolyn Bryant that this black boy, Till, had a

mind to possess her." Id at 273. While Brownmiller seems to categorize the case as one that evidences a conflict over possession, it is regarded in African American history as a tragic dramatization of the South's pathological hatred and fear of African Americans. Till's body, mutilated beyond recognition, was viewed by thousands so that, in the works of Till's mother, "the world could see what they did to my boy." Juan Williams, *Standing for Justice* in *Eyes on the Prize* 44 (Viking, 1987). The Till tragedy is also regarded as one of the historical events that bore directly on the emergence of the Civil Rights movement. "[W]ithout question it moved black America in a way the Supreme Court ruling on school desegregation could not match," Id. As Williams later observed, "the murder of Emmett Till had a powerful impact on a generation of blacks. It was this generation, those who were adolescents when Till was killed, that would soon demand justice and freedom in a way unknown in America before." Id at 57. Thus, while Brownmiller looks at the Till case and sees the vicious struggle over the possession of a white woman, African Americans see the case as a symbol of the insane degree to which whites were willing to suppress the Black race. While patriarchal attitudes toward women's sexuality played a supporting role, to place white women center stage in this tragedy is to manifest such confusion over racism as to make it difficult to imagine that the white antirape movement could be sensitive to more subtle racial tensions regarding Black women's participation in it.

55 See Anna Julia Cooper, *A Voice from the South* (Negro Universities Press, 1969; reprint of the Aldine Printing House, Ohio, 1892).

56 Id at 31.

57 In all fairness, I must acknowledge that my companion accompanied me to the back door. I remain uncertain, however, as to whether the gesture was an expression of solidarity or an effort to quiet my anger.

58 To this one could easily add class.

59 An anecdote illustrates this point. A group of female law professors gathered to discuss "isms in the Classroom." One exercise led by Pat Cain involved each participant listing the thee primary factors that described herself. Almost without exception, the white women in the room listed their gender either primarily or secondarily, none listed their race. All of the women of color listed their race first, and then their gender. This seems to suggest that identity descriptions seem to begin with the primary source of opposition with whatever the dominant norm is. See Pat Cain, *Female Jurisprudence: Grounding the Theories* 19–29 (unpublished manuscript on file with author)(explaining the exercise and noting that "no white woman ever mentions race, whereas every woman of color does" and that, similarly "straight women do not include 'heterosexual' . . . whereas lesbians who are open always include 'lesbian' ").

60 For a comparative discussion of Third World feminism paralleling this observation, see Kumari Jayawardena, *Feminism and Nationalism in the Third World*, 1–24 (Zed Books, 1986). Jayawardena states that feminism in the Third World has been 'accepted' only within the central struggle against international domination. Women's social and political status has improved most when advancement is necessary to the broader struggle against imperialism.

61 For a discussion of how racial ideology creates a polarizing dynamic which subordinates Blacks and privileges whites, see Kimberlé Crenshaw, *Race, Reform and Retrenchment: Transformation and Legitimation of Antidiscrimination Law* 101 Harv L Rev 1331, 1371–6 (1988).

62 Jack Matthews, *Three Color Purple Actresses Talk About Its Impact*, LA Times § at 1 (Dec. 20, 1985). But see Gene Siskel, *Does Purple Hate Men? Chicago Tribune* § 13 at 16 (Jan. 5 1986): Clarence Page, *Toward the New Black Cinema, Chicago Tribune* § 5 at 3 (Jan. 12, 1986).

63 A consistent problem with any negative portrayal of African Americans is that they are seldom balanced by positive images. On the other hand, most critics overlooked the positive transformation of the primary male character in *The Color Purple*.

64 Daniel P. Moynihan, *The Negro Family: The Case for National Action* (Office of Policy Planning and Research, United States of Department of Labor, 1965).

65 See Lee Rainwater and William L. Yancey, *The Moynihan Report and the Politics of Controversy* 427–9 (MIT Press, 1967) (containing criticisms of the Moynihan Report by, among others, Charles E. Silberman, Christopher Jencks, William Ryan, Laura Carper, Frank Riessman and Herbert Gans).

66 Id at 395–7 (critics included Martin Luther King, Jr., Benjamin Payton, James Farmer, Whitney Young, Jr., and Bayard Rustin).

67 One of the notable exceptions is Jacquelyne Johnson Jackson, *Black Women in a Racist Society*, in *Racism and Mental Health* 185–6 (University of Pittsburgh Press, 1973).

68 *The Vanishing Black Family* (PBS Television Broadcast, January 1986).

69 William Julius Wilson, *The Truly Disadvantaged: The Inner City, The Underclass and Public Policy* (University of Chicago Press, 1987).

70 Columnist Mary McGory, applauding the show, reported that Moyers found that sex was as common in the Black ghetto as a cup of coffee. McGrory, *Moynihan Was Right 21 Years Ago, Washington Post* B1 and B4 (Jan. 26, 1986). George Will argued that oversexed Black men were more of a menace than Bull Conner, the Birmingham Police Chief who in 1968 achieved international notoriety by turning fire hoses on protesting school children. George Will, *Voting Rights Won't Fix It, The Washington Post*, A-23 (Jan. 23, 1986). My guess is that the program has influenced

the debate about the so-called underclass by providing graphic support to pre-existing tendencies to attribute poverty to individual immorality. During a recent and memorable discussion on the public policy implications of poverty in the Black community, one student remarked that nothing can be done about Black poverty until Black men stop acting like "roving penises," Black women stop having babies "at the drop of a hat" and they all learn middle-class morality. The student cited the Moyers report as her source.

71 Although the nearly exclusive focus on the racist aspects of the program poses both theoretical and political problems, it was entirely understandable given the racial nature of the subsequent comments that were sympathetic to the Moyers view. As is typical in discussions involving race, the dialogue regarding the Moyers program covered more than just the issue of Black families; some commentators took the opportunity to indict not only the Black underclass, but the Black civil rights leadership, the war on poverty, affirmative action and other race-based remedies. See for example, Will, *Voting Rights Won't Fix It* at A-23 (cited in note 70).

72 Their difficulties can also be likened to the prevalence of an economic system and family policy that treat the nuclear family as the norm and other family units as aberrant and unworthy of societal accommodation.

73 Wilson, *The Truly Disadvantaged* at 96 (cited in note 69).

74 Id at 154 (suggestions include macroeconomic policies which promote balanced economic growth, a nationally oriented labor market strategy, a child support assurance program, a child care strategy, and a family allowances program which would be both means tested and race specific).

75 Nor does Wilson include analysis of the impact of gender on changes in family patterns. Consequently, little attention is paid to the conflict that may result when gender-based expectations are frustrated by economic and demographic factors. This focus on demographic and structural explanations represents an effort to regain the high ground from the Moyers/Moynihan approach, which is more psycho-social. Perhaps because psycho-social explanations have come dangerously close to victim-blaming, their prevalence is thought to threaten efforts to win policy directives that might effectively address deteriorating conditions within the working class and poor black communities. See Kimberlé Crenshaw, *A Comment on Gender, Difference, and Victim Ideology in the Study of the Black Family*, in *Racist Society*, in *Racism and Mental Health* 185–6 (University of Pittsburgh, 1973).

TEN

Radicalizing Feminism

Joy James

In order for us as poor and oppressed people to become a part of a society that is meaningful, the system under which we now exist has to be radically changed. This means that we are going to have to learn to think in radical terms. I use the term radical in its original meaning – getting down to and understanding the root cause. It means facing a system that does not lend itself to your needs and devising means by which you change that system. That is easier said than done. But one of the things that has to be faced is, in the process of wanting to change that system, how much have we got to do to find out who we are, where we have come from and where we are going?

Ella Baker, "The Black Woman in the Civil Rights Struggle"[1]

During the height of the black liberation and black power movements, veteran activist Ella Baker's cogent assessment of the political contradictions of liberalism among black elites advocating civil rights distinguished between attempts to become "a part of the American scene" and "the more radical struggle" to transform society. According to Baker,

In . . . struggling to be accepted, there were certain goals, concepts, and values such as the drive for the "Talented Tenth". That, of course, was the concept that proposed that through the process of education black people would be accepted in the American culture and they would be accorded their rights in proportion to the degree to which they qualified as being persons of learning and culture.[2]

For Baker, the common belief that "those who were trained were not trained to be part of the community, but to be leaders of the community" implied "another false assumption that being a leader meant that you were separate and apart from the masses, and to a large extent people were to look up to you, and that your responsibility to the people was to represent them." This precluded people from acquiring their own sense of values; but the 1960s, according to Baker, would usher in another view: "the concept of the right of the people to participate in the decisions that affected their lives."[3]

Despite agitational movements, the concept of African Americans participating in political decisions has historically been translated through corporate, state or philanthropic channels. A century ago, the vision and resources of the American Baptist Home Missionary Society (ABHMS) allowed wealthy, white Christian missionaries to create the black elite Talented Tenth as a shadow of themselves as influential, liberal leaders, and to organize privileged black Americans to serve as a buffer zone between white America and a restive, disenfranchised black mass. Funding elite black colleges such as Spelman and Morehouse (named after white philanthropists) to produce aspirants suitable for the American ideal, the ABHMS encouraged the development of race managers rather than revolutionaries.[4] To the extent that it followed and follows the founders' mandate, the Talented Tenth was, and remains, anti-revolutionary.[5] The formation of the Talented Tenth – supported by white influential liberals – historically included women. It therefore liberalized the proto-feminism of historical black female elites. Contemporary black feminist politics as pursued by elites evince an anti-revolutionary tendency reflective of the bourgeois ideology of "race uplift." Vacillating between race management and revolutionary praxes, black feminisms are alternately integrated into, or suppressed within, corporate-consumer culture.

Yet, as Baker noted, the 1960s ushered in a more democratic, grassroots-driven form of leadership. The "new wave" of black feminisms originating from the 1960s invariably connect with historical anti-racist struggles in the United States. Black women created (and continue to create) feminism out of militant national liberation or anti-racist movements in which they often functioned as unrecognized organizers and leaders. Equally, their contributions to American feminism are inadequately noted, even among those who document the history of contemporary radical feminism. Emerging from black militant groups, Afra-Americans shaped feminist politics. A critical examination of these sites of emergent feminism and their embedded contradictions reveals black feminisms' more radical dimensions. For instance, the Combahee River Collective traces its origin to political formations now generally considered as uniformly sexist:

> Black feminist politics [has] an obvious connection to movements for Black liberation, particularly those of the 1960s and 1970s. Many us were active in those movements (Civil Rights, Black nationalism, the Black Panthers), and all of our lives were greatly affected and changed by their ideologies, their goals, and their tactics used to achieve their goals. It was our experience and disillusionment within these liberation movements, as well as experience on the periphery of the white male left, that led to the need to develop a politics that was anti-racist, unlike those of white women, and anti-sexist, unlike those of Black and white men.[6]

The Combahee River Collective took its name from the guerrilla foray led by the black revolutionary Harriet Tubman on June 2, 1863. This freed hundreds of enslaved people in South Carolina's Port Royal region, and was the first and only military campaign in the United States planned and executed by a woman. During the Civil War, Tubman headed the intelligence service in the department of the South and was the first American woman to lead black and white troops in battle. Before making a name for herself as military strategist and garnering the people's title of "General Tubman," this formerly enslaved African woman had earlier proved herself "a compelling and stirring orator in the councils of the abolitionists and anti-slavers."[7] Tubman's distinct archetype for a black female warrior disputes conventional narratives that masculinize black history and resistance. Although males remain the icons for black rebellions embattled with white supremacy and enslavement, women engaged in radical struggles, including the strategy of armed self-defense. As fugitives with bounties on their heads, they rebelled, survived or became casualties of state and racial-sexual repression.

Despite being designated "outlaws" and turned into outcasts because of their militancy, historical or ancestral black women such as Tubman have managed to survive in political memory. A few have been gradually (marginally) accepted into an American society that claims their resistance by incorporating or "forgiving" their past revolutionary tactics. Tubman's antebellum, criminalized resistance to slavery, like Ida B. Wells's post-Reconstruction, anti-lynching call-to-arms, typifies a rebellion that later became legitimized through American reclamation acts. To recall or reclaim black women who bore arms to defend themselves and other African Americans and females against racial-sexual violence remains an idiosyncratic endeavor in a culture that condemns subaltern physical resistance to political dominance and violence, while supporting the use of weapons in the defense (or, in some cases, the expansion) of the nation-state, individual and family, home, and private property.

Seeking explicitly to foster black female militancy in the 1970s, Combahee black feminists selected an Afra-American military strategist and guerrilla fighter as their archetype. Their choice of Tubman over her better known contemporary, Sojourner Truth, suggests an intent to radicalize feminism. Truth, not Tubman, is closely identified with feminism because of the former's work as a suffragette and associations with the prominent white feminists of her day. Tubman is identified with black people – men, women and children – and military insurrection against the US government. Her associations with white men are better known than those with white women; for instance, she allegedly planned to participate in John Brown's raid on Harper's Ferry, despite the warnings of the prominent abolitionist and pro-feminist, Frederick Douglass. With this African warrior and freedom-fighter as their feminist model, the Combahee River Collective emerged in 1977 to contest the liberalism of the National Black Feminist Organization (NBFO) that preceded the Collective.

In its manifesto, the Collective expressed its "serious disagreements with NBFO's bourgeois-feminist stance and their lack of a clear political focus" and offered an activist alternative.[8] The Collective, which included [Barbara Smith,] Gloria Hull and Margo Okazawa-Rey, later went on to organize against a series of murders targeting black girls and women in the Boston area. Combahee's black feminist manifesto emphasized radical activism rather than liberal politics:

> Although we are feminists and Lesbians, we feel solidarity with progressive Black men . . . Our situation as Black people necessitates that we have solidarity around the fact of race, which white women of course do not need to have with white men, unless it is their negative solidarity as racial oppressors. We struggle together with Black men against racism, while we also struggle with Black men about sexism.[9]

Given the prevalence of anti-radical bias in American society, one must wade deeply into the mainstream to retrieve critiques such as the following, also issued by the Combahee River Collective:

> We realize that the liberation of all oppressed peoples necessitates the destruction of the political-economic systems of capitalism and imperialism as well as patriarchy. We are socialists because we believe that work must be organized for the collective benefit of those who do the work and create the products, and not for the profit of the bosses. Material resources must be equally distributed among those who create these resources. We are not convinced, however, that a socialist revolution that is not also a feminist and anti-racist revolution will guarantee our liberation.[10]

Ideology and Feminist Identity

How to maintain Combahee's integrative analyses – intersecting race, gender, sexuality and class – with more than rhetoric, that is, in viable political practice that organizes in non-elite communities, became a major challenge for feminists. All anti-racist and anti-sexist politics, notwithstanding the rhetoric, are not equally ambitious or visionary in their demands and strategies for transforming society. The majority culture's desire or need to bring "closure" or containment to the black revolutionary struggles that fuelled radical black feminism (such as Combahee) has filtered into black feminist ideology, altering its potential for transformation.[11] "Closure" itself is, likely, either an illusory or a conservative pursuit, given the continuance of the repressive conditions (impoverishment, abrogation of rights, racial and sexual denigration) that engendered revolutionary struggle.

Although the greatest opponent to anti-racist and feminist revolutionary struggles has been the counter-revolutionary state (embodied in the twentieth century by the United States[12]), black feminist writings have, by and large, paid insufficient attention to state repression and the conflictual ideologies and divergent practices found within black feminisms. This is partly because so much necessary energy has been focused on black feminisms' marginalization in European American and African American culture (in addition, the impact of black feminisms on Latina, African, Asian, Arab and Native American women could be more fully addressed), and partly because of the anti-radical tendencies found within black feminisms, tendencies that are often obscured.

Liberal, radical, and revolutionary black feminisms are often reductively presented as ideologically unified and uniformly "progressive," while black feminisms are simultaneously viewed as having little impact beyond black women. Sorting out progressive politics within black feminisms, one may distinguish between ideological trajectories that reveal black feminisms' at times compliant, often ambiguous, and sometimes oppositional, relationships to state hegemony. Delineating ideology works to contextualize black feminist attitudes towards institutional and political power. In the blurred political spectrum of a progressivism that broadly includes "liberal," "radical," "neoradical," and "revolutionary" politics and their overlap, all of these camps change character or shape-shift to varying degrees with the political context and era. For instance, no metanarrative can map radical or "revolutionary" black feminism, although the analyses of activist-intellectuals such as Ella Baker serve as cartography. Some reject, while others embrace, the self-proclaimed "revolutionary" that manifests through rhetorical, literary, cultural, or conference productions. "Revolutionary" denotes dynamic movement, rather than fixed stasis, within a political praxis relevant to changing material conditions and social consciousness. With a fluid rather than fixed appearance, the emergence of the revolutionary remains episodic. As conditions change, what it means to be a revolutionary changes (therefore the articulation of a final destination for radical or revolutionary black feminisms remains more of a motivational ideal, and the pronouncement of an arrival at the final destination a depoliticizing mirage).

Despite ideological fluidity and border crossings, one can make some valid or useful generalizations. Black feminisms that accept the political legitimacy of corporate state institutional and police power, but posit the need for humanistic reform, are considered liberal. Black feminisms that view (female and black) oppression as stemming from capitalism, neocolonialism and the corporate state that enforces both, are generally understood to be radical. Some black feminisms explicitly challenge state and corporate dominance and critique the privileged status of bourgeois elites among the "Left": those that do so by connecting political theory for radical transformation with political acts to abolish corporate state and elite dominance are revolutionary.

Differentiating between liberalism and radicalism – or even more so between "radical" and "revolutionary" – to theorize black feminist liberation politics is extremely difficult but essential for understanding some limitations of "left" politics and black feminisms. Part of the difficulty in delineating the "Left" (of black feminisms) stems from the resurgence of the Right and its modification of liberal and progressive thought.

New terminology denotes the pervasive influence of conservatism as "neo" becomes a standard political prefix for the era of post-Civil Rights and post-feminist movements. The efficacy of rightist conservatism has led to the coupling of reactionary with conservative politics to construct the rightist hybrid "neoconservative"; the merger of conservative with liberal politics to create the right-leaning "neoliberalism"; and the marriage of liberalism with radicalism to produce "neoradicalism" as a more statist or corporate form of radical politics. Alongside "neoconservatism" and "neoliberalism," one finds "neoradicalism." All denote a drift towards conservatism. This drift has engendered deradicalizing trends that include the hegemony of bourgeois intellectuals within neoradicalism and the commodification of the "revolutionary" as a performer who captures the attention and imagination of pre-radicalized masses, while serving as storyteller for the apolitical consumer. Responding to revolutionary struggles, the counter-revolutionary, antirevolutionary and neoradical surface to confront and displace those inspired and sustained by vibrant rebellions.

Neoradicalism, like liberalism, denounces draconian measures against women, poor and racialized peoples, and, similarly, it also positions itself as "loyal" opposition to the state. Therefore, what it denounces is not the state itself but its excesses – prison exploitation and torture, punitive measures towards the poor, environmental degradation, counter-revolutionary violence and contra wars. Abolition movements directed by neoradicals rarely extend their rhetoric to call for the abolition of capitalism and the corporate state. When led or advocated by those representative of the disenfranchised, the deradicalizing tendencies are muted by the appearance of the symbolic radical.

All black feminists, including those who follow conventional ideology to some degree, share an outsider status in a commercial culture. That marginalization is not indicative of, but is often confused for, an intrinsic or inherent radicalism. Ideological differences among Afra-Americans belie the construction of (black) women or, even more significantly, black feminists as a "class." Refusing to essentialize black women or feminism, writers such as bell hooks have noted the conflictual political ideologies found among black women. In 1991, hooks's "Must We Call All Women 'Sister'?" interrogated feminist championing of Anita Hill that made little mention of how this then Reaganite Republican had promoted anti-feminist, anti-gay/lesbian, anti-disabled and anti-civil rights policies at the Equal Employment Opportunity Commission (EEOC) under the supervision of Clarence Thomas.[13] The gender solidarity surrounding Hill obscured her support for ultraconservative policies. Prior to her courageous testimony at the Senate Judiciary Committee hearings (which eventually confirmed Thomas as a Supreme Court justice), she had implemented reactionary attacks on the gains of the civil rights and women's movements (gains that had enabled non-activists such as Hill and her former EEOC supervisor to attend Yale Law School).

The consequences of African Americans' failure to distinguish and discuss political ideologies among black public figures has been noted by legal theorist Kimberlé Crenshaw. Crenshaw argues against a racial uniformity in black solidarity that includes reactionaries. In July 1998, at a C-SPAN televised gathering of black lawyers critical of the American Bar Association's invitation to Thomas to keynote its annual meeting, Crenshaw gave [an incisive] critique of black support for Thomas. She contended that, because of his race, African Americans paid little attention to his right-wing politics and so failed to distinguish between "conservative" and "reactionary" ideologies. (Neo-nazi David Duke's endorsement of Thomas's appointment to the Court underscores the affinity right-wing ideologues felt for Thurgood Marshall's Republican replacement.[14]) According to Crenshaw, ideological distinctions eroded black opposition to former president George Bush's Supreme Court nominee, but if black Americans had maintained and sharpened the distinction between conservative and reactionary positions, more would have actively opposed Thomas's appointment to the Court.

Crenshaw's argument has merit. Conservativism has some respectability among black women and men immured in the "race uplift" of Booker T. Washington's black capitalism (but not fully compliant with his prohibitions against competing with whites). Reactionary politics, however, hold no respectable public place among African Americans. Historically viewed as an extension of white supremacy and racial dominance, reactionaries have been considered anathema to black and female lives. Yet African Americans seem unwilling, publicly and critically, to discuss black reactionaries in service to the state and to distinguish their counter-revolutionary service from the anti-revolutionary disavowals of black liberals and neoradicals. (In similar fashion, maintaining distinctions between revolutionaries and radicals appears to be equally problematic for Americans.)

Just as blurring the lines between black reactionaries and conservatives politically accommodates reactionaries by reclassifying them as respectable "conservatives," black feminists have erased the distinction between liberalism and the radicalism that incited some of black feminisms' most dynamic, militant formations (like the Combahee River Collective). Given that liberalism has accrued the greatest material resources and social legitimacy, the coalition of liberals and radicals to foment neoradicalism means that respectability has been designated to dual beneficiaries. Liberal black feminism garners the image of being on the "cutting edge" by appending itself to symbols of radicalism and hence increases its popularity as "transformative." Radicals are able to mainstream or maximize their visibility and the market for their rhetoric via legitimization through association with liberalism. The terms for merger may be weighted towards liberalism, for liberalism – and its offshoot neoliberalism – wields more material resources and legitimacy than radicalism or neoradicalism. Liberalism also allows black feminisms to increase their compatibility with mainstream American politics, as well as mainstream African American political culture.

African Americans generally do not favour political "extremism," as is attested by their strong fidelity to a Democratic Party that takes black voters for granted and that, under the Clinton presidency, increased police powers and punitive measures against the poor. Rather than rightist reactionary or leftist revolutionary politics, most black Americans support a progressive liberalism (left of center) that has greater social conscience and, therefore, moral content than that of the general society. This consequently places many African Americans outside the narrowly construed, conventional political spectrum. Due to a tendency to be more socially progressive and supportive of vigorous, sometimes outraged and sometimes outrageous, condemnations of white supremacy, African Americans are often portrayed as political "extremists" or outsiders.

Given that centrism remains the dominant political stance, some black feminisms reconfigure radicalism to fit within liberal paradigms. This enables an erasure of revolutionary politics and a rhetorical

embrace of radicalism without material support for challenges to transform or abolish, rather than modify, state corporate authority. An
analogy for black feminist erasures can be made with the framing of a
painting. The mounting or mat establishes the official borders for the
viewer. Often, matting crops off the original borders of the picture. If
incorrectly done, the mat encroaches upon the image itself and the
signature of the image-maker. In matting or framing black feminisms for
public discourse and display, the extreme peripheries of the initial
creation are often covered over. Placing a mat over the political vision
of black feminism establishes newer (visually coordinated) borders that
frequently blot out the fringes (revolutionaries and radical activists) to
allow professional or bourgeois intellectuals and radicals to appear
within borders as the only "insurgents." With layered or overlapping
mats that position rhetoric as representative of revolutionary struggle,
the resulting portrait will obscure radicals to portray liberals or neoradicals as gender and race "rebels."

Resisting and Reshaping Radicalism

Although a great impetus for the development of black feminism came
from black revolutionary movements, anti-radicalism within American
feminism (as well as masculinism among American radicals) obscured
black female militancy. Anti-radical sentiment among some black feminists (which has led some black feminist writers to dismiss black
women's ideological critiques of black feminist politics as "sectarian")
raises the issue of the place of revolutionary and anti-revolutionary
thought within progressive black feminism.

Black feminist liberation ideology challenges state power by addressing class exploitation, racism, nationalism and sexual violence with
critiques of, and activist confrontations with, corporate state policies.
The "radicalism" of feminism recognizes racism, sexism, homophobia
and patriarchy, but refuses to make "men" or "whites" or "heterosex-
uals" the problem in lieu of confronting corporate power, state authority
and policing. One reason to focus on the state, rather than on an
essentialized male entity, is that the state wields considerable dominance
over the lives of non-elite women. The government intrudes upon and
regulates the lives of poor or incarcerated females more than bourgeois
and non-imprisoned ones, determining their material well-being and

physical mobility, and affecting their psychological and emotional health. Never the primary economic providers for black females, given the history and legacy of slavery, un- and underemployment and racialized incarceration, the majority of black men exert little economic control over female life, although they retain considerable physical, sexual and psychological dominance.

Radical black feminists' liberation theories address their nemesis: political violence, in both its private and public manifestations; counter-revolutionary state police repression, and a liberal anti-revolutionary discourse that seeks to contain radical black feminism by portraying it as an idealistic maverick. Radicalizing potential based on incisive analyses; autonomy from mainstream and bourgeois feminism; independence from masculinist or patriarchal anti-racism; a (self) critique of neoradicalism, and, most importantly, activism (beyond "speech acts") that connects with "grassroots" and non-elite objectives and leadership all mark a transformative black feminism. Yet, radicalism remains problematic for many.

Revolutionary praxis or the radical sentiments of the movement era (roughly 1955–75, to include the black civil rights struggle, the American Indian Movement [AIM], Chicano and *Puertorriqueño* insurrections and militant feminism) were not discarded solely because they became "anachronistic." These praxes proved to be dangerous and costly in the face of state and corporate opposition and co-optation. The attacks launched against militancy had to do with its effectiveness, its potential to effect radical change.

Today one finds in American politics in general, and black feminisms in particular, the "mainstreaming" of radicalism as a form of resistance to radical politics in which formerly radical means, such as protest marches and demonstrations disrupting civic and economic affairs, are increasingly deployed for non-radical or liberal ends, such as the maintenance of affirmative action. Likewise, formerly radical causes – such as prisoners' rights activism and advocacy to abolish the prison industrial complex – are increasingly administered through conference research and social service centers financed by corporate philanthropy seeking to influence policy objectives.

In corporate culture, gender and race are filtered through class to juxtapose and contrast "workers" and "professionals." To the extent that corporate culture has infiltrated US progressivism, the polarities of worker/manager resurface to foster a resistance to, or reshaping of, radicalism embodied in a "corporate Left." Those able to raise large sums of money through corporate largesse to institutionalize their political formations and identities as astute "organizers," maintaining a political leadership that reflects the style of chief executives and mirrors state corporate sites (among which academia is included) would qualify as members of the corporate Left. Their status as sophisticated politicos goes unchallenged because of the material resources garnered. That these corporate sites and their corresponding political style are not known for their accountability to disenfranchised communities or democratic processes, but for funding alternative entities to diffuse radical movements, is viewed as irrelevant by some progressives. Joan Roelofs, however, argues that:

> One reason capitalism doesn't collapse, despite its many weaknesses and valiant opposition movements, is because of the "nonprofit sector." Yet philanthropic capital, its investment and its distribution, are generally neglected by the critics of capitalism ... Some may see a galaxy of organizations doing good works – a million points of light – but the nonprofit world is also a system of power which is exercised in the interest of the corporate world.[15]

Whether through the academy, government agencies or private foundations, an emergent "corporate Left" has helped to deradicalize feminism and anti-racism and so anti-racist feminism or feminist anti-racism. Distinguishing between the "revolutionary" and the post-movement hybrid "neoradical" places a finer point on analyses of progressive black feminist politics and their contradictions.

Questions of co-optation and integrity are audible to those who listen attentively for sounds of political independence from corporate (state) influence. The din can be confusing, given that conflictual allegiances abound in American politics and culture. For instance, the oxymoronic wit of PBS "public service announcements" that validate corporate state funders, while broadcasting acquiescence to business elites, reappears in progressive projects funded by corporate entities and severed from non-elite, community leadership. Searching for political independents, one finds that liberalism competes with and censures radicalism, while radicalism competes with and censures revolutionary praxis. Both forms of censorship seem to be guided by an amorphous notion of what constitutes responsible "Left" politics, delineated within a rapacious corporate world funding the political integration of "radicals" on terms favouring the maintenance of stability and accumulation of capital as prime directives.

Corporate culture oils radicalism's slide into neoradicalism. According to consumer advocate Ralph Nader, being raised in American culture often means "growing up corporate." (For those raised "black," growing up corporate in America means training for the Talented Tenth.) One need not be affluent to grow up corporate, one need only adopt a managerial style. When merged with radicalism, the managerial ethos produces a "neoradicalism" that, as a form of commercial "left" politics, emulates corporate structures and behaviour. As corporate funders finance "radical" conferences and "lecture movements," democratic power sharing diminishes. Radical rhetoricians supplant grassroots organizers and political managers replace vanguard activists. Within this context, feminist "radicals" are discouraged from both effective oppositional politics to social and state dominance and organic links to non-elite communities. Instead, they are encouraged, as progressives, to produce a "ludic feminism" which, according to Teresa Ebert, "substitutes a politics of representation for radical social transformation."[16] Ludic feminism has a curious relationship to black feminism because the latter has been shaped and contextualized by radical movements.

In the Politics of "Sisterhood"

In the late 1960s, liberal bourgeois feminism among white women gradually expanded to include black women. This emergent multiracial "sisterhood" transferred the nineteenth-century white missionary mandate (promoting an elite leadership to serve as interpreters of, representatives for, the racialized and marginalized non-elite) to white bourgeois feminists. The result was a political paradox: on the hand, black feminisms pushed white feminism (in its various ideologies) to repudiate ethnocentrism and racism and so, to some degree, "radicalized" America's dominant feminism. On the other hand, the financially-endowed white cultural feminism supported and 'mainstreamed' black feminism by rewarding liberal politics within it, and to some degree, deradicalized black feminist politics by normalizing its liberalism. This logically follows the historical trajectory of white radical feminism in contemporary American politics.

Amid the political battles waged by white middle-class women in the movement era, Alice Echols's *Daring to be Bad: Radical Feminism in America, 1967–1975* notes three forms of activism.[17] First emerged "politicos" who worked in civil rights organizations, such as the Student Nonviolent Coordinating Committee (SNCC), anti-war and radical youth groups, such as Students for a Democratic Society (SDS), and revolutionary or underground spin-offs, such as the Weathermen. Out of these formations emerged radical women who became disaffected because of the sexism of male-dominated organizations, and subsequently developed, as "radical feminists," organizations such as Redstockings that were opposed to the state's dehumanizing domestic and foreign policies.

From the gains or concessions that radical feminists were able to wrest in the 1960s from the corporate military industrial complex arose "cultural feminists" who benefited from the radicals' path-breaking work; according to Echols, cultural feminists, as liberal feminists, benefited from the militancy of radical feminists, whom they later excised in order to consolidate an image of respectability and to garner corporate support for hegemonic or mainstream feminism. Women such as Gloria Steinem, Robin Morgan and other founders of *Ms* came to represent the cultural feminism that, unlike its radical rivals, defined men, not the state, as the primary obstacle or "enemy" of women. Radical feminists acknowledged that men needed to change attitudes and behaviour, writes Echols, but emphasized structural critiques (of capitalism and the state). Radical feminists became increasingly marginalized and eventually supplanted by cultural feminists who expressed politics less critical of, and so more compatible with, the state and its financial centres. In fact, *Ms*.'s early funders were white corporate males who, while categorized as women's "oppressors," became the financiers of mainstream feminisms.[18]

Given their accommodationist politics and access to state and corporate resources, one could refer to such feminisms, whether conservative or liberal in ideology, as "state feminism." Echols's depiction of cultural feminism, or what is referred to here as state feminism, as supplanting radical feminism because of its compatibility with, or complementarity to, state hegemony resonates with the black liberation struggles of the time period she analyses.[19] This raises important questions about the aspirations and dimensions of today's black cultural feminism and its relationship to black radical feminism. For instance, one might ask if a cultural form of black feminism (one that essentializes African women or women of color) functions as a buffer against revolutionary (feminist) critiques that cite capitalism and the state as primary obstacles to black and, therefore, female advancement? Can cultural black feminism exist as a hybrid heavily invested in the political appearances of revolutionary symbolism and representations shaped by ludic feminism, rather than political organizing with non-elites for revolutionary praxes?

If the answer to either or both of the questions above is "yes" or even "perhaps," then neither race, gender nor class is the radicalizing impetus or deradicalizing tendency influencing black feminisms. Political ideologies shape feminist aspirations. Given that it is more assimilable, liberal black feminism remains more likely to be promoted into the political mainstream as representative or normative among gender progressive Afra-Americans. Like the general society, mainstream feminism allows scant political space for revolutionary anti-racists, even if they are white feminists, whose militant critiques of state power contest the assumptions (and funding) of liberal feminism. Cultural or liberal black feminism wields more influence in bourgeois, European American feminism than revolutionary white anti-racist feminism does. Compatible ideologies allow white liberal feminist politics transracial privileges that mask an alienation from, or antipathy towards, radical anti-racism. New forms of multiracial feminism allow dominant white feminists to "privilege" black female political celebrities over white female political prisoners. Revolutionary, anti-racist white women, rarely referenced by feminists (or black militants and white anti-racists), are even more isolated than the white radical feminists and groups described by Echols.

The low visibility granted anti-racist revolutionary white women in mainstream feminism coexists with their marginalization in discursive "critical white studies" and "abolition of whiteness" and "race traitor" movements, where whites challenge the existential (if not always material) benefits of white supremacy. There is little mention of whites who viewed racism, patriarchy and economic exploitation as embedded in state power and so who, as revolutionaries, resisted the state. Little is known among liberal feminists or anti-racists of Sylvia Baraldini, an Italian national convicted of aiding black revolutionary Assata Shakur to escape from prison, or white female revolutionaries Susan Rosenberg and Marilyn Buck, also convicted of assisting Shakur, who (along with black male revolutionaries) are serving between thirty- and seventy-year sentences. (Baraldini received an additional three years for refusing to testify before a Grand Jury investigating the Puerto Rican Independentista movement.[20]) Likewise, the case of Judi Bari, the white feminist Earth Firster!, garners little attention in liberal feminism, black or white or multicultural, perhaps because it points to the continuance of COINTELPRO (under the guidance of FBI veteran Richard Held) in policing white female radical environmentalists.[21] Bari, who died from breast cancer in March 1997, survived a May 1990 car bombing. A nonviolent activist, she offered analyses that made connections between the FBI repression of the Black Panther Party and the American Indian Movement and environmental radicals. The meeting and embrace between Bari and Ramona Africa, who survived the 1985 bombing of the African organization MOVE in Philadelphia in which eleven African Americans died, reflects radical forms of transracial "sisterhood" and political solidarity.

Revolutionary feminist politics are more likely to note the political ramifications of radical alliances for "sisterhood" and anti-racist feminist movements. Such politics are also more inclined to scrutinize coalitions between radical and liberal black feminisms and white radical and bourgeois feminisms. There has been considerable discussion about interracial conflict between black and white women; some focus on collaboration between the two groups, but greater analysis of the ramifications of cross-ideological alliances or coalitions between African- and European-American women is required.

Conclusion

The legacies of black female radicals and revolutionaries contest arguments that state repression and subaltern resistance are not "black women's issues" or are too "politicized" for "feminism." Such legacies also contradict contentions that feminism is inherently "bourgeois" and therefore incapable of an organic revolutionary politics. Yet, even the "revolutionary" is marketed in a corporate culture (where Revlon commercials once proclaimed that the corporation made "revolutionary cosmetics for revolutionary women"). Revolutionary black feminism transgresses corporate culture in its focus on female independence, community building/caretaking and resistance to state-dominance, corporate exploitation, racism and sexism. Emphasizing economic and political power rather than social service programs for the disenfranchised, it challenges basic social tenets as expressed in "law and order" campaigns, the respectability of political dissent channelled through lobbying and electoral politics, and in the acceptance of the corporate state as a viable vehicle for redressing disenfranchisement.

The blurred lines between revolutionary, anti-revolutionary and counter-revolutionary politics allow, in the United States, for the normative political and discursive "sisterhood" that embraces conservative and liberal women, yet rarely extends itself to radical or revolutionary women. Adherence to mainstream political ideology appears key in the normative appeal of anti-racism, feminism and anti-racist feminism. Because political marginalization usually follows challenges to repressive state policies and critiques of female or feminist complicity in those practices, the revolutionary remains on the margin, more so than any other exponent of black feminism.

The symbiotic relationship between subaltern black feminists and the "white" masculinist state contests any presumption of a unified politics. Seeking a viable community and society, anti-racist feminism can serve as either sedative or stimulant. Conflicting messages about the nature of political struggle and leadership can be found within black feminisms. Black feminisms function as a "shadow," both in the negative aspects attributed to them and in their subordinate status on the American scene. Ever present, often ignored but completely inescapable, their plurality is stereotypically seen as monolithic and depicted as the antithesis of the robust American "body." Fending their shadows as American alter, political, egos, black women paint varied portraits of the shadow boxer as radical; as lone warrior; successful corporate fund-raiser for, and beneficiary of, progressive issues; individual survivalist; and community worker, disciplined to the leadership of non-elites in opposing state corporate dominance.

The predicament of progressive black feminisms remains the struggle to maintain radical politics despite black feminisms' conflictual persona. Yet this, after all, is the shadow boxer's dilemma: to fight the authoritative body casting one off, while simultaneously struggling with internal conflict and contradictions.

Notes

1   Ella Baker, "The Black Woman in the Civil Rights Struggle," quoted in
    Joanne Grant, *Ella Baker: Freedom Bound* (New York: John Wiley, 1998),
    230.

2   Baker presented this speech in 1969 at the Institute for the Black World in
    Atlanta, Georgia. Ibid., 228.

3   Ibid. Harvard historian Evelyn Brooks Higginbotham documents how white
    Christian philanthropists such as Henry Morehouse and other leaders
    within the American Baptist Home Missionary Society (ABHMS) in 1896
    promoted the concept of the Talented Tenth as black elite race leaders.
    ABHMS funded the emergence of this elite to serve a population facing
    severe discrimination and persecution following the aborted Reconstruc-
    tion. ABHMS explicitly created the Talented Tenth with a dual purpose, to
    function as a model showcase for whites (and blacks), a living demon-
    stration that black intellectual and moral inferiority were myths and to
    counter revolutionary and anarchistic tendencies among an increasingly
    disenfranchised black populace. (See Evelyn Brooks Higginbotham, *Right-
    eous Discontent: The Women's Movement in the Black Baptist Church,
    1880–1920* (Cambridge, MA: Harvard University Press, 1993). In 1903,
    W. E. B. Du Bois popularized the term in *The Souls of Black Folk* with his
    essay "The Talented Tenth." A century after white liberal missionaries
    coined the phrase, the idea of the Talented Tenth is being revitalized by
    Harvard's black intellectual elites, such as Henry Louis Gates, Jr., whose
    The Future of the Race, co-authored with fellow Harvard professor Cornel
    West, and 1998 PBS/Frontline documentary *The Two Nations of Black
    America*, promote the formation of the Talented Tenth.

4   See *Righteous Discontent*, op. cit. Amnesty International documents over
    one hundred political prisoners currently in the United States. Today, for
    the US-based revolutionaries to exist as more than a cult of martyrs like the
    Gnostic Christians, the Talented Tenth, as "buffer zone," would grant the
    preferential option to the poor, imprisoned and militant.

5   The anti-revolutionary politics of liberals or neoradicals are not synony-
    mous with counter-revolutionary state destabilization, policies that include
    police repression, infiltration and co-optation. Whereas the anti-revolution-
    ary can also be the anti-reactionary or anti-right wing and seek a centrist
    or center-left politics, the counter-revolutionary is reactionary. Anti-revolu-
    tionaries, though, may be incorporated into state or corporate counter-
    revolutionary initiatives.

6   The Combahee River Collective Statement, in Barbara Smith, ed., *Home*

Girls: A Black Feminist Anthology (New York: Kitchen Table, Women of Color Press, 1983), 273. The manifesto was first printed in Gloria T. Hull, Patricia Bell Scott, and Barbara Smith, eds., *All the Women are White, All the Black Are Men, But Some of Us Are Brave: Black Women's Studies* (New York: Feminist Press, 1982).

7   Earl Conrad, "I Bring You General Tubman," *Black Scholar* vol. 1, no. 3–4 (Jan.–Feb. 1970), 4.

8   Combahee River Collective Statement, 279.

9   Ibid., 275–6.

10 Ibid.

11 For an example, see Patricia Hill Collins's discussion of organising in *Black Feminist Thought: Knowledge, Consciousness, and the Politics of Empowerment* (Boston: Unwin Hyman, 1990).

12 US counter-revolutionary initiatives have been extensive and costly in terms of human rights abuses. See Noam Chomsky, *The Culture of Terrorism* (Boston: South End Press, 1988).

13 bell hooks, "Must We Call All Women 'Sister'?," *Z Magazine* (February 1992).

14 At a 1997 New York University forum on black women writers, on a panel shared with Angela Davis, former Black Panther Elaine Brown referred to Maulana Karenga as an American "Buthelezi"; Kimberlé Crenshaw makes the same reference to Clarence Thomas in her July 1998 presentation.

15 Joan Roelofs, "The Third Sector as a Protective Layer for Capitalism," *Monthly Review*, vol. 47 (September 1995), 16–17.

16 Teresa L. Ebert, *Ludic Feminism and After: Postmodernism, Desire, and Labor in Late Capitalism* (Ann Arbor: University of Michigan Press, 1996), 3.

17 Alice Echols, *Daring to be Bad: Radical Feminism in America, 1967–1975* (Minneapolis: University of Minnesota Press, 1989). Echols's insightful text is somewhat limited by her failure to fully research and analyze the contributions of black feminist radicals such as Frances Beale, a founder of the Student NonViolent Coordinating Committee's Black Women's or Third World Women's Alliance, and Barbara Smith, a founder of the Combahee River Collective.

18 See Echols, ibid., for documentation on the initial funding for *Ms*.

19 Echols's descriptions of the strife between radical and liberal feminists parallel to a certain extent the black liberation movement's conflictual relationship between revolutionary nationalism, as found in the Black Panther Party (the Party advocated an end to imperialism, capitalism and racism, together with "power to the people," not the police) and the cultural nationalism of Us, with its emphasis on an "African" lifestyle. There was overlap between the two; for instance, the New York Chapter

of the Panthers synthesized an African (American) aesthetic with critiques of capitalism, government corruption, and police violence.

20　Imprisoned since the mid-1980s (the United Statse has denied the Italian government's request for extradition or leniency), Baraldini has spoken out from her jail cell in Danbury, Connecticut, on behalf of black death-row inmate and political prisoner, Mumia Abu-Jamal. [*Editors' note:* in 1999, Sylvia Baraldini was repatriated to Italy to serve her remaining sentence.] An internationalist and student radical in the 1960s and 1970s, she protested the Vietnam War, demonstrated for women's rights, and campaigned against apartheid and colonialism in Africa. Organizing to expose the Federal Bureau of Investigation (FBI)'s COINTELPRO malfeasance, she was a member of the Committee to Free the Panther 21 (defendants who were acquitted of all charges after years of harassment and incarceration in New York). Parole guidelines specify forty to fifty-two months' incarceration for the crimes for which Baraldini was convicted; Baraldini has served over four times that amount. Baraldini, Rosenberg, and Buck fall within the category of "political prisoner" as defined by Amnesty International. (Amnesty International has also declared US citizen Lori Berenson as a Peruvian political prisoner. The reporter and former MIT student went to Peru in 1994 to write about the Peruvian poor and the government's violations of their rights and welfare and was sentenced to life by a hooded military tribunal. See Rhoda Berenson's Mother's Day article about her daughter, "A Mother's Story," *Vogue*, May 1997.)

21　See Judi Bari, *Timber Wars* (Monroe, ME: Common Courage Press, 1994). Notorious for its anti-Panther violence, today COINTELPRO largely focuses on white radical peace or environmental activists and members of the Puerto Rican Independence Movement. Currently, the majority of US political arrests stem from anti-nuclear weapons or anti-School of the Americas demonstrations, while Grand Juries are used to derail Puerto Rican Independence activism. For evaluations of the political use of grand juries and the policing of the environmental and Puerto Rican Independence movements, see Elihu Rosenblatt, ed., *Criminal Injustice* (Boston, South End Press, 1996). [Also see Joy James, ed., *States of Confinement: Policing, Detention and Prisons* (New York: St Martin's Press, 2000).

Appendix

A Black Feminist Statement

The Combahee River Collective

We are a collective of Black feminists who have been meeting together since 1974.[1] During that time we have been involved in the process of defining and clarifying our politics, while at the same time doing political work within our own group and in coalition with other progressive organizations and movements. The most general statement of our politics at the present time would be that we are actively committed to struggling against racial, sexual, heterosexual, and class oppression and see as our particular task the development of integrated analysis and practice based upon the fact that the major systems of oppression are interlocking. The synthesis of these oppressions creates the conditions of our lives. As Black women we see Black feminism as the logical political movement to combat the manifold and simultaneous oppressions that all women of color face.

We will discuss four major topics in the paper that follows: (1) the genesis of contemporary Black feminism; (2) what we believe, i.e., the specific province of our politics; (3) the problems in organizing Black feminists, including a brief herstory of our collective; and (4) Black feminist issues and practice.

1   The Genesis of Contemporary Black Feminism

Before looking at the recent development of Black feminism, we would like to affirm that we find our origins in the historical reality of Afro-American women's continuous life-and-death struggle for survival and liberation. Black women's extremely negative relationship to the American political system (a system of white male rule) has always been determined by our membership in two oppressed racial and sexual castes. As Angela Davis points out in "Reflections on the Black Women's Role in the Community of Slaves," Black women have always embodied, if only in their physical manifestation, an adversary stance to white male rule and have actively resisted its inroads upon them and upon them and their communities in both dramatic and subtle ways. There have always been Black women activists – some known, like Sojourner Truth, Harriet Tubman, Frances E. W. Harper, Ida B. Wells Barnett, and Mary Church Terrell, and thousands upon thousands unknown – who had a shared awareness of how their sexual identity combined with their racial identity to make their whole life situation and the focus of their political struggles unique. Contemporary Black feminism is the outgrowth of countless generations of personal sacrifice, militancy, and work by our mothers and sisters.

A Black feminist presence has evolved most obviously in connection with the second wave of the American women's movement beginning in the late 1960s. Black, other Third World, and working women have been involved in the feminist movement from its start, but both outside reactionary forces and racism and elitism within the movement itself have served to obscure our participation. In 1973 Black feminists, primarily located in New York, felt the necessity of forming a separate Black feminist group. This became the National Black Feminist Organization (NBFO).

Black feminist politics also have an obvious connection to movements for Black liberation, particularly those of the 1960s and 1970s. Many of us were active in those movements (civil rights, Black nationalism, the Black Panthers), and all of our lives were greatly affected and changed by their ideology, their goals, and the tactics used to achieve their goals. It was our experience and disillusionment within these liberation movements, as well as experience on the periphery of the white male left, that led to the need to develop a politics that was antiracist, unlike those of white women, and the antisexist, unlike those of Black and white men.

There is also undeniably a personal genesis for Black feminism, that is, the political realization that comes from the seemingly personal experiences of individual Black women's lives. Black feminists and many more Black women who do not define themselves as feminists have all experienced sexual oppression as a constant factor in our day-to-day existence. As children we realized that we were different from boys and that we were treated differently – for example, when we were told in the same breath to be quiet both for the sake of being "ladylike" and to make us less objectionable in the eyes of white people. As we grew older we became aware of the threat of physical and sexual abuse by men. However, we had no way of conceptualizing what was so apparent to us, what we *knew* was really happening.

Black feminists often talk about their feelings of craziness before becoming conscious of the concepts of sexual politics, patriarchal rule, and, most importantly, feminism, the political analysis and practice that we women use to struggle against our oppression. The fact that racial politics and indeed racism are pervasive factors in our lives did not allow us, and still does not allow most Black women, to look more deeply into our own experiences and define those things that make our lives what they are and our oppression specific to us. In the process of consciousness-raising, actually life-sharing, we began to recognize the commonality of our experiences and, from the sharing and growing consciousness, to build a politics that will change our lives and inevitably end our oppression.

Our development also must be tied to the contemporary economic and political position of Black people. The post-World War II generation of Black youth was the first to be able to minimally partake of certain educational and employment options previously closed completely to Black people. Although our economic position is still at the very bottom of the American capitalist economy, a handful of us have been able to gain certain tools as a result of tokenism in education and employment which potentially enable us to more effectively fight our oppression.

A combined antiracist and antisexist position drew us together initially and as we developed politically we addressed ourselves to heterosexism and economic oppression under capitalism.

2   What We Believe

Above all else, our politics initially sprang from the shared belief that Black women are inherently valuable, that our liberation is a necessity not as an adjunct to somebody else's but because of our need as human persons for autonomy. This may seem so obvious as to sound simplistic, but it is apparent that no other ostensibly progressive movement has ever considered our specific oppression a priority or worked seriously for the ending of that oppression. Merely naming the pejorative stereotypes attributed to Black women (e.g., mammy, matriarch, sapphire, whore, bulldagger) let alone cataloguing the cruel, often murderous, treatment we receive, indicates how little value has been placed upon our lives during four centuries of bondage in the Western hemisphere. We realize that the only people who care enough about us to work consistently for our liberation is us. Our politics evolve from a healthy love for ourselves, our sisters, and our community which allows us to continue our struggle and work.

This focusing upon our own oppression is embodied in the concept of identity politics. We believe that the most profound and potentially the most radical politics come directly out of our own identity, as opposed to working to end somebody else's oppression. In the case of Black women this is a particularly repugnant, dangerous, threatening, and therefore revolutionary concept because it is obvious from looking at all the political movements that have preceded us that anyone is more worthy of liberation than ourselves. We reject pedestals, queenhood, and walking ten paces behind. To be recognized as human, levelly human, is enough.

We believe that sexual politics under patriarchy is as pervasive in Black women's lives as are the politics of class and race. We also often find it difficult to separate race from class from sex oppression because in our lives they are most often experienced simultaneously. We know that there is such a thing as racial-sexual oppression which is neither solely racial nor solely sexual, e.g., the history of rape of Black women by white men as a weapon of political repression.

Although we are feminists and lesbians, we feel solidarity with progressive Black men and do not advocate the fractionalization that white women who are separatists demand. Our situation as Black people necessitates that we have solidarity around the fact of race, which white women of course do not need to have with white men, unless it is their negative solidarity as racial oppressors. We struggle together with Black men against racism, while we also struggle with Black men about sexism.

We realize that the liberation of all oppressed peoples necessitates the destruction of the political-economic systems of capitalism and imperialism as well as patriarchy. We are socialists because we believe that work must be organized for the collective benefit of those who do the work and create the products and not for the profit of the bosses. Material resources must be equally distributed among those who create these resources. We are not convinced, however, that a socialist revolution that is not also a feminist and antiracist revolution will guarantee our liberation. We have arrived at the necessity for developing an understanding of class relationships that takes into account the specific class position of Black women who are generally marginal in the labor force, while at this particular time some of us are temporarily viewed as doubly desirable tokens at white-collar and professional levels. We need to articulate the real class situation of persons who are not merely raceless, sexless workers, but for whom racial and sexual oppression are significant determinants in their working economic lives. Although we are in essential agreement with Marx's theory as it applied to the very specific economic relationships he analyzed, we know that this analysis must be extended further in order for us to understand our specific economic situation as Black women.

A political contribution which we feel we have already made is the expansion of the feminist principle that the personal is political. In our consciousness-raising sessions, for example, we have in many ways gone beyond white women's revelations because we are dealing with the implications of race and class as well as sex. Even our Black women's style of talking, testifying in Black language about what we have experienced, has a resonance that is both cultural and political. We have spent a great deal of energy delving into the cultural and experiential nature of our oppression out of necessity because none of these matters have ever been looked at before. No one before has ever examined the multilayered texture of Black women's lives.

An example of the kind of revelation/conceptualization achieved through consciousness-raising occurred at a meeting when we discussed the ways in which our early intellectual interests had been attacked by our peers, particularly Black men. We discovered that all of us, because we were "smart," had also been considered "ugly," i.e., "smart-ugly." "Smart-ugly" crystallized the way in which most of us had been forced to develop our intellects at great cost to our "social" lives. The sanctions in the Black and white communities against Black women thinkers are comparatively much higher than those against white women, particularly ones from the educated middle and upper classes.

As we have already stated, we reject the stance of lesbian separatism because it is not a viable political analysis or strategy for us. It leaves out far too much and far too many people, particularly Black men, women, and children. We have a great deal of criticism and loathing for what men have been socialized to be in this society: what they support, how they act, and how they oppress. But we do not have the misguided notion that it is their maleness, per se – i.e., their biological maleness – that makes them what they are. As Black women we find any type of biological determinism a particularly dangerous and reactionary basis upon which to build a politic. We must also question whether lesbian separatism is an adequate and progressive political analysis and strategy, even for those who practice it, since it so completely denies any but the sexual sources of women's oppression, negating the facts of class and race.

3   Problems in Organizing Black Feminists

During our years together as a Black feminist collective we have experienced success and defeat, joy and pain, victory and failure. We have found that it is very difficult to organize around Black feminist issues, difficult even to announce in certain contexts that we *are* Black feminists. We have tried to think about the reasons for our difficulties, particularly since the white women's movement continues to be strong and to grow in many directions. In this section we will discuss some of the general reasons for the organizing problems we face and also talk specifically about the stages in organizing our own collective.

The major source of difficulty in our political work is that we are not just trying to fight oppression on one front or even two, but instead to address a whole range of oppressions. We do not have racial, sexual, heterosexual, or class privilege to rely upon, nor do we have even the minimal access to resources and power that groups who possess any one of these types of privilege have.

The psychological toll of being a Black woman and the difficulties this presents in reaching political consciousness and doing political work can never be underestimated. There is a very low value placed upon Black women's psyches in this society, which is both racist and sexist. As an early group member once said, "We are all damaged people merely by virtue of being Black women." We are dispossessed psychologically and on every other level, and yet we feel the necessity to struggle to change our condition and the condition of all Black women. In "A Black Feminist's Search for Sisterhood," Michele Wallace arrives at this conclusion:

> We exist as women who are Black who are feminists each stranded for
> the moment, working independently because there is not yet an environ-

ment in this society remotely congenial to our struggle – because, being on the bottom, we would have to do what no one else has done: we would have to fight the world.[2]

Wallace is not pessimistic but realistic in her assessment of Black feminists' position, particularly in her allusion to the nearly classic isolation most of us face. We might use our position at the bottom, however, to make a clear leap into revolutionary action. If Black women were free, it would mean that everyone else would have to be free since our freedom would necessitate the destruction of all the systems of oppression.

Feminism is, nevertheless, very threatening to the majority of Black people because it calls into question some of the most basic assumptions about our existence, i.e., that gender should be a determinant of power relationships. Here is the way male and female roles were defined in a Black nationalist pamphlet from the early 1970s:

> We understand that it is and has been traditional that the man is the head of the house. He is the leader of the house/nation because his knowledge of the world is broader, his awareness is greater, his understanding is fuller and his application of this information is wiser. . . . After all, it is only reasonable that the man be the head of the house because he is able to defend and protect the development of his home. . . . Women cannot do the same things as men – they are made by nature to function differently. Equality of men and women is something that cannot happen even in the abstract world. Men are not equal to other men, i.e., ability, experience, or even understanding. The value of men and women can be seen as in the value of gold and silver – they are not equal but both have great value. We must realize that men and women are a complement to each other because there is no house/family without a man and his wife. Both are essential to the development of any life.[3]

The material conditions of most Black women would hardly lead them to upset both economic and sexual arrangements that seem to represent some stability in their lives. Many Black women have a good understanding of both sexism and racism, but because of the everyday constrictions of their lives cannot risk struggling against them both.

The reaction of Black men to feminism has been notoriously negative. They are, of course, even more threatened than Black women by the possibility that Black feminists might organize around our own needs.

They realize that they might not only lose valuable and hardworking allies in their struggles but that they might also be forced to change their habitually sexist ways of interacting with and oppressing Black women. Accusations that Black feminism divides the Black struggle are powerful deterrents to the growth of an autonomous Black women's movement.

Still, hundreds of women have been active at different times during the three-year existence of our group. And every Black woman who came, came out of a strongly felt need for some level of possibility that did not previously exist in her life.

When we first started meeting early in 1974 after the NBFO's first eastern regional conference, we did not have a strategy for organizing, or even a focus. We just wanted to see what we had. After a period of months of not meeting, we began to meet again late in the year and started doing an intense variety of consciousness-raising. The over-whelming feeling that we had is that after years and years we had finally found each other. Although we were not doing political work as a group, individuals continued their involvement in lesbian politics, steril-ization abuse and abortion rights work, Third World Women's Inter-national Women's Day activities, and support activity for the trials of Dr. Kenneth Edelin, Joanne Little, and Inez Garcia. During our first summer, when membership had dropped off considerably, those of us remaining devoted serious discussion to the possibility of opening a refuge for battered women in a Black community. (There was no refuge in Boston at that time.) We also decided around that time to become an independent collective since we had serious disagreements with NBFO's bourgeois-feminist stance and their lack of a clear political focus.

We also were contacted at that time by socialist feminists, with whom we had worked on abortion rights activities, who wanted to encourage us to attend the National Socialist Feminist Conference in Yellow Springs. One of our members did attend and despite the narrowness of the ideology that was promoted at that particular conference, we became more aware of the need for us to understand our own economic situation and to make our own economic analysis.

In the fall, when some members returned, we experienced several months of comparative inactivity and internal disagreements which were first conceptualized as a lesbian–straight split but which were also the result of class and political differences. During the summer those of us who were still meeting had determined the need to do political work and to move beyond consciousness-raising and serving exclusively as an emotional support group. At the beginning of 1976, when some of the women who had not wanted to do political work and who also had voiced disagreements stopped attending of their own accord, we again looked for a focus. We decided at that time, with the addition of new members, to become a study group. We had always shared our reading with each other, and some of us had written papers on Black feminism for group discussion a few months before this decision was made. We began functioning as a study group and also began discussing the possibility of starting a Black feminist publication. We had a retreat in the late spring which provided a time for both political discussion and working out interpersonal issues. Currently we are planning to gather a collection of Black feminist writing. We feel that it is absolutely essential to demonstrate the reality of our politics to other Black women and believe that we can do this through writing and distributing our work. The fact that individual Black feminists are living in isolation all over the country, that our own numbers are small, and that we have some skills in writing, printing, and publishing makes us want to carry out these kinds of projects as a means of organizing Black feminists as we continue to do political work in coalition with other groups.

4   Black Feminist Issues and Practice

During our time together we have identified and worked on many issues of particular relevance to Black women. The inclusiveness of our politics makes us concerned with any situation that impinges upon the lives of women and those of Third World and working people in general. We are of course particularly committed to working on those struggles in which race, sex, and class are simultaneous factors in oppression. We might, for example, become involved in workplace organizing at a factory that employs Third World women or picket a hospital that is cutting back on already inadequate health care to a Third World community, or set up a rape crisis center in a Black neighborhood. Organizing around welfare or daycare concerns might also be a focus. The work to be done and the countless issues that this work represents merely reflect the pervasiveness of our oppression.

Issues and projects that collective members have actually worked on are sterilization abuse, abortion rights, battered women, rape, and health care. We have also done many workshops on Black feminism on college campuses, at women's conferences, and most recently for high school women.

One issue that is of major concern to us and that we have begun to publicly address is racism in the white women's movement. As Black feminists we are made constantly and painfully aware of how little effort white women have made to understand and combat their racism, which requires among other things that they have a more than superficial comprehension of race, color, and Black history and culture. Eliminating racism in the white women's movement is by definition work for white women to do, but we will continue to speak to and demand accountability on this issue.

In the practice of our politics we do not believe that the end always justifies the means. Many reactionary and destructive acts have been done in the name of achieving "correct" political goals. As feminists we do not want to mess over people in the name of politics. We believe in collective process and a nonhierarchical distribution of power within our own group and in our vision of a revolutionary society. We are committed to a continual examination of our politics as they develop through criticism and self-criticism as an essential aspect of our practice. In her introduction to *Sisterhood Is Powerful* Robin Morgan writes: "I haven't the faintest notion what possible revolutionary role white heterosexual men could fulfill, since they are the very embodiment of reactionary-vested-interest-power."

As Black feminists and lesbians we know that we have a very definite revolutionary task to perform and we are ready for the lifetime of work and struggle before us.

Notes

1 This statement is dated April 1977.
2 Michele Wallace, "A Black Feminist's Search for Sisterhood," The *Village Voice* (28 July 1975), 6–7.
3 Mumininas of Committee for Unified Newark, *Mwanamke Mwananchi* (*The Nationalist Woman*) (Newark, NJ, 1971), 4–5.

African American Women in Defense of Ourselves

As women of African descent, we are deeply troubled by the recent nomination, confirmation and seating of Clarence Thomas as an Associate Justice of the US Supreme Court. We know that the presence of Clarence Thomas on the Court will be continually used to divert attention from historic struggles for social justice through suggestions that the presence of a Black man on the Supreme Court constitutes an assurance that the rights of African Americans will be protected. Clarence Thomas' public record is ample evidence this will not be true. Further, the consolidation of a conservative majority on the Supreme Court seriously endangers the rights of all women, poor and working class people and the elderly. The seating of Clarence Thomas is an affront not only to African American women and men, but to all people concerned with social justice.

We are particularly outraged by the racist and sexist treatment of Professor Anita Hill, an African American woman who was maligned and castigated for daring to speak publicly of her own experience of sexual abuse. The malicious defamation of Professor Hill insulted all women of African descent and sent a dangerous message to any woman who might contemplate a sexual harassment complaint.

We speak here because we recognize that the media are now portraying the Black community as prepared to tolerate both the dismantling of affirmative action and the evil of sexual harassment in order to have any Black man on the Supreme Court. We want to make clear that the media have ignored or distorted many African American voices. We will not be silenced.

Many have erroneously portrayed the allegations against Clarence Thomas as an issue of either gender or race. As women of African descent, we understand sexual harassment as both. We further understand that Clarence Thomas outrageously manipulated the legacy of lynching in order to shelter himself from Anita Hill's allegations. To deflect attention away from the reality of sexual abuse in African American women's lives, he trivialized and misrepresented this painful part of African American people's history. This country, which has a long legacy of racism and sexism, has never taken the sexual abuse of Black women seriously. Throughout US history Black women have been sexually stereotyped as immoral, insatiable, perverse; the initiators in all sexual contacts – abusive or otherwise. The common assumption in legal proceedings as well as in the larger society has been that Black women cannot be raped or otherwise sexually abused. As Anita Hill's experience demonstrates, Black women who speak of these matters are not likely to be believed.

In 1991, we cannot tolerate this type of dismissal of any one Black woman's experience or this attack upon our collective character without protest, outrage, and resistance.

As women of African descent, we express our vehement opposition to the policies represented by the placement of Clarence Thomas on the Supreme Court. The Bush administration, having obstructed the passage of civil rights legislation, impeded the extension of unemployment compensation, cut student aid and dismantled social welfare programs, has continually demonstrated that it is not operating in our best interest. Nor is this appointee. We pledge ourselves to continue to speak out in defense of one another, in defense of the African American community and against those who are hostile to social justice no matter what color they are. No one will speak for us but ourselves.

Open Letter from Assata Shakur

My name is Assata Shakur, and I am a twentieth century escaped slave. Because of government persecution, I was left with no other choice than to flee from the political repression, racism and violence that dominate the US government's policy towards people of color. I am an ex-political prisoner, and I have been living in exile in Cuba since 1984.

I have been a political activist most of my life, and although the US government has done everything in its power to criminalize me, I am not a criminal, nor have I ever been one. In the 1960s, I participated in various struggles: the black liberation movement, the student rights movement, and the movement to end the war in Vietnam. I joined the Black Panther Party. By 1969 the Black Panther Party had become the number one organization targeted by the FBI (Federal Bureau of Investigation)'s COINTELPRO program. Because the Black Panther Party demanded the total liberation of black people, J. Edgar Hoover called it the "greatest threat to the internal security of the country" and vowed to destroy it and its leaders and activists.

In 1978, my case was one of many cases bought before the United Nations Organization in a petition filed by the National Conference of Black Lawyers, the National Alliance Against Racist and Political Repression, and the United Church of Christ Commission for Racial Justice, exposing the existence of political prisoners in the United States, their political persecution, and the cruel and inhuman treatment they receive in US prisons. According to the report:

> The FBI and the New York Police Department (NYPD) in particular, charged and accused Assata Shakur of participating in attacks on law enforcement personnel and widely circulated such charges and accusations among police agencies and units. The FBI and the NYPD further charged

her as being a leader of the Black Liberation Army which the government and its respective agencies described as an organization engaged in the shooting of police officers. This description of the Black Liberation Army and the accusation of Assata Shakur's relationship to it was widely circulated by government agents among police agencies and units. As a result of these activities by the government, Ms. Shakur became a hunted person; posters in police precincts and banks described her as being involved in serious criminal activities; she was highlighted on the FBI's most wanted list; and to police at all levels she became a "shoot-to-kill" target.

I was falsely accused in six different "criminal cases" and in all six of these cases I was eventually acquitted or the charges were dismissed. The fact that I was acquitted or that the charges were dismissed did not mean that I received justice in the courts, that was certainly not the case. It only meant that the "evidence" presented against me was so flimsy and false that my innocence became evident. This political persecution was part and parcel of the government's policy of eliminating political opponents by charging them with crimes and arresting them with no regard to the factual basis of such charges.

On May 2, 1973 I, along with Zayd Malik Shakur and Sundiata Acoli, were stopped on the New Jersey Turnpike, supposedly for a "faulty tail light." Sundiata Acoli got out of the car to determine why we were stopped. Zayd and I remained in the car. State trooper [James] Harper then came to the car, opened the door and began to question us. Because we were black, and riding in a car with Vermont license plates, he claimed he became "suspicious." He then drew his gun, pointed it at us, and told us to put our hands up in the air, in front of us, where he could see them. I complied and in a split second, there was a sound that came from outside the car, there was a sudden movement, and I was shot once with my arms held up in the air, and then once again from the back. Zayd Malik Shakur was later killed, trooper Werner Foerster was killed, and even though trooper Harper admitted that he shot and killed Zayd Malik Shakur, under the New Jersey felony murder law, I was charged with killing both Zayd Malik Shakur, who was my closest friend and comrade, and charged in the death of trooper Forester. Never in my life have I felt such grief. Zayd had vowed to protect me, and to help me to get to a safe place, and it was clear that he had lost his life, trying to protect both me and Sundiata. Although he was also unarmed, and the gun that killed trooper Foerster was found under Zayd's leg, Sundiata Acoli, who was captured later, was also charged with both deaths. Neither Sundiata Acoli nor I ever received a fair trial. We were both convicted in the news media way before our trials. No news media was ever permitted to interview us, although the New Jersey police and the FBI fed stories to the press on a daily basis. In 1977, I was convicted by an all-white jury and sentenced to life plus thirty-three years in prison. In 1979, fearing that I would be murdered in prison, and knowing that I would never receive any justice, I was liberated from prison, aided by committed comrades who understood the depths of the injustices in my case, and who were also extremely fearful for my life.

The US Senate's 1976 Church Commission report on intelligence operations inside the USA revealed that "The FBI has attempted covertly to influence the public's perception of persons and organizations by disseminating derogatory information to the press, either anonymously or through 'friendly' news contacts." This same policy is evidently still very much in effect today.

On December 24, 1997, The New Jersey State called a press conference to announce that New Jersey State Police had written a letter to Pope John Paul II asking him to intervene on their behalf and to aid in having me extradited back to New Jersey prisons. The New Jersey State Police refused to make their letter public. Knowing that they had probably totally distorted the facts, and attempted to get the Pope to do the devil's work in the name of religion, I decided to write the Pope to inform him about the reality of' "justice" for black people in the state of New Jersey and in the United States.

In January of 1998, during the Pope's visit to Cuba, I agreed to do an interview with NBC [National Broadcasting Company] journalist Ralph Penza around my letter to the Pope, about my experiences in the New Jersey court system, and about the changes I saw in the United States and its treatment of Black people in the last twenty-five years. I agreed to do this interview because I saw this secret letter to the Pope as a vicious, vulgar, publicity maneuver on the part of the New Jersey State Police, and as a cynical attempt to manipulate Pope John Paul II. I have lived in Cuba for many years, and was completely out of touch with the sensationalist, dishonest, nature of the establishment media today. It is worse today than it was thirty years ago. After years of being victimized by the "establishment" media it was naive of me to hope that I might finally get the opportunity to tell "my side of the story." Instead of an interview with me, what took place was a "staged media event" in three parts, full of distortions, inaccuracies and outright lies. NBC purposely misrepresented the facts. Not only did NBC spend thousands of dollars promoting this "exclusive interview series" on NBC, they also spent a great deal of money advertising this "exclusive interview" on black radio stations and also placed notices in local newspapers.

Distortions and Lies in the NBC Series

In an NBC interview [New Jersey Governor Christine] Whitman was quoted as saying that "this has nothing to do with race, this has everything to do with crime." Either Gov. Whitman is completely unfamiliar with the facts in my case, or her sensitivity to racism and to the plight of black people and other people of color in the United States is at a sub-zero level. In 1973 the trial in Middlesex County had to be stopped because of the overwhelming racism expressed in the jury room. The court was finally forced to rule that the entire jury panel had been contaminated by racist comments like "If she's black, she's guilty." In an obvious effort to prevent us from being tried by "a jury of our peers" the New Jersey courts ordered that a jury be selected from Morris County, New Jersey where only 2.2 percent of the population was black and 97.5 percent of potential jurors were white. In a study done in Morris County, one of the wealthiest counties in the country, 92 percent of the registered voters said that they were familiar with the case through the news media, and 72 percent believed we were guilty based on pretrial publicity. During the jury selection process in Morris County, white supremacists from the National Social White People's Party, wearing swastikas, demonstrated carrying signs reading "SUPPORT WHITE POLICE." The trial was later moved back to Middlesex County where 70 percent thought I was guilty based on pretrial publicity. I was tried by an all-white jury, where the presumption of innocence was not the criteria for jury selection. Potential jurors were merely asked if they could "put their prejudices aside," and "render a fair verdict." The basic reality in the United States is that being black is a crime and black people are always "suspects" and an accusation is usually a conviction. Most white people still think that being a "black militant" or a "black revolutionary" is tantamount to being guilty of some kind of crime. The current situation in New Jersey's prisons underlines the racism that dominates the politics of the state of New Jersey in particular and in the US as a whole. Although the population of New Jersey is approximately 78 percent white, more than 75 percent of New Jersey's prison population is made up of blacks and Latinos. Eighty percent of the women in Jersey prisons are people of color. That may not seem like racism to Gov. Whitman, but it reeks of of racism to us.

The NBC story implied that Gov. Whitman raised the reward for my capture based on my interview with NBC. The fact of the matter is that she has been campaigning since she was elected into office to double the reward for my capture. In 1994, she appointed Colonel Carl Williams who immediately vowed to make my capture a priority.* In 1995, Gov. Whitman sought to match a $25,000 departmental appropriation sponsored by an "unidentified legislator." I watched a tape of Gov. Whitman's "testimony" in her interview with NBC. She gave a very dramatic, exaggerated version of what happened, but there is no evidence whatsoever to support her claim that trooper Foerster had "four bullets in him at least, and then they got up and with his own gun, fired two bullets into his head." She claimed that she was writing Janet Reno for federal assistance in my capture, based on what she saw in the NBC interview. If this is the kind of "information" that is being passed on to [Attorney General] Janet Reno and the Pope, it is clear that the facts have been totally distorted. Whitman also claimed that my return to prison should be a condition for "normalizing relations with Cuba." How did I get so important that my life can determine the foreign relations between two governments? Anybody who knows anything about New Jersey politics can be certain that her motives are purely political. She, like [Robert] Torrecelli [D., NJ] and several other opportunistic politicians in New Jersey, came to power as part-time lobbyists for the [former Cuban dictator] Batista faction – soliciting votes from rightwing Cubans. They want to use my case as a barrier for normalizing relations with Cuba, and as a pretext for maintaining the immoral blockade against the Cuban people.

In what can only be called deliberate deception and slander NBC aired a photograph of a woman with a gun in her hand implying that

---

* Editors' note: In 1999, Whitman was forced to remove Williams from his post supervising New Jersey state police troopers after he made a number of racially controversial claims, asserting that people of color had a greater tendency toward criminality.

the woman in the photograph was me. I was not, in fact, the woman in the photograph. The photograph was taken from a highly publicized case where I was accused of bank robbery. Not only did I voluntarily insist on participating in a lineup, during which witnesses selected another woman, but during the trial, several witnesses, including the manager of the bank, testified that the woman in that photograph was not me. I was acquitted of that bank robbery. NBC aired that photograph on at least five different occasions, representing the woman in the photograph as me. How is it possible that the New Jersey State Police, who claim to have a detective working full time on my case, Governor of New Jersey Christine Whitman, who claimed she reviewed all the "evidence," or NBC, which has an extensive research department, did not know that the photograph was false? It was a vile, fraudulent attempt to make me look guilty. NBC deliberately misrepresented the truth. Even after many people had called in, and there was a massive fax, and e-mail campaign protesting NBC's mutilation of the facts, Ralph Penza and NBC continued to broadcast that photograph, representing it as me. Not once have the New Jersey State Police, Gov. Whitman, or NBC come forth and stated that I was not the woman in the photograph, or that I had been acquitted of that charge.

Another major lie and distortion was that we had left trooper Werner Foerster on the roadside to die. The truth is that there was a major cover-up as to what happened on May 2, 1973. Trooper Harper, the same man who shot me with my arms raised in the air, testified that he returned to the State Police Headquarters which was less than 200 yards away, "To seek aid." However, tape recordings and police reports made on May 2, 1973 prove that not only did trooper Harper give several conflicting statements about what happened on the turnpike, but he never once mentioned the name of Werner Foerster, or the fact that the incident took place right in front of the trooper headquarters. In an effort to hide his tracks and cover his guilt he said nothing whatsoever about Foerster to his superiors or to his fellow officers.

In a clear attempt to discredit me, Col. Carl Williams [as head] of the New Jersey State Police was allowed to give blow by blow distortions of my interview. In my interview I stated that on the night of May 2, 1973 I was shot with my arms in the air, then shot again in the back. Williams stated "that is absolutely false. Our records show that she reached in her pocketbook, pulled out a nine millimeter weapon and started firing." However, the claim that I reached into my pocketbook and pulled out a gun while inside the car was even contested by trooper Harper. Although on three official reports, and when he testified before the grand jury he stated that he saw me take a gun out of my pocketbook, he finally admitted under cross-examination that he never saw me with my hands in a pocketbook, never saw me with a weapon inside the car, and that he did not see me shoot him.

The truth is that I was examined by three medical specialists: (1) A neurologist who testified that I was paralyzed immediately after the being shot. (2) A surgeon who testified that "It was absolutely anatomically necessary that both arms be in the air for Mrs. Chesimard [Shakur] to receive the wounds." The same surgeon also testified that the claim by trooper Harper that I had been crouching in a firing position when I was shot was "totally anatomically impossible." (3) A pathologist who testified that "There is no conceivable way that it [the bullet] could have traveled over to hit the clavicle if her arm was down." He said: "It was impossible to have that trajectory." The prosecutors presented no medical testimony whatsoever to refute the above medical evidence.

No evidence whatsoever was ever presented that I had a 9-millimeter weapon, in fact New Jersey State Police testified that the 9-millimeter weapon belonged to Zayd Malik Shakur based on a holster fitting the weapon that was recovered from his body. There were no fingerprints, or any other evidence whatsoever that linked me to any guns or ammunition.

The results of the Neutron Activation test to determine whether or not I had fired a weapon were negative. Although Col. Williams refers to us as the "criminal element" neither Zayd, or Sundiata Acoli or I were criminals, we were political activists. I was a college student until the police kicked down my door in an effort to force me to "cooperate" with them and Sundiata Acoli was a computer expert who had worked for NASA, before he joined the Black Panther Party and was targeted by COINTELPRO.

In an obvious maneuver to provoke sympathy for the police, the NBC series juxtaposed my interview with the weeping widow of Werner Foerster. While I can sympathize with her grief, I believe that her appearance was deliberately included to appeal to people's emotions, to blur the facts, to make me look like a villain, and to create the kind of lynch mob mentality that has historically been associated with white women portrayed as victims of black people. In essence the supposed interview with me became a forum for the New Jersey State Police,

Foerster's widow, and the obviously hostile commentary of Ralph Penza. The two initial programs together lasted 3.5 minutes: me 59 seconds, the widow 50 seconds, the state police 38 seconds, and Penza 68 seconds. Not once in the interview was I ever asked about Zayd, Sundiata or their families. As the interview went on, it was painfully evident that Ralph Penza would never see me as a human being. Although I tried to talk about racism and about the victims of government and police repression, it was clear that he was totally uninterested.

I have stated publicly on various occasions that I was ashamed of participating in my trial in New Jersey because it was so racist, but I did testify. Even though I was extremely limited by the judge as to what I could testify about, I testified as clearly as I could about what happened that night. After being almost fatally wounded I managed to climb in the back seat of the car to get away from the shooting. Sundiata drove the car five miles down the road and carried me into a grassy area because he was afraid that the police would see the car parked on the side of the road and just start shooting into it again. Yes, it was five miles down the highway where I was captured, dragged out of the car, stomped and then left on the ground. Although I drifted in and out of consciousness I remember clearly that both while I was lying on the ground, and while I was in the ambulance, I kept hearing the state troopers ask "is she dead yet?" Because of my condition I have no independent recollection of how long I was on the ground, or how long it was before the ambulance was allowed to leave for the hospital, but in the trial transcript trooper Harper stated that it was while he was being questioned, some time after 2:00 am that a detective told him that I had just been brought into the hospital. I was the only live "suspect" in custody, and prior to that time Harper had never told anyone that a woman had shot him.

As I watched Gov. Whitman's interview the one thing that struck me was her "outrage" at my joy about being a grandmother, and my "quite nice life" as she put it here in Cuba. While I love the Cuban people and the solidarity they have shown me, the pain of being torn away from everybody I love has been intense. I have never had the opportunity to see or to hold my grandchild. If Gov. Whitman thinks that my life has been so nice, that fifty years of dealing with racism, poverty, persecution, brutality, prison, underground, exile and blatant lies has been so nice, then I'd be more than happy to let her walk in my shoes for a while so she can get a taste of how it feels. I am a proud black woman, and I'm not about to get on the television and cry for Ralph Penza or any other journalist, but the way I have suffered in my lifetime, and the way my people have suffered, only God can bear witness to.

Col. Williams . . . stated "we would do everything we could go get her off the island of Cuba and if that includes kidnapping, we would do it." I guess the theory is that if they could kidnap millions of Africans from Africa 400 years ago, they should be able to kidnap one African woman today. It is nothing but an attempt to bring about the re-incarnation of the Fugitive Slave Act. All I represent is just another slave that they want to bring back to the plantation. Well, I might be a slave, but I will go to my grave a rebellious slave. I am and I feel like a maroon woman. I will never voluntarily accept the condition of slavery, whether it's de facto or ipso facto, official or unofficial. In another recent interview, Williams talked about asking the federal government to add to the $50,000 reward for my capture. He also talked about seeking "outside money, or something like that, a benefactor, whatever." Now who is he looking to "contribute" to that "cause"? The Ku Klux Klan, the Neo-nazi parties, the white militia organizations? But the plot gets even thicker. He says that the money might lure bounty hunters. "There are individuals out there, I guess they call themselves 'soldiers of fortune,' who might be interested in doing something, in turning her over to us." Well, in the old days they used to call them slave-catchers, trackers, or patter-rollers, now they are called mercenaries. Neither the governor nor the state police say one word about "justice." They have no moral authority to do so. The level of their moral and ethical bankruptcy is evident in their eagerness to not only break the law and hire hoodlums, all in the name of "law and order." But you know what gets to me, what makes me truly indignant? With the schools in Paterson, NJ falling down, with areas of Newark looking like a disaster area, with the crack epidemic, with the wide-spread poverty and unem-ployment in New Jersey, these depraved, decadent, would-be slave-masters want federal funds to help put this "nigger wench" back in her place. They call me the "most wanted woman" in Amerika. I find that ironic. I've never felt very "wanted" before. When it came to jobs, I was never the "most wanted," when it came to economic opportunities I was never the "most wanted," [nor] when it came to decent housing. It seems like the only time Black people are on the "most wanted" list is when they want to put us in prison.

But at this moment, I am not so concerned about myself. Everybody has to die sometime, and all I want is to go with dignity. I am more concerned about the growing poverty, the growing despair that is rife in Amerika. I am more concerned about our younger generations, who represent our future. I am more concerned that one-third of young blacks are either in prison or under the jurisdiction of the "criminal in-justice system." I am more concerned about the rise of the prison-industrial complex that is turning our people into slaves again.* I am more concerned about the repression, the police brutality, violence, the rising wave of racism that makes up the political landscape of the US today. Our young people deserve a future, and I consider it the mandate of my ancestors to be part of the struggle to ensure that they have one. They have the right to live free from political repression. The US is becoming more and more of a police state and that fact compels us to fight against political repression. I urge you all, every single person who reads this statement, to fight to free all political prisoners. As the concentration camps in the US turn into death camps, I urge you to fight to abolish the death penalty. I make a special, urgent appeal to you to fight to save the life of Mumia Abu-Jamal, the only political prisoner who is currently on death row.†

It has been a long time since I have lived inside the United States. But during my lifetime I have seen every prominent black leader, politician or activist come under attack by the establishment media. When African Americans appear on news programs they are usually talking about sports, entertainment or they are in handcuffs. When we have a protest they ridicule it, minimize it, or cut the numbers of the people who attended in half. The news is big business and it is owned and operated by affluent white men. Unfortunately, they shape the way that many people see the world, and even the way people see themselves. Too often

---

* Editors' note: The Thirteenth Amendment to the US Constitution legalizes slavery and involuntary servitude for those convicted of crimes.

† Editors' note: Due to class bias and racially driven sentencing, of the nearly 2 million people incarcerated in US jails, prisons and detention centers, approximately 70% are African, Latino, Native or Asian American; over 3,000 people in prison are awaiting execution. Racial disparities in sentencing (those convicted of killing whites are four times more likely to be sentenced to death) have led the American Bar Association to call for a moratorium on the death penalty. See Mumia Abu-Jamal, *Live from Death Row* (Reading, MA: Addison-Wesley, 1995); Joy James, ed., *States of Confinement: Policing, Detention and Prisons* (New York: St Martin's Press, 2000).

black journalists, and other journalists of color mimic their white counterparts.

They often gear their reports to reflect the foreign policies and the domestic policies of the same people who are oppressing their people. In the establishment media, the bombing and murder of thousands of innocent women and children in Libya or Iraq or Panama is seen as "patriotic," while those who fight for freedom, no matter where they are, are seen as "radicals," "extremists," or "terrorists."

Like most poor and oppressed people in the United States, I do not have a voice. Black people, poor people in the US have no real freedom of speech, no real freedom of expression and very little freedom of the press. The black press and the progressive media has historically played an essential role in the struggle for social justice. We need to continue and to expand that tradition. We need to create media outlets that help to educate our people and our children, and not annihilate their minds. I am only one woman. I own no TV stations, or radio stations or newspapers. But I feel that people need to be educated as to what is going on, and to understand the connection between the news media and the instruments of repression in Amerika. All I have is my voice, my spirit and the will to tell the truth. But I sincerely ask, those of you in the Black media, those of you in the progressive media, those of you who believe in truth and freedom, to publish this statement and to let people know what is happening. We have no voice, so you must be the voice of the voiceless.

Free all political prisoners. I send you love and revolutionary greetings from Cuba, one of the largest, most resistant and most courageous palenques (maroon camps) that has ever existed on the face of this planet.

Bibliography

Apetheker, Bettina. *Women's Legacy: Essays on Race, Sex, and Class in American History*. Amherst: University of Massachusetts Press, 1982.

Baca Zinn, Maxine and Bonnie Thornton Dil, eds. *Women of Color in U.S. Society*. Philadelphia: Temple University Press, 1994.

Barkely Brown, Elsa. "African American Women's Quilting: A Framework for Conceptualizing and Teaching African-American Women's History," *Signs* 13, (1989).

Boyce Davies, Carole. *Black Women, Writing, and Identity: Migrations of the Subject*. London and New York: Routledge, 1994.

Cade, Toni, ed. *The Black Woman: An Anthology*. New York: Signet, 1970.

——edited with preface by Toni Morrison. *Deep Sightings & Rescue Missions*. New York: Vintage, 1996.

Cannon, Katie C. *Black Womanist Ethics*. Atlanta: Scholars Press, 1988.

Carby, Hazel. *Reconstructing Womanhood: The Emergence of the Afro-AmericanWoman Novelist*. New York: Oxford University Press, 1987.

Christian, Barbara. *Black Feminist Criticism: Perspectives on Black Women Writers*. New York: Pergamon, 1985.

Clark Hine, Darlene. *Black Women in America: An Historical Encyclopedia*, 2. vols, Brooklyn, N.Y.: Carlson, 1993.

Collins, Patricia Hill. *Black Feminist Thought: Knowledge, Consciousness, and the Politics of Empowerment*. Boston: Unwin Hyman, 1990.

——*Fighting Words: Black Women & The Search for Justice*. Minneapolis: University of Minnesota Press, 1998.

Cott, Nancy. *The Grounding of Modern Feminism*. New Haven: Yale University Press, 1987.

Davis, Angela. *Angela Davis: An Autobiography* New York: Random House, 1974.

——*Women, Race, and Class*. New York: Random House, 1981.

——*The Angela Y. Davis Reader*, ed. with intro. by Joy James. Oxford: Blackwell, 1998.

——*Blues Legacies and Black Feminism*. New York: Vintage Books, 1999.

DuCille, Ann. *The Coupling Convention: Sex, Text, and Tradition in Black Women's Fiction*. New York: Oxford University Press, 1993.

Ebert, Teresa. *Ludic Feminism and After*. Ann Arbor: University of Michigan Press, 1996.

Evans, Mari, ed. *Black Women Writers*. New York: Anchor, 1984.

Gates Jr., Henry Louis, ed. *Reading Black, Reading Feminist*. New York: Penguin, 1990.

Giddings, Paula. *When and Where I Enter: The Impact of Black Women on Race and Sex in America*. New York: William Morrow, 1984.

Grant, Jacquelyn. *White Women's Christ and Black Women's Jesus: Feminist Christology and Womanist Response*. Atlanta: Scholars Press, 1989.

Guy-Sheftall, Beverly, ed. *Words of Fire: An Anthology of African-American Feminist Thought*. New York: The New Press, 1995.

Harley, Sharon and Rosalyn Terborg-Penn. *The Afro-American Woman*. New York: Kennikat Press, 1978.

hooks, bell. *Ain't I a Woman? Black Women and Feminism*. Boston: South End Press, 1981.

——*Black Looks: Race and Representation*. Boston: South End Press, 1992.

——*Feminist Theory: From Margin to Center*. Boston: South End Press, 1984.

——*Talking Back: Thinking Feminist, Thinking Black*. Boston: South End Press, 1989.

——*Yearning: Race, Gender, and Cultural Politics*. Boston: South End Press, 1990.

Hull, Gloria T., Patricia Bell Scott, and Barbara Smith, eds. *All the Women Are White, All the Blacks Are Men, But Some of Us Are Brave: Black Women Studies*. Old Westbury, New York: Feminist Press, 1982.

James, Joy. *Resisting State Violence: Radicalism, Gender & Race in US Culture*. Minneapolis: University of Minnesota Press, 1996.

——*Transcending the Talented Tenth: Black Leaders and American Intellectuals*. New York: Routledge, 1997.

——*Shadowboxing: Representations of Black Feminist Politics*. New York: St. Martin's Press, 1999.

Jordan, June. *Civil Wars*. Boston: Beacon Press, 1981.

——*On Call: Political Essays*. Boston: South End Press, 1985.

Joseph, Gloria and Jill Lewis, eds., *Common Differences: Conflicts in Black andWhite Feminist Perspectives*. Garden City, NY: Anchor, 1981.

Ladner, Joyce. *Tomorrow's Tomorrow*. New York: Doubleday, 1971.

Lerner, Gerda, ed. *Black Women in White America: A Documentary History*. New York: Pantheon, 1972.

Lorde, Audre. *Sister Outsider: Essays and Speeches*. Trumansburg, New York: Crossing Press, 1984.

McDowell, Deborah. *"The Changing Same": Black Women's Literature, Criticism, and Theory.* Bloomington: Indiana University Press, 1995.

Moody, Anne. *Coming of Age in Mississippi.* New York: Dell, 1968.

Morrison, Toni, ed. *Race-ing Justice, En-gendering Power: Essays on Anita Hill, Clarence Thomas, and The Construction of Social Reality.* New York: Pantheon/Random House, 1992.

——*Playing in the Dark: Whiteness and the Literary Imagination.* New York:Vintage, 1993.

Painter, Nell. *Sojourner Truth: A Life, A Symbol.* New York: W.W. Norton, 1996.

Pryse, Marjorie and Hortense J. Spillers, eds. *Conjuring: Black Women, Fiction, and Literary Tradition.* Bloomington: Indiana University Press, 1985.

Sharpley-Whiting, T. Denean, *Frantz Fanon: Conflicts & Feminisms.* Lanham, MD and New York: Rowman & Littlefield Press, 1998.

——*Black Venus: Sexualized Savages, Primal Fears, and Primitive Narratives.* Durham, N.C.: Duke University Press, 1999.

Sharpley-Whiting, T. Denean et al., eds. *Spoils of War: Women of Color, Cultures, and Revolutions.* Lanham, MD and New York: Rowman & Littlefield, 1997.

Shakur, Assata. *Assata: An Autobiography.* Chicago: Lawrence Hill, 1987.

Smith, Barbara, ed. *Home Girls: A Black Feminist Anthology.* New York: Kitchen Table/Women of Color Press, 1983.

Spelman, Elizabeth. *The Inessential Woman: Problems of Exclusion in Feminist Thought.* Boston: Beacon Press, 1988.

Sudbury, Julia. *"Other Kinds of Dreams": Black Women's Organizations and the Politics of Transformation.* London: Routledge, 1998.

Truth, Sojourner. *Autobiography of Sojourner Truth.* New York: Oxford University Press, 1994.

Vaz, Kim Marie, ed. *Black Women in America.* Thousand Oaks, CA: Sage, 1995.

Wall, Cheryl, ed. *Changing Our Own Words: Essays on Criticisms, Theory, and Writing by Black Women.* New Brunswick: Rutgers University Press, 1989.

Walker, Alice. *In Search of Our Mothers' Gardens:Womanist Prose.* San Diego: Harcourt Brace Jovanovich, 1983.

Wallace, Michele. *Black Macho and the Myth of the Superwoman.* New York: Dial Press, 1978.

——*Invisibility Blues.* London: Verso, 1990.

Wells, Ida B. *Crusade for Justice.* Chicago: University of Chicago Press, 1970.

White, Deborah Grey. *Arn't I A Woman? Female Slaves in the Plantation South.* New York: W. W. Norton, 1985.

Williams, Delores. *Sisters in the Wilderness: The Challenge of Womanist God-Talk*. New York: Orbis Books, 1993.

Wing, Adrien Katherine, ed. *Critical Race Feminism*. New York: New York University Press, 1997.

Zack, Naomi, ed. *RACE/SEX: Their Sameness, Difference and Interplay*. New York: Routledge, 1997.

Index

Note: Information in notes is signified by n after the page number.